FROM SHADOW TO PROMISE

Old Testament Interpretation

from Augustine to the Young Luther

FROM SHADOW TO PROMISE

Old Testament Interpretation

from Augustine to the Young Luther

JAMES SAMUEL Nesbitt PREUS

The Belknap Press of

Harvard University Press

Cambridge, Massachusetts

1969

© Copyright 1969 by the President and Fellows of Harvard College
All rights reserved

Distributed in Great Britain by Oxford University Press, London
Library of Congress Catalog Card Number 60-12732
Printed in the United States of America

TO BETTE RAE

PREFACE

Few scholars can claim real competence both as Reformation historians and as Medievalists. But a growing number are venturing to understand and interpret the two periods together. Many of them, I suspect, are motivated by the ecumenical movement, a necessary task of which is to explain and reverse some of the centrifugal forces, unleashed in the sixteenth century, which scattered Christians into hostile camps. Among such scholars, I owe most to my teacher, Professor Heiko Augustinus Oberman, now of the University of Tübingen, whose enthusiasm, scholarly insight, and criticism helped shape this study in its earlier form as a doctoral dissertation at Harvard Divinity School. Further, I thank Professor Gerhard Ebeling, of the University of Zürich, not only for his fine published articles on the young Luther, but also for the patient hearing he gave me during his visit to Cambridge in the spring of 1966. Finally, I owe a debt from an earlier time to the man who first taught me how to go to the sources, Professor Edmund Smits of Luther Theological Seminary, Saint Paul, Minnesota.

J.S.P.

Cambridge, Massachusetts
October 1968

CONTENTS

Introduction 1

PART ONE. MEDIEVAL HERMENEUTICS TO 1513

I. *Augustine* 9
II. *Hugh of Saint Victor* 24
III. *Three Scholastic Theologians* 38
IV. *The Prologue Literature: Nicholas of Lyra* 61
V. *Two Nominalist Theologians* 72
VI. *Paul of Burgos* 86
VII. *James Perez of Valencia* 102
VIII. *Late Scholastic Developments* 123
IX. *Three Late Medieval Contemporaries* 133

PART TWO. LUTHER'S FIRST PSALMS COURSE, 1513–1515

X. *A Medieval Luther* 153
XI. *Luther's Development: A Projection* 166
XII. *The Senses and Structure of Scripture* 176
XIII. *The New Hermeneutical Divide* 200
XIV. *The Discovery of the Faithful Synagogue* 212
XV. *Tropology, Promise, and Faith* 226

Conclusion	267
Appendix: Occurrences of Pactum and Promissio in the Dictata	275
Bibliography	285
Index	295

FROM SHADOW TO PROMISE

"Mira permutatio, ut verba prevaleant rebus . . . !"
— Luther, 1515

ABBREVIATIONS

ARG	*Archiv für Reformationsgeschichte.* Leipzig and Gütersloh, 1903 ff.
CChr	*Corpus Christianorum, Series Latina.* Turnholti, 1953 ff.
CSEL	*Corpus Scriptorum Ecclesiasticorum Latinorum.* Vienna, 1866 ff.
EvTh	*Evangelische Theologie.* Munich, 1941 ff.
HTR	*Harvard Theological Review.* Cambridge, Mass., 1908 ff.
JThC	*Journal for Theology and the Church.* New York, 1964 ff.
KuD	*Kerygma und Dogma.* Göttingen, 1955 ff.
LCC	*Library of Christian Classics.* Philadelphia, 1953 ff.
PG	*Patrologia Graeca,* ed. J. P. Migne. Paris, 1857–1866.
PL	*Patrologia Latina,* ed. J. P. Migne. Paris, 1844–1855.
RGG	*Die Religion in Geschichte und Gegenwart,* 3rd ed. Tübingen, 1957–1965.
Sent.	The cited author's *Books of Sentences,* or commentary thereon.
WA	D. *Martin Luthers Werke: Kritische Gesamtausgabe.* Weimar, 1883 ff. Cited by volume, page, and line.
ZKG	*Zeitschrift für Kirchengeschichte.* Stuttgart, 1876 ff.
ZKT	*Zeitschrift für Katholische Theologie.* Innsbruck, 1876 ff.
ZThK	*Zeitschrift für Theologie und Kirche.* Tübingen, 1891 ff.

The numbering of Psalms follows the *Biblia Vulgata* throughout.

INTRODUCTION

It may seem odd that defense should be required for the thesis that Martin Luther's earliest writings betray a decisively medieval character, given the fact that he began his career as a professor in a medieval university. So attractive, however, is the lure of Luther's genius and originality that scholars have frequently insisted on finding a hidden uniqueness in almost everything Luther said, no matter how early. A generation of scholars and enthusiasts (with a few notable exceptions) willingly adopted Karl Holl's brilliant half-truth that the whole of the later Luther was already present in his first Psalms course (1513–1515). The fact that the entire medieval tradition was there too did not receive much attention.

It eventually had to be recognized that as a medieval doctor of Bible, Luther began his career steeped in the presuppositions, methods, and problems of medieval exegesis. Therefore, it is insufficient in a study of the young Luther merely to provide a mini-sketch of the "medieval background," or to embellish the exposition of Luther's early ideas with ever-longer footnotes containing select medieval texts, as though Luther were only remotely related to the medieval world of thought. According to that procedure, the tradition is seen and used merely as a backdrop, considered essentially past and done with, rather than as the real matrix and context of Luther's own life and thought, within which he struggled to develop his own theological position, and from which he never sought entirely to escape.

This is a study of the young Luther, but it differs from most others in that it offers a serious reconstruction of major issues of medieval hermeneutics *remoto Luthero* — with Luther left out of explicit consideration. Such a procedure, I believe, is indispensable to an adequate exposition of the Reformation's theological origins. From a *terminus a quo* that is really medieval, one begins where Luther began, and can hope to trace with some accuracy the steps of his development and departure from the tradition. The medieval theology may appear in the end to have been reduced to the unhappy role of a foil for Luther. But I do not wish to convey thereby the impression of a thousand years of hopeless incompetence being finally set right, in the fullness of time, by the Wittenberg professor. Indeed, contemporary hermeneutical discussion among heirs of the reformers shows signs of reappropriating neglected medieval insights. My intent is rather to make clear the logic of the medieval hermeneutical discussion, to show approximately where it stood at the end of the Middle Ages, and to trace Luther's gradual development of a new hermeneutic.

My material is organized around the focal concept of "promise." I became intrigued by the possibility that through this motif certain lines of continuity between Luther and the tradition, not sufficiently acknowledged, could be brought to light. It is well known that for Luther, "promise" was practically synonymous with "the Gospel." Less well known, but plain enough from a reading of recent studies, is the important role played by promise and *pactum* (or *pactio*) in the theology of Nominalism — particularly in its theology of justification and the sacraments. Were there roots here of the "theology of promise" found in Luther and Melanchthon, and of the covenant theology that was to develop later in the Reformed tradition?

In the early stages of my investigation, some lines of continuity seemed evident in late-medieval discussions of God's *acceptatio* of the viator and in the problem of how the sacraments confer grace. A fundamental theological idea operative in both these contexts, especially in the Franciscan tradition, was that only God's merciful promise or pact, proffered to man out of God's boundless freedom, could be designated the real "cause" both of God's bestowal of grace on the occasion of the Church's celebration of the sacraments and of God's acceptance of the merits of the viator as "fully worthy" (*condignum*) of eternal life. As my research progressed, however, these doctrinal contexts did not prove to be the right place to begin. While studying Luther's *Dictata super Psalterium*, the literary remains of his first course as a professor of Bible, I was unexpectedly (though it now seems inevitably) drawn into the area of hermeneutics, particularly the problems of Old Testament interpretation. It is these problems that shape the book.

The medieval hermeneutical tradition, the subject of Part I, can be characterized as an authentic attempt to establish the *sensus litteralis* of Scripture as its principal meaning, and to give it a theologically normative role in the formation of Christian theology. In his own way, Luther was trying to do the same thing. One stumbling block in this enterprise was the Old Testament — as it had been since the days of Marcion and still is. Does it really belong in the canon? How can the Christian community hope to discover abiding theological meaning in the literal, historical sense of the Old Testament text? What is the theological and religious relevance, for the Christian church, of the lives of the Old Testament people — their history as God's convenant people, the word that they heard, and their faith?

These questions were difficult for the medieval hermeneutical tradition to answer, for a good solution demands both that justice be done to the Old Testament's grammatical-historical meaning and that the theological and religious appropriateness of its place in the Christian canon of Scripture be shown. What frequently happened to the Old Testament (and perhaps still does happen) was that one of these demands was maintained at the expense of the other. Success in both requirements depended on many factors. First was the need to preserve a connection between the literal sense of Scripture, on the one hand, and the formation of normative religious and theological ideas, on the other. One had to bring into the process the Old Testament as well as the New.

Moreover, nothing so clearly threatened an effective theological role for the Old Testament in the Church as the Christ in the New Testament. An apparently praiseworthy christocentricity (who would have thought to challenge it?), together with an emphasis on grace and the Spirit, tended to subvert the Old Testament's theological function in canon and Church. Was not Christ the *telos* of the law and the prophets? But such concentration on Christ tended to set the supposedly authentic theological meaning of the Bible in opposition to the literal sense of the Old Testament. Another problem for hermeneuticians was to keep terminology honest and well-defined, so that one knew exactly what was meant by "literal" and "spiritual" and "historical." Careful distinctions tended to break down toward the end of the Middle Ages.

A further question that had to be faced was how to view the Old Testament history as a whole. Here is where the motif of promise enters. Was the Old Testament a *figura* — that is, were its people essentially figures and shadows, albeit unaware, of the Christians to come, so that in the latter alone appeared *veritas* and *lux?* Or was it a history with its own integrity under the promise — that is, were the Old Testament people, living in convenant with God, as authentic and spiritual in their faith and hope as is the Church? The answer made a great deal of difference to Old Testament interpretation, because in the latter case the Old Testament could function theologically and literally at the same time; in the former, it could only be a *figura*, which had passed away, of the Christian *veritas,* the New Testament.

As Part II will show, the notion of promise has served as a

good instrument for laying open the anatomy of Luther's involvement with these problems in the medieval tradition, as well as his gradual break from aspects of that tradition. Although I trace significant developments in Luther's thought, I do not presume to point to any particular passage or idea and assert, "Here, in essence, is the birth of Reformation theology." The threadbare arguments about Luther's so-called "Turmerlebnis" — more likely the creation of the old Luther than the experience of the young one — are not rehearsed, nor is a new solution proposed. As far as possible, I have tried to begin on premises that everyone can accept. For example, I assume that there is such a thing as "Reformation theology" — a theological complex that is neither medieval nor (at the present level of understanding) quite compatible with it. Further, "promise" is perhaps the best one-word synonym, in Luther's mature theological vocabulary, for "the Gospel" and hence lies at the very heart of Reformation theology. Another assumption of mine is that Gerhard Ebeling has made a convincing case that one cannot describe the emergence of the new theology without at the same time accounting for and describing the emergence of a new hermeneutic.[1] Finally, even though the *Dictata* as a whole reveals a Luther whose theological vision is in a state of flux, even of confusion, it is not yet incompatible with medieval theology. At the same time, new ideas abound, some of which, in retrospect, are harbingers of his later theology.

Few people would challenge the assertion that the Reformation meant a kind of rediscovery of the Old Testament in the Western church. In their different ways, the Reformers loved it and exploited it in an unprecedented manner. The Covenant

1. Ebeling ("Die Anfänge von Luthers Hermeneutik," *ZThK* 48 [1951], esp. pp. 178 f.) argues that an inseparable logical and temporal connection exists between developments in Luther's hermeneutical method and in his explication of the theological contents of the Bible.

theology of the later Reformed tradition was rooted in the Old Testament. It may seem surprising, now, to allow Luther much credit for this Old Testament recovery, given his rigorous christocentricity, his many unkind words about Moses, and the Marcionite leanings, both suspected and real, among representatives of the Lutheran tradition. But it is my contention that what separates Luther most decisively from the medieval hermeneutical tradition, and further, what best explains the genesis of his Reformation theology, depends on his peculiar appropriation of the Old Testament — his theological recovery of its history, its word, and its faith for the Church. The role played by *promissio,* God's promise, is decisive in this hermeneutical and theological event. I try to show further that correct understanding of these developments in the realm of hermeneutics is an indispensable presupposition for a proper understanding of Luther's development of a new theology of justification and the sacraments.

PART ONE: MEDIEVAL HERMENEUTICS TO 1513

I. AUGUSTINE

An examination of the Western hermeneutical tradition must begin, as must all historical studies of medieval theology, with Saint Augustine. While I have no intention of making a detailed and exhaustive analysis of his hermeneutical thought,[1] I wish to construct a sort of platform from which to launch the medieval discussion. This will clarify the categories and terms of the problems to be encountered.

A complex of problems came to expression in Augustine's *On Christian Doctrine*[2] and, through it, in *On the Spirit and the Letter*.[3] The first is a programmatic essay on hermeneutics which, along with certain writings of Jerome, a fourth century contemporary, provided the theoretical basis for most later medieval speculation on the method of interpreting the Bible. In the other work, Augustine gave expression to his equally formative and seminal doctrine of grace. As will be shown, the hermeneutical theory and the doctrine of grace are closely related to each other.

The single locus that provides the point of departure, and which will be a recurring point of reference, is Augustine's handling of the third rule of the Donatist Tyconius (d. c400), whose seven "keys" for understanding the obscurities of Scripture Augustine had adopted, revised at points, and incorpo-

---

1. On Augustine's hermeneutics, see Jean Pépin, "S. Augustin et la fonction protreptique de l'allégorie," *Recherches Augustiniennes* 1 (1958), 243–286; Gerhard Ebeling, *Evangelische Evangelienauslegung* (Munich, 1942), pp. 119–126; Maurice Pontet, *L'Exégèse de S. Augustin Prédicateur* (Paris, 1944); Gerhard Strauss, *Schriftgebrauch, Schriftauslegung, und Schriftbeweis bei Augustin* (Tübingen, 1959).
2. Latin quotations of *On Christian Doctrine* are from CSEL 80; English (cited as "tr.") from the Library of Liberal Arts edition, trans. D. W. Robertson (New York, 1958).
3. Latin citations are from CSEL 60; English from LCC 8: *Augustine: Later Works*, trans. John Burnaby (Philadelphia, 1955).

rated into his own work, thus bequeathing them to the medieval church.[4] By way of background, one should note that Tyconius and Augustine stand in that line of Christian apologists attempting to defend the divine authority of the whole Bible, and particularly of the Old Testament. It is also well known that Augustine himself for a time embraced the Manichaean view of the Old Testament (which was the same view, *mutatis mutandis,* as that of Marcion), whereby its crudity and the patent "immorality" of its God and its saints proved that it was no revelation of the God and Father of Jesus Christ. The answer of the Church to this reproach was allegorical or typological exegesis, whereby the Old Testament was demonstrated to have been speaking in figures, types, and parables of things to come. In a very important — perhaps fatal — sense, however, the Fathers agreed with Marcion: taken in its literal, historical meaning, the Old Testament has little to offer as a book for Christians.[5] Therefore, various kinds of figurative interpretation emerged, and the learned Tyconius laid down his rules for just such an interpretation.

Before knowing about Tyconius, Augustine had already been rooted out of his anti-Old Testament views by the allegorical preaching of Saint Ambrose at Milan. From Ambrose, Augustine first learned the secrets of allegorical interpretation: the Old Testament was not at all what it seemed; rather, it was a book of mysteries — *evangelical* mysteries, in fact.[6] In order to unveil these mysteries, one needed guidelines by

4. I shall not go into Tyconius' own third rule at this time, since his thought played no role in the medieval tradition independent of Augustine's rendition and interpretation of it. See F. C. Burkitt's Introduction in his edition of Tyconius' *Book of Rules* (*Texts and Studies,* ed. J. A. Robinson, III, no. 1), Cambridge, 1894.

5. Granted that the "prophecies," on which the early Church based its defense of the Old Testament as a Christian book, could in part be construed as literal-historical interpretation, this still left the bulk of the Old Testament unaccounted for.

6. Augustine relates his experience of hearing Ambrose in the *Confessions,* VI, c.4 (*CSEL* 33, 119).

which to recognize the texts that should be given figurative interpretation, and how such interpretation could properly be controlled and attained. Tyconius' rules provided such a series of "keys," as he called them; their whole intention was to aid in the intepretation of passages wherein, as Augustine would observe, "one thing was said, but another understood."
Tyconius entitled his third rule "Of Promises and the Law." At this point, Augustine abandons his model, writing that he prefers to call it "Of Spirit and Letter" or "Of Grace and Commandment." He observes that Tyconius' treatment is inadequate to the later problems raised by the Pelagian controversy.[7] For my purpose, it is necessary to draw attention to only a few elements of Augustine's brief treatment of this rule. At the outset, Augustine maintains that "spirit and letter" should not be regarded as an exegetical rule or key for solving problems encountered in reading Scripture; rather, it is a "great question" — a fundamental theological issue which, in response to the Pelagian heresy, he has dealt with at length elsewhere.[8] He refers to his *On the Spirit and the Letter*. Beyond the hint that "spirit and letter" have nothing special to do with the difference between the "spiritual" and "literal" senses of Scripture, which is also borne out in *On the Spirit and the Letter*,[9] he leaves here no clue as to how this rule might be applied specifically to exegesis.

Further on, however, there appears another comment on this third rule: "All of these rules except one, which is called

7. Augustine, *De doctrina christiana* (cited hereafter as *De doc. chr.*) III, 33, 46 (*CSEL* 80, 107; tr. 107): "Tertia regula est De promissis et lege, quae alio modo dici potest de spiritu et littera, sicut eam nos appellavimus, cum de hac re scriberemus; potest etiam sic dici: de gratia et mandato." Tyconius "labored well" on this problem, Augustine observes, but "being without an enemy, was less attentive" (p. 108; tr. 108).
8. *De doc. chr.* III, 33, 46 (*CSEL* 80, 107 f.; tr. 107): "Haec autem magis mihi videtur magna quaestio quam regula quae solvendis quaestionibus adhibenda est. Haec est quam non intellegentes Pelagiani vel condiderunt suam heresim vel auxerunt."
9. The biblical verse around which this discussion centers is 2 Cor.

'Of Promises and the Law,' cause one thing to be understood from another, a situation proper to figurative locutions."[10] Again, Augustine has set this rule off from all the others, but now he is more specific: the third rule does *not* imply or bear on the figurative interpretation of particular passages of Scripture. "Spirit" and "figurative," then, must not be confused.[11]

One inference that can be drawn from this comment on Rule Three, regarding the biblical text, is that God's "promise" and God's "law," as well as material regarding grace and commandment, are to be found in the plain literal sense of the Bible. Moreover, in this same treatise Augustine has already laid down a principle to that effect which later becomes axiomatic for most medieval interpretation of Scripture: "Among those things which are said openly (*aperte*) in Scripture are to be found all those teachings which involve faith, the mores of living, and that hope and charity which we have discussed in the previous book." [12] Again, "Hardly anything (*nihil fere*) may be found in these obscure places which is not found very plainly (*planissime*) said elsewhere." [13]

3:6: "The letter kills; the spirit makes alive." "Letter" in Augustine's exposition is the killing law that demands righteousness and manifests sin, without giving "spirit" or grace by which sin may be overcome.

10. *De doc. chr.* III, 37, 56 (*CSEL* 80, 117; tr. 116): "Hae autem omnes regulae, excepta una quae vocatur De promissis et lege, aliud ex alio faciunt intellegi, quod est proprium tropicae locutiones."

11. This, in essence, is the basis of Ebeling's fundamental distinction between what he calls an "Origenistic" and an "Augustinian" reading of 2 Cor. 3:6. See "Die Anfänge," pp. 182-187. According to Ebeling, the root failure of medieval hermeneutics was not to maintain this distinction, which led to the victory of an "Origenistic" identification of "spiritual" with "figurative." One was thus misled into thinking that the various forms of figurative exegesis were *eo ipso* "spiritual."

12. *De doc. chr.* II, 9, 14 (*CSEL* 80, 42; tr. 42): "In his enim quae aperte in scripturis posita sunt, inveniuntur illa omnia quae continent fidem moresque vivendi, spem scilicet atque caritatem, de quibus libro superiore tractavimus."

13. *De doc. chr.* II, 6, 8 (*CSEL* 80, 37; tr. 38): "Nihil enim fere de illis obscuritatibus eruitur, quod non planissime dictum alibi repperiatur." The "fere" leaves Augustine a small loophole for justifying those things

A Two-Value Literal Sense

Thus, Augustine holds that the articles of faith, along with that which Christians are to love and to hope, are practically (*fere*) all given in the plain passages of Scripture. The Bible's normative theological content is therefore part of its "clear" sense. But the first of the above two passages shows that there are also plenty of other things said *aperte* or openly in Scripture. What is to be done with that material? Is it, so to speak, neutral? Not at all! Augustine's fundamental view of the Bible does not allow for neutral passages. The whole Bible, having been "written for our learning (*doctrina*)," is edifying; all of it, in the intention of its divine author, teaches faith, hope and love.

Therefore, the goal of all exegesis is to teach faith, hope, and love, the greatest of which is love.[14] The consequence is: "whatever appears in the divine Word that does not properly pertain to virtuous behavior or to the truth of faith, you must take to be figurative."[15] In practice, this means that whenever the interpreter encounters a passage which does not literally teach faith or love, his task is to interpret it figuratively: he must raise it to the level of the edifying. For the passage that in its literal meaning does not edify must (according to Augustine's understanding of the divine intention) be a *figura* of something that does edify — a *signum* of some spiritual or theological *res* whose true meaning must be revealed as *credenda*, *diligenda*, or *speranda*, that is, as *doctrina*, *lex*, or *promissio*.[16]

---

that the Church believes and does without plain scriptural warrant, such as baptizing infants.

14. De doc. chr. I, 35, 39–40, 44; III, 10, 15.
15. *De doc. chr.* III, 10, 14 (CSEL 80, 88; tr. 88): "quicquid in sermone divino neque ad morum honestatem neque ad fidei veritatem proprie referri potest, figuratum esse cognoscas."
16. These last three terms are my own schematic way of designating the kind of material in Scripture that Augustine would call normative be-

This situation has interesting consequences in terms of Scripture's grammatical meaning. The outcome is that the clear sense of Scripture comprises in itself two distinct levels of value: some of it is edifying (teaching faith, hope, and love) in itself (*proprie*), and some of it is not. And what is not edifying is to be interpreted as having "said one thing, but meant another." It is to be "allegorized."[17] The *norm* (or to use later terminology, the *norma normans*) for that allegorization process is the other part of the grammatical sense — that which already clearly teaches faith, love, and hope.

Perhaps the following diagram will be helpful in illustrating the situation. The solid line represents the literal sense of the whole Bible. The upper level represents the goal of all exegesis, which is to show all Scripture teaching faith, love, and hope. The literal, grammatical sense reaches this upper level in part and, insofar as it does, is normative. The broken line on the upper level represents the spiritual or figurative interpretation to which the nonedifying part of the letter must be raised. It is important to notice that in content, the resulting spiritual sense (that is, the unedifying literal sense made edifying) is the same as the normative literal sense.

There is much potential for confusion in this. "Literal sense," on its two different levels, can designate both that which must be given figurative interpretation because it is unedifying, and that which need not, or must not, be interpreted figuratively, because it is normative as it stands, or one might even say, because it is already spiritual. Furthermore, the unedifying literal sense, on the bottom level, is regarded as a *figura* or *signum*.

---

cause it is "edifying," that is, it teaches faith, love, and hope. As shall be seen, they correspond to the three-fold spiritual sense: *allegoria, tropologia,* and *anagoge*. Ebeling summarizes this matter in "The New Hermeneutics and the Young Luther," *Theology Today* 21 (1964), 37 f.

17. "Allegoria" is Augustine's comprehensive term for figurative interpretation; the word does not yet have the specialized meaning referred to in the preceding note.

AUGUSTINE | 15

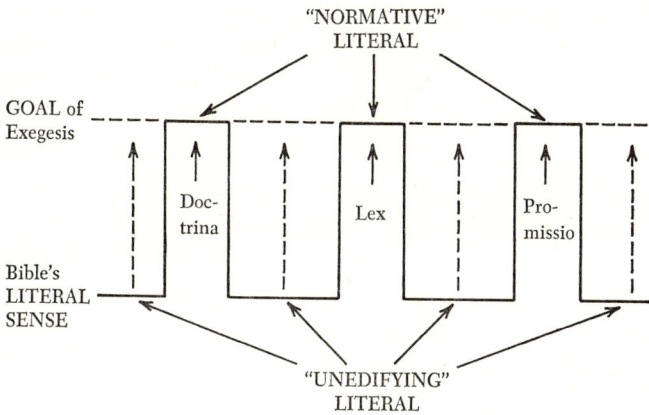

The Place of the Old Testament

Now some question must be raised about the Old Testament: is it not appropriate now to transpose these two levels of value into Old Testament/New Testament terms, on the ground that what Christians believe, love, and hope is *all* contained in the New Testament? Is it not the case, or almost so, that the whole Old Testament is *de littera* unedifying (at best a *norma normata,* or rather *normanda*) and therefore subject to figurative interpretation by the New Testament as its *norma normans?* Does not this view of Augustine's tend radically to reduce, quantitatively, the amount of the Old Testament that can be left standing, and understood properly, in its grammatical sense?

Indeed, a possibility for future hermeneutical development has appeared: the Old Testament may now rather easily be equated *in toto* with the unedifying letter, a *figura* that must not be read in its literal sense, but must be raised to the level of the normative literal sense, which the New Testament provides. When this happened, as it sometimes did in medieval thought, one could assert, without qualification, that the whole Old Testament is allegory (that is, a letter to be allegorized); or that the Old Testament, spiritually understood, is the same as the New Testament; or even that the New Testament is the "true" literal sense of the Old Testament. All such alternatives appear in texts to be dealt with later. And all have the same general effect: to be rid of the Old Testament as a theologically relevant text in its own right. For the division between unedifying and edifying, between "mere" letter (with a bad connotation) and "spirit" (meaning theologically relevant and edifying), now falls between the two testaments. In the medieval hermeneutic, as shall be shown, many factors worked in favor of locating the "hermeneutical divide," as I shall call it, between the testaments.

One final question must be put to Augustine: does the Old Testament have any of that still-relevant theological content in its literal sense? Even on the slender basis of his two writings mentioned, it is clear that the answer is Yes, primarily because the Old Testament *lex* is still binding, its commandments still "right to observe as they are written." [18]

The Function of Promissio

The place of the Old Testament *promissio*, however, is ambiguous, and different from the place of *lex* and *doctrina*.[19]

18. Augustine, *De spiritu et littera liber unus* (cited hereafter as *De sp. et lit.*) 24 (*CSEL* 60, 178; tr. 214). The phrase refers to the nine precepts of the Decalogue (the Sabbath excepted) "quae sic recte observantur, ut scripta sunt." Cf. *De sp. et lit.* 36 (*CSEL* 60, 189; tr. 221 f.): "the old covenant contained precepts of righteousness such as we are still enjoined to observe, especially those which are set forth in the two tables with a literal and not allegorical significance ([vetus testamentum] talia contineat praecepta iustitiae, qualia nunc quoque observare praecipimur, quae maxime duabus illis tabulis sine figura adumbratae significationis expressa sunt)." This still-binding nature of the commandment is what gives the law its "killing" power and demands grace.

19. I omit reference to *doctrina* in Augustine himself; it will appear frequently enough in later sources. What is presented here is sufficient to show that Augustine does not transpose the two-level situation of the biblical letter into an absolute Old Testament/New Testament division, even though much of what he argues points in that direction.

This arises in part from the intrinsic nature of promise itself. *Lex* and *doctrina* have the character of eternal verities (that which is always to be done and believed). Examples are the Old Testament command to love God and neighbor, and the doctrine of the oneness of God. The essential matter of these truths is never changed but merely perfected in the New Testament dispensation. The command of love is perfected by the New Testament grace and Spirit, which makes it effectively operative — fulfillable — among Christians; the doctrine of the one God is filled out and deepened by becoming explicitly Trinitarian.

Promise is different. Christians live, in part, under the same *lex* and *doctrina* (*mutatis mutandis*) as the Old Testament people. But they live under different promises. For promise has an intrinsic historical and temporal meaning: it points to a time of fulfillment. It cannot be an eternal verity in the same sense that *lex* and *doctrina* can be.[20] The consequence seems to be that the Old Testament promises are irrelevant to the Christian virtue of hope, which depends entirely on the New Testament.

The Promises of Temporalia. — According to Augustine, the Old Testament promises of earthly things (*temporalia* or *visibilia*) are clearly irrelevant now; they belong, therefore, to the part of the text that must be interpreted figuratively: "The promises of the old covenant are earthly promises. Certain of its ordinances (*sacramenta*) were shadows (*umbrae*) of things to come, such as circumcision, the sabbath and other observances of days, rules . . . It is true that apart from these, the old covenant contained precepts of righteousness such as we are still enjoined to observe." [21]

20. For example, Jer. 31:31: "The days are coming when I shall make a New Covenant." When this prophecy is fulfilled, it is done with; one lives in its fulfillment and under a different promise now.

21. *De sp. et lit.* 36 (*CSEL* 60, 189; tr. 221 f.): "Veteris testamenti promissa terrena sunt, licet — exceptis sacramentis, quae umbrae erant futurorum, sicut est circumcisio et sabbatum et aliae dierum observationes

Here promise, in contrast to the "precepts of righteousness," is subject to figurative interpretation, since the promises referred to are temporary and of no theological significance now. Thus, after listing some of the commandments, Augustine continues: "Nevertheless, the promises there announced . . . are earthly and temporal, good things of this corruptible flesh, even though they may be figures (*figurentur*) of the eternal and heavenly goods belonging to the New Covenant. Whereas now there is promised a good of the heart itself, a good of the mind, a spiritual good which is an intelligibile good." [22] This use and understanding of the Old Testament promises tends to place the hermeneutical divide sharply between the two covenants, so that all the Old Testament promises are mere *figurae* of the New Testament promises (just as the phenomenal world is a *figura* of the intelligible world).

The Promise of Christ. — There is a different, a second Old Testament promise which does not function at all in this way for Augustine. This is the promise of the New Covenant, or of Christ: "It holds good that the grace of God in the New Covenant was promised also through the prophet, and that this grace is defined [in Jeremiah] as consisting in the writing of God's laws in the hearts of men" [23] Here is an Old Testament promise that tends to fit into the normative-literal sense — at least to the extent that it is not the *figura* of something else, not

---

et quarundam . . . ritus . . . talia contineat praecepta iustitiae, qualia nunc quoque observare praecipimur."

22. *De sp. et lit.* 36 (*CSEL* 60, 189 f.; tr. 222): "tamen, quia in eo . . . promissa terrena et temporalia recitantur, quae bona sunt huius corruptibilis carnis, quamvis eis sempiterna atque caelestia ad novum scilicet testamentum pertinentia figurentur, nunc ipsius cordis bonum promittitur, mentis bonum, spiritus bonum, hoc est intelligibile bonum." The translation omits the last phrase referring to "intelligible good," a phrase that gives a Platonic connotation to Augustine's understanding of the proper objects of Christian hope.

23. *De sp. et lit.* 49 (*CSEL* 60, 204; tr. 233): "constat gratiam dei promissam esse testamento novo etiam per prophetam eandemque gratiam

subject to figurative interpretation. Presumably, it would be linked with hope. At least Augustine would have said that the Old Testament people should have taken it literally, and with ultimate seriousness, and should have placed all their hope in the promise of the coming grace.

Even though that particular promise is now fulfilled for Christians, they too wait for the coming Christ. Thus, the Old Testament promise can in a sense be the *figura* of a New Testament promise (that is, Christ's first advent signifying his second advent), but with this essential difference: the coming Christ himself is the object of faith and hope for both the Old Testament and the New Testament people. In this respect, therefore, one would not view the Old Testament faith, in comparison to the Christian, as inferior and "carnal," as one would in respect to the "earthly" promises. For here, exactly the same *res* is promised: Christ himself.

The point is that it makes a great deal of difference in the interpretation of the Old Testament which of these two approaches predominates. For under the first, whereby the Old Testament promises are *figurae* of the promises to Christians, the outcome is always an unfavorable contrast of the Old Testament faith to the Christian. For example, Augustine writes, "Just as the law of works, written on tables of stone, and its reward in the land of promise which the house of Israel according to the flesh received . . . belongs to the Old Covenant; so also the law of faith written in the heart, and its [promised] [24] reward in the immediate vision of God which the spiritual house of Israel shall enjoy . . . belongs to the new covenant.[25]

---

in eo definitam, ut scribantur leges dei in cordibus hominum." Cf. paragraph 40.

24. In Augustine's next paragraph, "promise" appears specifically in connection with the vision of God; hence, insertion of it here does not go beyond Augustine's meaning.

25. *De sp. et lit.* 41 (CSEL 60, 194; tr. 225): "Sicut ergo lex facto-

Under this interpretation, the Old Testament people are only a *figura* of the Christians, because the Old Testament text is taken as a *figura* of the New Testament text. Christians are their true literal sense just as the New Testament is the true literal sense of the Old Testament. The question of the theological and religious value of existence under the Old Covenant has dropped below the interpretive horizon, for one is now dealing with things of which the Old Testament people could not themselves have been aware. No historical relation between them and the New Testament people is envisioned. Indeed, one would not exaggerate too much in saying that, in this view, redemptive history really begins only with the coming of Christ. Everything before it is *figura*. The hermeneutical divide is placed emphatically at the advent of Christ.

In contrast, under the other view (wherein the Old Testament promise points to the future convenant, or to Christ), redemptive history begins in the Old Testament period, and its people, like the Christians, live under the promise of Christ. Israel, rather than being a shadow of which Christianity is the first reality, now can be the vine onto which Christians are ingrafted as branches. The Old Testament functions both historically and theologically in the canon.

The same difference can be pointed to in regard to the *lex*. One can emphasize the essential sameness of the command, and so envisage a certain parallel between the existence of the Old Testament people and Christians, or one can emphasize the fact that *caritas,* grace, and Spirit, which are necessary for the law's effective operation, are not given until the coming of Christ, who alone unveils the meaning of the figures, dis-

---

rum scripta in tabulis lapideis mercesque eius terra illa promissionis, quam carnalis domus Israhel . . . accepit, pertinet ad testamentum vetus, ita lex fidei scripta in cordibus mercesque eius species contemplationis, quam spiritalis [sic] domus Israhel . . . percipiet, pertinet ad testamentum novum."

penses the Spirit, and establishes the Church and its grace-giving sacraments.

The Senses of Scripture

This stage-setting is sufficient for a study of the medieval sources — with one exception. It became standard to designate the various forms of figurative exegesis as the allegorical, tropological (or moral), and anagogical. This particular breakdown of spiritual senses into three parts derives not from Augustine but from John Cassian (d. 435), his contemporary. Although Augustine did not use this terminology, it was later adjusted to fit his hermeneutical rule whereby Scripture intends to teach faith, love, and hope — *credenda, diligenda, speranda.*[26]

Cassian writes: "There are three genera of spiritual *scientia: tropologia, allegoria, anagoge,* of which it is said in the book of Proverbs [22:20]: 'But you, write those things for yourself *tripliciter* upon the breadth of your heart.' "[27] Cassian's elaboration of the meaning of the senses concludes that allegory is what Paul used in Galatians 4, when he explained Abraham's two sons as two testaments: "those things which were in fact done are said to have prefigured the form of another mystery."

26. Augustine had designated four senses of Scripture: *historia, allegoria, analogia,* and *aetiologia. Historia,* he wrote, "is when *res gesta* are remembered, whether divinely or humanly done." Allegory designates the understanding of things said figuratively ("cum figurate dicta intelliguntur"). Analogy demonstrates the *congruentia* of the Old and new Testaments, and etiology accounts for the causes of things said and done. *De genesi ad litteram imperfectus liber,* c.2, n.5 (PL 34, 222). The same schema is given in *De utilitate credendi,* c.3 (PL 42, 68 f.).

27. John Cassian, *Conlationes* XIV, c.8: "De spiritali scientiae" (CSEL 13/2, 404): "Spiritalis autem scientiae genera sunt tria, tropologia, allegoria, anagoge, de quibus in Proverbiis ita dicitur: 'tu autem discribe tibi ea tripliciter super latitudinem cordis tui.' " Origen had used this same passage, based on the LXX reading, to legitimate his threefold sense of Scripture: R. P. C. Hanson, *Allegory and Event* (London, 1959), p. 235.

Tropology is "the moral explanation pertaining to the cleansing of life and to actual instruction," and anagogy has to do with "spiritual mysteries arising to more sublime and sacred secrets of heaven." Cassian then gives his famous example of Jerusalem, whereby historically it is a city of the Jews, allegorically the *ecclesia Christi*, tropologically the soul of man, and anagogically the heavenly City of God.[28]

Anagogy, which would relate, systematically, to hope, and therefore to *promise,* has a peculiar definition here in that it may be construed either in a mystical sense (so that it reveals the "secrets of heaven" seen by the great contemplatives), or in an eschatological sense (so that it points to the promise of Christ's second advent, or to the coming City of God).[29] In the first case, emphasis would fall on special spiritual endowments of a gifted elite; in the second, upon God's promise of the future, and the common hope in it. Both of these dimensions will crop up in interesting ways as the study progresses.

Summary

The key issues upon which the whole study turns are now apparent. One is the function of the Bible's literal sense in the formation of Christian religious and theological thought:

28. *Conlationes* XIV, c.8 (*CSEL* 13/2, 404 f.): "ea quae in veritate gesta sunt alterius sacramenti formam praefigurasse dicuntur. Anagoge vero de spiritalibus mysteriis ad sublimiora quaedam et sacratiora caelorum secreta . . . tropologia est moralis explanatio ad emundationem vitae et instructionem pertinens actualem . . . Igitur praedictae quattuor figurae in unum ita, si volumus, confluunt, ut una atque eadem Hierusalem quadrifarie possit intellegi: secundum historiam civitas Iudaeorum, secundum allegoriam ecclesia Christi, secundum anagogen civitas dei illa caelestis . . . secundum tropologiam anima hominis, quae frequenter hoc nomine aut increpatur aut laudatur a domino."

29. These two interpretations are by no means mutually exclusive if medieval mysticism is understood as one form of "realized eschatology," for the goal of both the mystic and the ordinary *viator* was the *visio dei*; the mystic only caught a glimpse of it a little before the time. The mere

whether terminology can be kept clear, or whether it will succumb to the potential for confusion already present in Augustine's hermeneutical statement. Second, can the whole canon really function in the theological enterprise, or will the letter-spirit distinction be transposed into Old Testament/New Testament terms, thus threatening a loss of the theological as well as grammatical-historical meaning of the Old Testament. The third question is the function of the Old Testament promise: whether, as "promise of Christ" or some other inviolable divine commitment to his people it can contribute to and inform the Christian theological expression of faith and hope; or whether, as mere promise of *temporalia,* it will be relegated to the status of *signum tantum,* mere sign. A further issue is the resulting view of the Old Testament history as a whole: does redemptive history, with authentic word of God and faith, begin in the Old Testament, or only with the coming of Christ? Finally, what effect, if any, will the ambiguity of the earliest definition of anagogy have on the function of promise in biblical interpretation?

---

promissio, meanwhile, would have to suffice for ordinary folk. Augustine certainly had both elements in his theology, but he did not include *anagoge* as one of his four senses, and I have not had a chance to determine how the mystical and echatological elements are related in his theology.

II. HUGH OF SAINT VICTOR

Prior to Saint Thomas, the most important medieval voice in the hermeneutical discussion was that of Hugh of Saint Victor (d. 1141). He belonged to a school of biblical scholars whose characteristics have been made well known through the research of Beryl Smalley. Smalley's admiration for the Victorine school arises largely from its careful attention to the literal and historical meaning of the Old Testament, and its quiet insistence on the literal meaning as the foundation for all interpretation.[1] In this enterprise, the members of the school were in contact with Jewish scholarship, whose most learned representative of the day was Rabbi Shelomo Izhaki, better known simply as Rashi (d. 1105).[2] Hugh provides an informative link between Augustine and the so-called "High" Middle Ages.

Tyconius' Third Rule

First, on the third rule of Tyconius, Hugh repeats verbatim the summation given by Isidore of Seville in the seventh century. Hugh writes: "The third rule concerns the letter and the spirit, that is, the law and grace: law through which are set forward precepts to be done; grace through which we are aided in order that we may do them."[3] With Augustine, then, it is

---

1. Beryl Smalley, *The Study of the Bible in the Middle Ages* (2nd ed., Notre Dame, 1964), esp. pp. 83–106. See my Bibliography for further studies by her.
2. Herman Hailperin, *Rashi and the Christian Scholars* (Pittsburgh, 1963), p. 25.
3. *Didascalicon: de studio legendi* (cited hereafter as *Didasc.*) V, c.4 (ed. C. H. Buttimer [Washington, D.C., 1939], p. 99, lines 6–9): "Tertia

understood that letter and spirit are not primarily concerned with the literal and figurative interpretation of Scripture passages. However, a hermeneutical consequence has been drawn, almost inevitably, from Augustine's interpretation of letter and spirit as law and grace, which itself suggests two stages in redemptive history: "the law is to be understood (*sentienda*) not only historically (*historice*), but also spiritually (*spiritualiter*)." [4] Just as the grace of Christ followed the law of Moses, so in the interpretation of Scripture the law is to be understood not only historically, in its Old Testament sense, but "spiritually," in terms of New Testament grace which is now present.[5] The direction being taken is plain: the Augustinian interpretation of spirit and letter as grace and law is working toward a hermeneutical principle that justifies a figurative reading of the Old Testament law, whereby its letter is elevated to the theologically normative sense given in the New Testament.

regula est de littera et spiritu, id est de lege et gratia: lege per quam praecepta facienda admonentur; gratia per quam ut operemur juvamur." Isidore's (d. 636) version (*PL* 83, 582 A) is virtually identical.

4. *Didasc.* V, c.4 (p. 99, lines 9–11): "vel quod lex non tantum historice, sed etiam spiritualiter sentienda sit." In the next and final sentence concerning the third rule, "namque et historice oportet fidem tenere, et spiritualiter legem intelligere," Isidore and Hugh seem to be giving, in primitive form, the distinction between *fides historica* (the facts of the faith that even the devils believe) and *fides caritate formata* (faith informed and made alive by grace, which includes spiritual understanding of the law and the aid of grace to fulfill it).

5. In this I disagree with Wilfrid Werbeck, who following the Origen-Augustine distinction of Ebeling, observes that Isidore has fallen back into the "Origenistic" understanding of 2 Cor. 3:16 (*Jacobus Perez von Valencia* [Tübingen, 1959], p. 94). It seems rather than the interpretation given by Isidore-Hugh is perfectly consistent with Augustine, for just as grace has followed upon the law in *Heilsgeschichte,* and qualified it, so also in hermeneutics spiritual understanding (informed by the New Testament) is to be applied to the literal sense of the Old Testament law. One cannot challenge this hermeneutical consequence without also threatening the Augustinian understanding of spirit and letter upon which it is based.

The Senses of Scripture

Later scholastic texts report that Cassian's breakdown of the Scriptural senses, along with his famous illustration of Jerusalem, was transmitted through "Beda." Although the Venerable Bede did in fact know this schema, the quotation found in most scholastic texts is instead taken from the twelfth-century *Gloss* (later known as the *Glosa ordinaria*), which emanated from the school of Anselm of Laon. The four senses are: "history, which tells the *res gestae*; allegory, in which one thing is understood from another; tropology, i.e. moral pronouncement, which deals with the ordering of morals; anagogy, through which we are led to higher things in order to be drawn up to the highest and heavenly things." [6]

It should be noted that "allegory" is still understood in Augustine's general sense of "figurative," whereby "one thing is said, another meant." Furthermore, the anagogical sense has not been specifically tied to the future (via promise) so much as to transcendent, heavenly realities. This means again that the anagogical sense can be construed as mystical as well as eschatological, no sharp distinction having been made between them.

In fact, Hugh of Saint Victor simply drops out the anagogical as a separate sense: Scripture, he says, presents its material according to a "triplex intelligentia": history, allegory, and tro-

6. The text is given by J. P. Migne as Strabus, *Prothemata glossae ordinariae* (PL 113, 63 B), although it is clear that Walafrid Strabus had little to do with the *Gloss* in its present form (see Smalley, *The Study of the Bible*, pp. 56–60): "historia, quae res gestas loquitur; allegoria, in qua aliud ex alio intelligitur; tropologia, id est moralis locutio, in qua de moribus ordinandis tractatur; anagoge . . . per quem de summis et coelestibus tractaturi, ad superiora ducimur . . . Verbi gratia, Hierusalem." This passage is quoted by Alexander of Hales, Henry Totting of Oyta, and others. Totting's modern editor refers us to Bede, *De Tabernaculo* I, c.6 (PL 91, 410), and *In Cantica Canticarum allegorica exposita* IV (PL 91, 1142) for evidence that Cassian's fourfold scheme was known to Bede.

pology. History is the narration of the *res gestae*. Allegory occurs "when through that which is said to have been done, something else is done, whether in the past or in the present or in the future." ⁷ To tropology belong things which are signs of other things that are to be done (*faciendum esse*).⁸

Earlier I pointed out that, according to Saint Augustine, Scripture's edifying intention limited or defined its contents according to what it clearly taught was to be believed, loved, and hoped (the "normative-literal" sense). In Hugh, as in following interpreters, this view is simplified somewhat: faith and love predominate, and in summary statements of what Scripture is about, the element of hope is often dropped out.

7. The inclusion of "in the future" under allegory indicates that eschatological interpretation is included under this rubric, not under a separate, anagogical category. Aquinas made a note of this in *Summa Theologiae* (cited hereafter as *ST*) I q.1 a.10 ad 2 (Ottawa, 1953, I, 10b). Hugh elsewhere explains himself more fully, dividing *allegoria* into "simple allegory" and anagogy. But I cannot see the point of Hugh's distinction without emending the Migne text to read "visible" (italicized below) instead of "invisible"; that is the only way any distinction appears between "simple allegory" and anagogy. If my suggestion is accepted, then "simple allegory" occurs when "through something visibly done, something else *visibly* done is signified (cum per visibile factum aliud *visibile* factum significatur)"; and "anagogy" means (etymologically) *"sursum ductio,* when through something visibly done, something invisibly done is declared (per visibile invisibile factum declaratur)." (*De scripturis et scriptoribus* [cited hereafter as *De script.*] c.3; *PL* 175, 12 B). With such an emendation, the distinction between the two emerges clearly as between a typology of historical realities, on the one hand, and on the other, the visible as sign of an invisible, transcendent, or eschatological mystery.

8. Hugh of St. Victor, *De Sacramentis christianae fidei* (cited hereafter as *De sacr.*), Prol., c. 4 (*PL* 176, 184 C f.): "De hac autem materia tractat divina Scriptura secundum triplicem intelligentiam: hoc est historiam, allegoriam, tropologiam. Historia est rerum gestarum narratio, quae in prima significatione litterae continetur; allegoria est cum per id quod factum dicitur, aliquid aliud factum sive in praeterito sive in praesenti, sive in futuro significatur; tropologia est cum per id quod factum dicitur, aliquid faciendum esse significatur." Cf. *Didasc.* V, c.2 (p. 95, lines 15 f.); in the same place Hugh notes also that not all the senses are found in every scriptural text (p. 95, lines 17–19; p. 96, lines 15–21).

Thus, "Either a *factum* signifies another *factum* and is allegory, or a *factum* signifies a *faciendum*, and is a *moralitas*. Toward these two things — the cognition of the truth (i.e., the wholeness of faith) and the love of goodness (i.e., the perfection of good works) — we are instructed. Holy Scripture is thus to be read on account of these two things, so that we might sincerely believe, and act well." [9]

One might expect that an interpreter with sympathies to mystical theology (and Hugh was such a person *par excellence*) would then tend to replace "hope" with mystical experience — the medieval equivalent of realized eschatology. This would tend to subordinate the promise of the future as a central element of Scripture in favor of whatever might lend itself to opening up of heavenly secrets. The more universally applicable virtue of hope would then be subordinated to a virtue available to a gifted few, a spiritual elite.

Role of the Sensus Historicus

It is essential to investigate the motive behind Hugh's well-known concern for the historical sense of Scripture and to find out exactly how the historical-literal sense is related to the spiritual senses. Hugh has a sharp rebuke for contemporary allegorizers of the Bible,[10] and he gives theological grounds

9. *De script.* c.16 (PL 175, 24 A): "aut factum significat factum et est allegoria; aut factum faciendum significat, et est moralitas. *In his duobus* ad cognitionem veritaits, id est integritatem fidei, et ad amorem bonitatis, id est ad perfectionem bonorum operum, instruimur. *Propter quae duo* legenda est divina Scriptura, scilicet ut credamus sincere, et bene operemur." (Italics mine.) Cf. *De sacr.* Prol. c.6 (PL 176, 185 D), on "recta fides" and "bona operatio."

10. *De script.* c.5 (PL 175, 13 B): "They say, 'We read the Scripture, but we do not read the letter (Scripturam legimus, sed non legimus litteram). We don't care about the letter; we teach allegory.' But how do you read the Scripture without reading the letter? For if you take away the letter, what is Scripture (Si enim littera tollitur, Scriptura quid est)? 'We,' they reply, 'read the letter, but not according to the letter. For we

for attention to the literal sense: one must not think he can despise the meaning of the letter, since it has been put there by the Spirit himself to lead us to spiritual things. "Do not therefore despise the humility of the word of God, for through humility you will be enlightened to divinity." [11]

How does the Bible lead one through the letter to the spirit? In his explanation, Hugh sets forth a theory for which Thomas Aquinas is more famous, the theory of *double signification*. For its proponents this theory provides the hallmark of the Bible in contrast to all other books. Explaining the importance of the literal sense, Hugh writes, "As long as you remain ignorant of the letter, do not go around boasting about your understanding of Scripture. For to be ignorant of the letter is to be unaware of what the letter signifies, and of what is signified by the letter. For that which is signified by the first [i.e., by the letter] signifies still a third thing. Since therefore those things which the letter signifies are signs for spiritual understanding, how can they be [this kind of] signs for you when they are not yet signified to you?" [12] Thus, the word signifies a thing (which I shall call "res^I"), which in turn is the sign of another ("third") thing ("res^{II}"). The importance of the thing signified by the words and of the "third thing" is clarified later in the same writing: "In other writings, the phi-

---

read allegory, and we expound the letter not according to the letter, but according to allegory.' But what is it to expound the letter without pointing out what the letter signifies (Quid ergo est litteram exponere, nisi id quod significat littera demonstrare)?"

11. *De script.* c.5 (PL 175, 14 D): "Noli igitur in verbo Dei despicere humilitatem, quia per humilitatem, illuminaris ad divinitatem." Note that this is very close to a christological analogy.

12. *De script.* c.5 (PL 175, 13D f.): "Noli itaque de intelligentia Scripturarum gloriari, quandiu litteram ignoras. Litteram autem ignorare est ignorare quid littera significet, et quid significetur a littera. Nam quod significatur a primo, tertium significat. Cum igitur res illae quas littera significat, spiritualis intelligentiae signa sint, quomodo signa tibi esse possunt, quae necdum tibi significata sunt?"

losopher knows only a signification of *words*; but in the sacred pages the signification of *things* is surely more remarkable than the signification of words. For simple use establishes the latter, but the former is dictated by nature. In the one case we have the voice of men; here we have the voice of God to men. The signification of words comes from man's good pleasure; the signification of things is natural [meaning "providential"], arising from the operation of the Creator who wishes certain things to be signified by other things." [13] The matter is summed up in the prologue of Hugh's *On the Sacraments*: "It is apparent how much Divine Scripture excels all other writings in subtlety and profundity, not only in its subject matter, but also in its method of treatment, since indeed in other writings words alone are found to have meaning, but in it not only words but also things are significative." [14]

Hugh's great concern for the literal meaning is thus clear. Only by proper understanding of the literal sense (word →

13. *De script.* c.14 (*PL* 175, 20 D f.): "Philosophus in aliis scripturis solam *vocum* novit significationem; sed in sacra pagina excellentior valde est rerum significatio quam vocum; quia hanc usus instituit, illam natura dictavit. Haec hominum vox est, illa Dei ad homines [so far, almost verbatim of *Didasc.* V, c.3; p. 96, which, however, adds at this point: "Haec (vox hominum) prolata perit, illa creata subsistit"]. Significatio vocum est ex placito hominum: significatio rerum *naturalis* est, et *ex operatione creatoris volentis quasdam res per alias significari.*" (Italics mine.) See also *De script.* c.3 (*PL* 175, 11 D f.). This notion provides the clue to understanding the close interrelationship between redemptive history as sacramental (one *event* signifies another), the fourfold hermeneutical structure that Thomas brought into conformity with it (so that one *sense* signifies another), and the understanding of the sacraments themselves (wherein the outward thing signifies invisible grace).

14. *De sacr.* Prol., c.5 (*PL* 176, 185 A): "Unde apparet quantum divina Scriptura caeteris omnibus scripturis non solum in materia sua, sed etiam in modo tractandi, subtilitate et profunditate praecellat; cum in caeteris quidem scripturis solae voces significare inveniantur; in hac autem non solum voces, sed etiam res significativae sint." Except for the last word, I have followed the translation of R. J. Deferrari, *Hugh of Saint Victor on the Sacraments of the Christian Faith* (Cambridge, Mass., 1951), p. 5.

res^I) can proper *theological* understanding of Scripture arise, because such understanding demands a grasp of the significative relations between *things* (res^I → res^{II}), which is the allegorical sense. Allegorical, or theological, interpretation is bound to go awry if the literal meaning is misunderstood. Hugh even advises memorizing the whole course of biblical history, paying special attention to persons, occurrences, times, and places.[15]

The Old Testament as Umbra. — Hugh nevertheless admits that sometimes the literal meaning makes little sense, or appears "incongrua." This is especially the case, he observes, with the Old Testament.[16] In the spiritual meaning, by contrast, everything is harmonious and clear.[17] But how does one arrive at the proper "allegorical" reading of Scripture (by "allegorical," Hugh means both theological and spiritually edifying)? One proceeds, he answers, in a different order than when reading historically. For historical reading follows the order of time (*ordo temporis*), while allegorical reading belongs to the order of *cognitio*.[18] Explaining this distinction,

15. *Didasc.* VI, c.3 (p. 114, lines 5-10): "Don't despise these things too much! Those who do gradually fade out. If you first refuse to learn the alphabet, you will not be able to hold your own with the grammarians. I know some fellows who want to philosophize right away, saying that fables ought to be left to pseudo-apostles. But their knowledge takes the shape of an ass. Don't imitate these types!"
16. *Didasc.* VI, c.9 (p. 126, lines 15 f.): "aliquando talis est littera, ut nisi in aliam resolvatur, nihil significare, vel incongrua esse videatur." In the next chapter (p. 126, lines 26 ff.), Hugh distinguishes between *significatio* and *sensus*: certain places in Scripture, although the *significatio verborum* is plain ("aperta"), seem to make no sense ("nullus tamen sensus esse videtur"). He gives examples, then concludes: "multa huiusmodi invenies in scripturis, et maxime in Veteri Testamento, secundum idioma illius linguae dicta" (p. 128, lines 15-17). Hugh does not here refer in any derogatory manner to the *doctrina* or mores of the Old Testament, however. And he allows the interpreter to leave no stone unturned in explicating the literal meaning of the text.
17. *Didasc.* VI, c.11 (p. 128, lines 20-23).
18. *Didasc.* VI, c.6 (p. 123, lines 9-13): "Non idem ordo librorum

Hugh makes it clear that the relevant theological content of Scripture, its *doctrina,* is found in the New Testament. "Now the consequence is that in this sort of reading, the New Testament, in which the manifest truth is proclaimed, is preferable to the Old, where one finds the same truth foretold, but occultly adumbrated in figures." [19] It is Christ, the Lion of the tribe of Judah (Rev. 5:5), who alone can break the seals of the Old Testament: "by fulfilling what was promised, he opened up what was hidden." [20]

The Old Testament period is, then, one of figure and of promise. When the promise is fulfilled, the Old Testament figures can be identified and filled with New Testament content, real *doctrina.* For the Old Testament has no doctrinal relevance of its own. The briefly mentioned promise of Christ, which is now "exhibita" and therefore no longer in existence,[21] plays no role for the present.

Clearly, Hugh's hermeneutical divide between unedifying and edifying is firmly fixed between the Old and New Testaments. Understanding, "cognition," really begins only with the appearance of Christ. The theological relevance of the Old Testament appears only at the end of the order of its own time, because theological relevance is limited to *doctrina,* which for Christians first emerges in the time of Christ.

---

in historica et allegorica lectione servandus est. historia ordinem temporis sequitur. ad allegoriam magis pertinet ordo cognitionis, quia . . . doctrina semper non ab obscuris, sed apertis, et ab iis quae magis nota sunt exordium sumere debet."

19. *Didasc.* VI, c.6 (p. 123, lines 13-17): "unde consequens est, ut Novum Testamentum, in quo manifesta praedicatur veritas, in hac lectione Veteri praeponatur, ubi eadem veritas figuris adumbrata occulte praenuntiatur. eadem utrobique veritas, sed ibi occulta, hic manifesta."

20. *Didasc.* VI, c.6 (p. 124, line 17): "implendo quae promissa erant, aperuit quae latebant."

21. *Didasc.* VI, c.6 (p. 123, lines 16 f.): "ibi occulta, hic manifesta; ibi promissa, hic exhibita." And a few lines later (p. 124, line 17): "implendo quae promissa erant, aperuit quae latebant."

But what does this mean for understanding the Old Testament history? It must mean that just as one cannot, according to Hugh, understand the Bible as a whole by *reading* it in the *ordo temporis,* the temporal order, so the Old Testament people, who of necessity *lived* in temporal order, cannot have lived in an understanding of what God's intention was, since they were without benefit of him who unlocks the meaning of their own history.[22] In fact, their own understanding was bound to be confused by the fact that although the words they heard were referring to things present or discernible to them (res[I]), the words did not yet advise them that these present *res* were themselves signs of other, future things (that is, New Testament things, res[II]). And so they were unaware that their whole history was an allegory. Just as, hermeneutically, one thing is said, but another understood, so with the Old Testament people, one thing was said and heard and understood, but something else was really meant. Only those few who were specially inspired, or who survived until the actual appearance of Christ, could have detected the allegorical character of their own history, for knowledge of the nativity, preaching, passion, resurrection, and ascension of Christ are absolute conditions for penetrating the mysteries of the ancient figures.[23]

The motive of Hugh's intense concern for understanding the literal, historical sense is thus apparent: the Old Testa-

22. Understood from this perspective, the following statement of Hugh's nicely illustrates my point (*Didasc.* VI, c.6; p. 124, lines 13-15): "Who do you think was able to understand these things, before they were completed? They were 'sealed' [Rev. 5:1-5], and no one could break the seals except the 'lion of the tribe of Judah.' "

23. *Didasc.* VI, c.6 (p. 125, lines 4-7): "nisi prius nativitatem Christi, predicationem, passionem, resurrectionem atque ascensionem, et caetera quae in carne et per carnem gessit, agnoveris, veterum figurarum mysteria penetrare non valebis." My concern here is not to impugn this understanding of the meaning of the advent of Christ for the Christian community or for exegesis of the New Testament. Rather, I wish to expose as sharply as possible the conquences of the emerging medieval hermeneutic for the exegesis of the Old Testament.

ment history, and consequently historical exegesis of the Old Testament, are important not because the Old Testament, its word, or faith are of religious or theological significance in the present, but because they are a sign and figure of the normative history, word, and faith that appears elsewhere, namely, in the time of Christ and the Church, and therefore in the New Testament.

Understanding the New Testament. — An important new question now arises: Is there also an allegorical or spiritual sense of the *New* Testament? Are the *res gestae Christi,* like those of the Old Testament patriarchs, also signs of still "higher" truth? If they are not, then we have the peculiar consequence that the Old Testament is more unique and divine than the New, for Hugh has already pointed out that what makes the Bible unique among books is the significative character of the events and things related therein! This would seem to necessitate a new level of spiritual interpretation, based on the occurrence of new *res* (res^{III}).

On the other hand, Hugh has also maintained that in the New Testament, Christian *doctrina* is clearly set forth (recalling the old Augustinian dictum that whatever is said obscurely in one place is found clearly in another): the New Testament says clearly that which the Old says obscurely. This seems to argue for the superiority of the New Testament, on the ground that it is edifying in its literal sense.

These are two different — and quite contradictory — ways of explaining the uniqueness of the Bible. With one having primary reference to the Old Testament, and the other related to the New, they can lead to quite different assessments of the place of the Bible in the church. For if one takes the New Testament uniqueness as a model, the groundwork is laid for a biblicism of the sort that arises — often but not exclusively — in medieval heretical circles. But if the New Testament is like the Old, in turn significative of something beyond itself, the way is open for locating its spiritual sense in, say, the Church, or in the spiritual man.

Summary

What conclusions can now be drawn, and how is the discussion advanced? In general, Hugh's systematic development in the directions suggested by Augustine is favorable for the further detailed study of the Old Testament history, but at the same time it systematically empties that history of theological meaning by reducing the Old Testament words and events to *figurae* and *signa* of New Testament words and events.[24] History is the *fundamentum,* as Hugh frequently wrote, but knowledge of it is necessary only for the sake of the spiritual, theological *aedificium* which is to be erected upon it.

In particular, certain conclusions may be noted. First, the theological meanings of the Old Testament words and events must wait upon the occurrence of the New Testament events before they can be understood properly. What was "sealed up" is broken open only by the appearance of Christ, and now clearly unveiled for the first time in the words of the New Testament. The Old Testament word, then, functions as a sign of the New Testament word.

Therefore, the Old Testament promises of *temporalia,* as *umbrae* of the New Testament promises of *eternalia,* can be expected to come to the fore, because they fit this schema perfectly. This expectation will be confirmed as the investigation proceeds, revealing the predominance of a concept of Old

---

24. This point must be made, despite widespread scholarly admiration of the Victorines for their attention to the *sensus historicus,* which undoubtedly makes them, together with Nicholas of Lyra, most attractive among medieval biblical scholars. But it was perhaps just their inability to invest theological meaning and relevance into the historical-critical enterprise itself that prevented this demanding sort of exegetical method from prevailing in the medieval period.

Testament promises whereby they are only promises of *temporalia* to which the people somewhat misguidedly adhered, not aware that their promises were only passing *figurae* of future New Testament promises of *spiritualia*. The Old Testament promise of Christ does not fit such a framework at all; as a result, it will be seen to play only a minor role in discussions and evaluations of the Old Testament.

As with Augustine, there are *two* levels of literal sense in the Bible, which are transposed into Old Testament-New Testament terms by Hugh. *Historia* (especially the Old Testament history) tends to find its place at the lower, unedifying level. The *doctrina* clearly given in the New Testament is equivalent to the normative-literal sense. The question remains open whether the New Testament will now function as truly normative, on the basis of its clear *doctrina,* or whether, in consistency with the unique significative character of the biblical events, it will be viewed as a book whose theological meaning for the future (that is, for us) is also obscure, therefore needing to be unlocked by a hermeneutical key lying beyond its scope, such as the Spirit-endowed Church, or *homo spiritualis*.

For Augustine, "letter" and "spirit" meant law and grace, and the hermeneutical transposition into Old Testament-New Testament terms was quite natural: what was really meant and intended in the Old Testament law was that very grace which has now appeared, which allows both spiritual understanding of the law (reflected in allegorical exegesis), and its true fulfillment in Christian life (reflected in tropological application).

By reducing the essential content of Scripture to credenda and agenda (*doctrina, lex*), and by subsuming anagogy under allegory, Hugh has encouraged the tendency to move away from emphasis upon the biblical promise and the virtue of hope.

One final consideration merits attention, and will recur:

formally, in this hermeneutical structure, words have the same function as they have in the medieval sacraments. They authoritatively describe the significance of the historical events, just as the sacramental *verba* describe the significance of the cultic events. In both cases, words give events "form"; biblical history is revealed to be a sacramental history. Thus, Hugh can speak for a host of medieval theologians when he says, "These things literally done, which represent spiritual things of this kind [that is, of the kind designated in allegory and anagogy], are called *sacramenta*." [25]

25. *De script.* c.3 (PL 175, 12 C).

III. THREE SCHOLASTIC THEOLOGIANS

Peter Lombard

In the third book of his *Sentences,* Peter Lombard provides several interesting insights into the literal and spiritual senses of Scripture and sets the scholastic standard for the function of the concept of *promise* in describing the relation between the Old and New Testaments. His discussion on these points, at the threshold of Book IV, which concerns the sacraments, is in a sense equivalent to comment in other types of literature on Tyconius' third rule, since the problem of spirit and letter is addressed, and the hermeneutical implications of Augustine's law-grace interpretation are made clear.

In the midst of his discussion of the commandment "Non occides," Lombard attempts to show the difference between its literal and spiritual meanings. According to the letter, it forbids killing, but according to the spirit, it prohibits even the will to kill. But this deepening, this *superadditio,* of the commandment is given in the letter of the Gospel, for "the letter of the Gospel expresses something which the letter of the law did not express." In fact, "the letter of the Gospel expresses the spiritual understanding, that is, the understanding which spiritual men have, and according to which one lives spiritually."[1]
The Gospel letter is thus at once literal and spiritual: its theo-

1. Peter Lombard, *Libri IV Sententiarum,* Bk. III (cited hereafter as III *Sent.*) d. 37 c.3 (2nd ed. [Quaracchi, 1916], II, 718): "huic mandato secundum litteram fit superadditio in Evangelio, quia littera Evangelii exprimitur, quod legis littera non exprimebatur. Evangelii littera exprimit intelligentiam spiritualem, id est, quam spirituales habent, et secundum quam spiritualiter vivitur."

logical meaning is clearly given in its grammatical sense. The letter of the *law,* by contrast, expresses only the "carnal" sense — in other words, that which carnal men have and live by.[2] Here again is a clear example of the literal sense of the New Testament providing the spiritual understanding of the Old; the New Testament "spirit" (that is, true meaning) is patent in its letter. The New Testament, therefore, contains the normative-literal correction and perfection of the unedifying Old Testament letter.

Despite this difference between the Testaments, however, Lombard finds a fundamental unity between them: the Decalogue and the Gospel are united in the *moralia* they teach (the prohibition of killing, after all, remains), although they are diverse in *caeremonialia*.[3] This distinction regarding the Old Testament law repeats the thought of Augustine, and is part of the medieval consensus. Although the moral law receives a certain *superadditio,* it is not essentially changed. Grace merely allows it to function properly, so that it ceases to be a "killing letter." [4]

    2. III *Sent.* d. 37 c.4 (II, 718): "littera Legis sensum carnalem [exprimit], id est, quem carnales habent, et secundum quem carnaliter vivitur; cui facta est superadditio."
    3. III *Sent.* d. 40 c.3 (II, 734): "Praecepta etiam diversa quantum ad caeremonialia: nam quantum ad moralia sunt eadem, sed plenius in Evangelio continentur."
    4. III *Sent.* d. 40 c.2 (II, 734): "Si vero quaeritur, quam dicat Apostolus litteram occidentem, ea certe est Decalogus, qui non dicitur littera occidens, eo quod mala sit Lex, sed quia, prohibens peccatum, auget concupiscentiam et addit praevaricationem, nisi liberet gratia, quae gratia non sic abundat in Lege, ut in Evangelio; Lex ergo bona est, et tamen occidit sine gratia." This, in summary, is what Augustine teaches in *De sp. et lit.*: without grace, the law kills; with grace, it is the same as the Gospel. Artur Landgraf gives further texts from Lombard that explicate this position more fully in "Die Gnadenökonomie des Alten Bundes nach der Lehre der Frühscholastik," *ZKT* 57 (1933), 237 f.; for other twelfth-century theologians, see pp. 230 ff.

Where the old and new dispensations substantially differ, however, is in promises and sacraments. Here, Lombard picks up an idea that has already been encountered in Saint Augustine: the promises of the Old Testament are earthly; those of the new are heavenly. Lombard writes: "The promises are different: there, earthly things are promised; here, heavenly. The sacraments are also different, because those were only signifying grace, while these confer it." [5]

Because it appeared in Lombard's *Sentences* just at the end of the third book, this manner of comparing and contrasting the Old and New Testaments became standard for his many commentators. It also played a prominent role in commentaries on the Psalms. Helping and promoting this notion of promise, as against that in which the Old Testament contains inviolable promises, was the hermeneutical schema of *signum* and *res*, laid out by Hugh of Saint Victor and summarized in neat and coherent scientific theory by Saint Thomas.

Bonaventura

Before turning to Aquinas, one should observe some striking continuities between Hugh and Aquinas' Franciscan contemporary Bonaventura. The continuity appears in their treatment of the anagogical sense of Scripture. It will be recalled that Hugh incorporated this as a part of allegorical interpretation having to do with heavenly mysteries, suggesting a mystical rather than futuristic notion of *anagoge*. This tendency is repeated in Alexander of Hales and accentuated further by Bonaventura. Unlike Hugh, Bonaventura includes the anagogical as a separate sense. But he defines it as "that by which we are taught how God is to be adhered to" [6] — a definition

5. III *Sent.* d. 40 c.3 (II, 734): "diversa sunt promissa: ibi terrena, hic caelestia promittit; diversa etiam Sacramenta, quia illa tantum significant, haec conferunt gratiam." Cf. Landgraf, "Die Gnadenökonomie," pp. 234 ff., for the widespread consensus on this point.

6. Bonaventura, *De reductione artium ad theologiam* 5, in *Tria Opus-*

which, rather than supporting a more eschatological view, gives special place to mysticism.

Bonaventura describes Scripture's three-fold spiritual content as follows: "The whole of Holy Scripture teaches these three things, namely, the eternal generation and incarnation of Christ [*sensus allegoricus*], the order of living [*moralis*] and the union of God and the soul [*anagogicus*]."[7] The great teachers of the anagogical sense, Bonaventura continues, are the contemplatives. Dionysius the Areopagite and Richard of Saint Victor are the classic representatives of this spiritual art.[8]

Thus, one might expect the concept of promise to support the desire for mystical union rather than the hope for the future. This is in fact the case in Bonaventura's expansion of Lombard's Book III, Distinction 40. In the first question, Bonaventura answers an Objection that seeks to minimize the difference between the old and the new laws by pointing out that *both* have promises and threats. In response, Bonaventura points out that only *promissiones temporales* were made in the old law, while in the new there are "promissiones aeternae, quibus Dominus promittit semetipsum nobis in praemium: eternal promises, in which the Lord promises himself to us as the reward."[9]

In the next Question, the effect of this eternal promise of

---

cula (Quaracchi, 1938), p. 372 (cited hereafter as *De reduct. art.*): "In omnibus enim sacrae Scripturae libris praeter *litteralem* sensum, quem exterius verba sonat, concipitur triplex sensus *spiritualis*, scil. *allegoricus*, quo docemur quid sit credendum de Divinitate et humanitate; *moralis*, quo docemur quomodo vivendum sit; et *anagogicus*, quo docemur, qualiter est Deo adhaerendum." (Italics mine.)

7. *De reduct. art.* 5 (p. 372): "Unde tota sacra Scriptura haec tria docet, scil. Christi aeternam generationem et incarnationem, vivendi ordinem et Dei et animae unionem."

8. *De reduct. art.* 5 (p. 373).

9. III *Sent.* d. 40 a. un. q. 1 ad 5, in *Opera Omnia* (Quaracchi, 1882–1902), III, 886. Continuing an Augustinian vein, Bonaventura adds that the threats and promises of the old law generated *timor* rather than *amor*.

the new law is described: it excites man to love (*amor*) of eternal things, and this love is the *amor caritatis*.[10] In the old law it was different. On the basis of its promises, man was not stirred to spiritual love. Furthermore, the Old Testament precepts did not direct him to "iustitia interior," nor did its sacraments act as effective aids for fulfilling the law. Therefore, the Old Testament man did not attain justification.[11]

The above, it is important to know, is part of Bonaventura's answer to the question of how one is to understand the letter as "killing" and the spirit as "life-giving" (again, 2 Cor. 3:6 is the problem). Here, very decisively, the question has been answered in Old Testament/New Testament terms. The hermeneutical divide between letter and spirit has been drawn emphatically between the Old and New Testaments, and at the expense of the old dispensation.

Yet like Lombard before him, Bonaventura does not wish to suggest a difference in the content of the two laws; rather, it is the manner in which they are *observed* and *understood* that counts. According to its literal observance, the law was killing because it served only to make guilt manifest, and because it did not provide the help of grace. Instead, it provided the occasion for concupiscence, and so dragged one down to death.[12]

---

10. III *Sent.* d. 40 a. un. q. 2 concl. 1 (III, 888): "in Lege nova . . . promissa excitant hominem ad amorem aeternorum, qui est amor caritatis."

11. III *Sent.* d. 40 a. un. q. 2 concl. 2 (III, 888): "in Lege erant promissa temporalia et precepta exterius regulantia et sacramenta figuralia; et sic ratione promissorum non excitabatur homo ad amorem spiritualem, ratione preceptorum non dirigebatur ad iustitiam interiorem, ratione Sacramentorum non adiuvabatur, ut posset faciliter Legem ipsam implere: et ideo deerat sibi iustificatio."

12. III *Sent.* d. 40 a. un. q. 2 concl. 3 (III, 888): "Et quia erat ibi ostensio culpae, et non aderat adiutorium gratiae; dabatur per consequens occasio ipsi concupiscentiae, ut traheret ad mortem; et ideo Lex Moysaica secundum litteralem sensum dicitur lex occidens per occasionem, non per causam." The word "occasio" is in reference to Rom. 7:8: "Occasione autem accepta, peccatum per mandatum operatum est in me omnem concupiscentiam"; cf. vs. 11.

By contrast, the old law can also be dealt with "according to spiritual understanding (*intellectus*), and thus, in a way, it agrees with the evangelical law, and those who were observing the law spiritually were evangelical men, for the law was pregnant with the Gospel." [13] Thus, in the time of the old dispensation, the law, if it was spiritually understood, functioned in exactly the same way as the Gospel functions now: it was leading to salvation via spiritual understanding and fulfillment. For the difference lies totally in the aid of grace that was normally absent in the old law, but which the new law carries with it, of itself.[14]

This aid of grace, this spiritual *intellectus* of the old law, was reserved for "special persons" of the old dispensation, Bonaventura observes. For those persons, there was simply no *differentia* in the two laws.[15] For them, "the law was *conformis* to the Gospel." [16]

13. III *Sent.* d. 40 a. un. q. 2 concl. 2 (III, 888): "Lex vetus dupliciter potest observari et intellegi, videlicet secundum intellectum spiritualem; et sic quodam modo concordat cum lege evangelica, et qui spiritualiter Legem observabant viri evangelici erant, quia lex praegnans erat Evangelio." There was already a broad consensus on this point in the twelfth century; see Landgraf, "Die Gnadenökonomie," pp. 223–226. Landgraf quotes Praepositinus (d. c1210) as follows: "Erant tamen aliqui qui spiritualiter intelligebant [mandata] et illi iustificabantur et non pertinebant ad vetus testamentum, immo ad novum" (pp. 225 f.).

14. III *Sent.* d. 40 a. un. q. 2 ad 2 (III, 889). Bonaventura is here answering the objection that the same problem confronts one in the new law: everything depends on how the law is observed and understood. He replies: "dicendum quod non est simile hunc et inde, quia Lex secum portat onus et non habet annexum adiutorium secundum suum litteralem sensum. *Evangelium vero de se adiutorium habet ipsius gratiae*; et ita non praebet mortis occasionem." (Italics mine.) This is very close to the sacramental idea of *ex opere operato* with regard to the presence of grace in the Gospel word.

15. III *Sent.* d. 40 a. un. q. 1 resp. (III, 885): "est notandum, quod cum comparamus has leges ad invicem, hoc potest esse dupliciter: vel secundum statum communem, vel habito respectu ad statum specialis personae. Si habito respectu specialis personae, sic penes haec duo non est differentia."

16. III *Sent.* d. 40 a. un. q. 2 ad 5 (III, 889). Here, Bonaventura is

One may conclude, therefore, that the law was not really intended by God to be a "killing" law; rather, it was put at the service of a few spiritual men to lead them to salvation. This becomes clear when the question is raised why God should give such a thing as a "killing law." Bonaventura answers: "The Lord, in laying down the law, even though he gave it to the carnal in order to shatter their hardness, so that in a certain way they might be led by the hand to grace by recognizing their infirmity, nevertheless He *principally* gave it for the sake of those who were understanding it spiritually — who were being saved and were meriting through the keeping of this very law." [17]

Thus, so far as Old Testament existence is concerned, God gave special *intellectus* to special persons, which allowed them an advantage *coram Lege*. Without this special grace, however, the law would be misunderstood. In the same way, hermeneutically, what is commanded in the old law must be understood "spiritually" — in light of New Testament grace and Spirit.

I have gone to such length on this point in order to fill out the salient features of the medieval understanding of the rela-

---

answering the objection, brought from Bede, that the law saved prior to the time of the Gospel: "dicendum, quod Beda intelligit non de observantia litterali, sed de observantia spirituali, secundum quam Lex conformis erat Evangelio. Nos autem dicimus, Legem occidentem esse secundum observationem litteralem." Cf. the "concordat" in n. 13 above. Bonaventura's editors cite Augustine as the source of this view (III, 888, n. 8): "Spiritualiter intellecta [Lex vetus], Evangelium est." *Serm.* 25 c.2 n. 2: (PL 38, 168).

17. III *Sent.* d. 40 a. un. q. 2 ad 3 (III, 889): "dicendum, quod Dominus in latione Legis, etsi daret eam carnalibus ad confringendam eorum duritiam, ut quodam modo manuducerentur ad gratiam recognoscendo infirmitatem suam, *principaliter* tamen dabat eam propter *spiritualiter intelligentes*, qui salvabantur et merebantur in ipsius Legis observatione." (Italics mine.) The editors (III, 889, n. 5) again cite Augustine as originator of the first of the above uses of the law (to expose weakness and drive to grace): Augustine, *Ep.* 145, n. 3; *Ep.* 196, c.2, n. 5 f.; *De sp. et lit.* c.9, n. 15.

tion of the two testaments. Just as it has been shown that a schema according to which the Old Testament is *signum* and *figura* of the New Testament does not lend itself to a direct promise-fulfillment relationship, nor to the development of an understanding of the Old Testament people whereby their existence under the Mosaic and Abrahamic dispensation is at the same time of both historical and theological interest; so here is a further barrier to such a development in Old Testament exegesis. The Old Testament people have been divided into two camps: the carnal, ordinary folk who do not really understand what is going on (that is, who are living a kind of allegorical history which is leading them nowhere and will be edifying for Christians only *ex post facto incarnationis*), and the spiritual elite — the "special persons" who do not really *belong* to the old covenant any more, and therefore do not await the new with longing and hope in its promise, since they already participate in the new age. Furthermore, when the law, insofar as it is understood and observed spiritually, is the same as the gospel, it does not function as Paul's "pedagogue-until-Christ"; rather, aided by a premature grace, it already functions as the way of merit and salvation.

Needless to say, this classic medieval exposition of the relationship between law and gospel considerably narrows the scope of Old Testament exegesis — in fact, it all but eliminates that book from the sphere of theological interpretation and construction. For existence under the old covenant is viewed either as carnal, involving a misunderstanding of the law's intention (a misunderstanding which arises, however, from its literal meaning), or as spiritual in virtue of a proleptic membership in the New Testament community, in which case not the Old Testament but the New provides the entire theological content. Only in the New Testament is misunderstanding of the law prevented by the annexation of grace to the message.

As a consequence of this view, the Old Testament promises can nowhere function to awaken a theologically significant faith or hope for the new dispensation. There is no historical connection between the people of the two dispensations. Old Testament promises appear only in unfavorable comparison with the New Testament promises. Finally, the proper function of the New Testament promises is to provide incentive to fulfill the law; their role is to excite that *amor* which the law requires for its true fulfillment.

Thomas Aquinas

In Saint Thomas, the hermeneutic of Hugh and the law-grace theology of Bonaventura are encountered in harmonious combination. The focus here will be on the hermeneutical theory, wherein Aquinas furnished a scientific schema appropriate to the theological ideas we have already encountered. Before plunging into his abstract theory, however, I must briefly show his agreement with Bonaventura and Lombard regarding those key theological issues: the relations of letter and spirit, law and grace, Old Testament and New.

Old and New Testaments. — Thomas elaborates on the comparison of the two testaments, using several organic analogies: the New is the same as the Old in species, but perfect as against the imperfection of the other. The analogies of seed and tree, and of boy and man, are used to illustrate the relationship.[18]

---

18. *ST* I–II q. 91 a. 5 corp. (II, 1213a f.): The question is whether the two laws are "una tantum"; the answer includes the following analysis of the ways in which two things may be distinguished: "dupliciter . . . inveniuntur aliqua distingui. Uno modo, sicut ea quae sunt omnino specie diversa, ut equus et bos. Alio modo, sicut perfectum et imperfectum in eadem specie, sicut puer et vir. Et hoc modo lex divina distinguitur in legem veterem et legem novam." Cf. *ST* I–II q. 107 a. 3 corp. (II, 1342a), where the question is whether the new law is "contained" (*contineatur*) in the old. Thomas answers that containment can be understood *dupliciter,* spatially or "virtually": "Alio modo virtute, sicut effectus in causa, vel

The promises are of some importance for Thomas in contrasting the two laws: as with Lombard, the law is a principle of *continuity* between the testaments, while promise is a mark of their *discontinuity*.[19] Thomas bases this assertion on a quotation of Augustine's, to the effect that the Old Testament promises temporal things, while the New promises eternal life.[20] According to Thomas, in agreement with Bonaventura, the function of the New Testament promises is to support *caritas* rather than hope.[21]

Thomas adds an interesting dimension to this discussion in answer to an Objection that doubts whether this distinction can really be maintained, since it is a fact that in the Old Testament one can find promises of eternal things, and in the New one can find temporal promises.[22]

---

complementum in completo; sicut genus continet species potestate, et sicut tota arbor continetur in semine. Et per hunc modum nova lex continetur in veteri." Cf. the same article, ad 2 (1342b): "Nihil tamen prohibet maius in minori virtute contineri, sicut arbor continetur in semine."

19. This is crystal clear in Thomas' comment on Heb. 8:6-8, in *Opera Omnia* (Parma, 1852 ff.), XIII, 731b): "Ibi [in veteri testamento] promittebantur temporalia . . . Hic autem caelestia . . . Sic ergo istud melius est quantum ad id, quod Dominus hominibus promittit . . . quaedam vero [sunt], quae ad rectitudinem vitae, et ista sunt praecepta moralia, quae manent . . . Et sic manent praecepta eadem, sed promissa diversa. Item sacramenta sunt diversa; quia ibi erat figura tantum, hic autem figurae veritas expressa." Cited in Kenneth Hagen, "Luther's Lectures on Hebrews in the Light of Medieval Commentaries on Hebrews" (ThD dissertation, Harvard Divinity School, 1966).

20. *ST* I-II q. 91 a. 5 corp. (II, 1213b): "Et ideo Aug. dicit in IV *Contra Faust.*, quod 'temporalium rerum promissiones in Testamento veteri continentur, et ideo vetus appellatur; sed aeternae vitae promissio ad novum pertinet Testamentum.' " (The editors cite the Augustine quotation as IV *C. Faust.* c.2; *PL* 42, 217 f.) The same passage, slightly altered, is quoted in *ST* I-II q. 107 a. 1 obj. 2 (II, 1338a).

21. *ST* I-II q. 107 a. 1 ad 2 (II, 1339b): "Et ideo . . . lex nova . . . dicitur lex amoris. Et dicitur habere promissa spiritualia et aeterna, quae sunt obiecta virtutis, praecipue caritatis."

22. *ST* I-II q. 107 a. 1 obj. 2 (II, 1338a-b): "[Videtur quod lex nova non sit alia a lege veteri] Quia etiam in novo testamento promittuntur aliqua promissa temporalia . . . Et in veteri testamento sperabantur

Thomas' answer shifts attention from *promissio* to *caritas*: the latter is of decisive importance in contrasting the old and new laws. The spiritual grace poured into men's hearts constitutes the *principalitas* of the *nova lex*, for this leads man to do good works not on the basis of "extrinsic" promises and threats, but rather out of an internal, habitual love of virtue.[23] This shows a shift from the position which Thomas had taken in his *Sentence* commentary, where the question was answered on the basis of the quality of the reward.

Thomas admits, as did Bonaventura, that there were "some" in the old dispensation who "were in the main expecting spiritual and eternal promises." But they did not in fact really belong to the age in which they were living. They had "caritas and the grace of the Holy Spirit," and thus "they belonged to the new law." [24]

As with Lombard and Bonaventura, then, the old law, spiritually understood, functioned in the same way as the

---

promissa spiritualia et aeterna, secundum illud *Ad Hebr*. 11 [:16]: 'Nunc autem meliorem patriam appetunt, idest celestem,' quod dicitur de antiquis Patribus." His discussion here is an advance over that of his earlier commentary on Lombard, III *Sent*. d. 40 q. 1 a. 4 (Parma, 1858, VII/1, 449): he answers affirmatively the question as to whether in the old law only *temporalia* were promised: "non spiritualis promissio, sed temporalis in ea fieri debuit."

23. *ST* I–II q. 107 a. 1 ad 2 (II, 1339b): "Illi . . . qui habent virtutem [that is, infused grace, the *habitus virtutis*], inclinantur ad virtutis opera agenda propter amorem virtutis, non propter aliquam poenam aut remunerationem extrinsecam. Et idea lex nova, cuius principalitas consistit in ipsa spirituali gratia indita cordibus, dicitur lex amoris."

24. *ST* I–II q. 107 a. 1 ad 2 (II, 1339b): "Fuerunt tamen aliqui in statu veteris testamenti habentes caritatem et gratiam Spiritus Sancti, qui principaliter expectabant promissiones spirituales et aeternas. Et secundum hoc pertinebant ad legem novam." Cf. III *Sent*. d. 40 q. 1 a. 4 quaestiunc. III (VII/1, 449): Whatever there were of "eternal" or "spiritual" promises were hidden under the figure of *temporalia* – at least this was the case with the promise "generally made to everyone in the old law (de promissione communiter omnibus facta in veteri lege), non autem de illa quae fiebat specialiter ad aliquos perfectos viros, qui ad legem novam pertinebant."

Gospel. The "letter" of the law of which Paul speaks in 2 Cor. 3:6 "kills" only *accidentaliter*: "The letter of the law is said to kill . . . but not insofar as its moral commands are concerned, except accidentally, in that from that very law which prohibits sin, there was brought no help of grace against sin." [25] One can also say that its ceremonies are "killing" now, for they have been abrogated. But the basic thought is that the law was *intended* not to kill but to be accompanied by the sacraments of the church, through which grace is infused and justification is attained.[26]

Thus, Thomas' doctrine of justification by grace *alone* prevents any theological value from being accorded to the existence of the Old Testament people. The question therefore arises — a question that will be of vital importance in the study of Luther: is it necessary to qualify, or even to subvert, the absolute requirements of new age grace, as Thomas understands it, in order to allow the Old Testament to function theologically? Or, to anticipate a bit more: will it be necessary to state the doctrine of justification without recourse to the notion of sacramentally infused grace, in order to state it at all with regard to the Old Testament people?

As it stands, the situation of the Old Testament people is this: Thomas divides them, as does Bonaventura, into those on one side who seem unaware of their role in redemptive history, unaware that their life under the Mosaic dispensation is in *figura futurae;* [27] and those elite few on the other side who

25. III *Sent.* d. 40 q. 1 a. 3 (VII/1, 448): " 'Occidere' . . . legis littera dicitur . . . quantum ad moralia non, nisi accidentaliter, inquantum ex ipsa lege peccatum prohibente, et auxilia gratiae contra ipsum non ferente, infirmus periculum mortis sumebat."

26. III *Sent.* d. 40 q. 1 a. 3 (VII/1, 448): The law of Moses provided only *iustitia acquisita*; "iustitia autem infusa a solo Deo effective est; unde lex per opera eam inducere non potest: sed per legem novam talis inducitur iustitia, quia *per sacramenta ejus gratia confertur,* quae justificat formaliter." (Italics mine.)

27. The term comes from *ST* I–II q. 107 a. 2 ad 1 (II, 1341a).

"belong to the New Covenant" before its time and already enjoy its grace and gifts. The result is that no theological value is left to the situation of living before the time of Christ's grace, under the mere promise, whereby one would really belong to the old age in fact but to the new in faith and hope.[28]

For Thomas, then, the time before grace is a time of unequivocal not-having; having the promise is not theologically meaningful, because promises and threats are "extrinsic" and therefore inferior to inner grace. The time of promise is simply and without further comment contrasted to the time of fulfillment.[29] The old ceremonies were supported by the fact that they prefigured the promised future. Now that the promise is fulfilled, they have no place, for the time of promise is past.[30]

The Hermeneutical Theory.[31] — Thomas advanced the

28. It is not my purpose to urge that Thomas should have suggested this third alternative. I make the observation simply because in Perez of Valencia and in Luther just such an idea is found.

29. *ST* I–II q. 107 a. 2 corp. (II, 1340b): "lex nova exhibet quod lex vetus promittebat . . . Unde lex nova dicitur lex veritatis; lex autem vetus umbrae vel figurae." The old law could not justify, but it prefigured man's justification in its ceremonies, and promised that justification in words ("figurabat quibusdam caeremonialibus factis, et promittebat verbis").

30. *ST* I–II q. 107 a. 2 ad 1 (II, 1341a), where the Old Testament promises and ceremonies belong in the same category: "ex hoc ipso quod caeremonialia praecepta sunt impleta, perfectis his quae figurabantur, non sunt ulterius observanda; quia si observarentur, adhuc significaretur aliquid ut futurum et non impletum. *Sicut etiam promissio* futuri doni locum iam non habet, promissione iam impleta per doni exhibitionem." (Italics mine.)

31. I strive for brevity here, since Thomas' hermeneutical theory is well known. See Smalley, *The Study of the Bible*, pp. 292–308; Ebeling, *Evangelienauslegung*, pp. 128 ff., and "The Hermeneutical Locus of the Doctrine of God in Peter Lombard and Thomas Aquinas," *JThC* 3 (1967), 70–111 (originally in *ZThK* 61 [1964], 283–326); P. Synave, "La Doctrine de S. Thomas d'Aquin sur le sens littéral des Écritures," *Revue Biblique* 35 (1926), 40–65; T. F. Torrance, "Scientific Hermeneutics According to St. Thomas Aquinas," *Journal of Theological Studies* 13 (1962), 259–289; P. C. Spicq, *Esquisse d'une histoire de l'exégèse Latine au Moyen age* (Paris, 1944), pp. 273–288.

thinking of Augustine and Hugh of Saint Victor by insisting upon the univocity of the biblical words. Both predecessors had allowed multiple meanings to words, so that their spiritual senses were discerned by unveiling their multiple meanings. But Thomas is confronted by an Objection that such a theory generates "confusion and deception, and takes away argumentative rigor" (an important point for a dogmatic theologian), and he concedes the point. Words in the Bible do not have more than one meaning. The spiritual senses, therefore, "are not multiplied by the fact that one *vox* signifies many things, but because the things themselves, signified by the *voces,* are able to be the *signa* of other things." [32] Thus, distinguishing sharply what *things* do from what *words* do, Thomas provides a clear-cut definition of the *sensus litteralis* whereby words themselves mean one thing only. The *spiritual* senses are derived not from the words but from the connection between the things signified by the words (res^I) and a second thing (res^{II}).[33]

32. *ST* I q. 1 a. 10 obj. 1 (I, 10a); ad 1 (I, 10b): the Objection runs: "Multiplicitas enim sesuum in una scriptura parit confusionem et deceptionem, et tollit arguendi firmitatem." Thomas replies, "sensus [spirituales] isti non multiplicantur propter hoc quod una vox multa significet, sed quia ipsae res significatae per voces, aliarum rerum possunt esse signa. Et ita etiam nulla confusio sequitur in Sacra Scriptura, cum omnes sensus fundentur super unum, scilicet litteralem, ex quo solo potest trahi argumentum."

33. *ST* I q. 1 a. 10 corp. (I, 10a): "Illa ergo prima significatio, qua voces significant res, pertinet ad primum sensum, qui est sensus historicus vel litteralis. Illa vero significatio, qua res significatae per voces iterum res alias significant, dicitur sensus spiritualis." Cf. *Quaestiones Quodlibetales* (cited hereafter as *Quodlib.*) VII q. 6 a. 1 corp. (Parma, 1859, IX, 563): "in sacra Scriptura manifestatur veritas dupliciter. Uno modo secundum quod res significantur per verba: et in hoc consistit sensus litteralis. Alio modo secundum quod res sunt figurae aliarum rerum: et in hoc consistit sensus spiritualis." The *Quodlib.* was written earlier than the *ST*, according to the chronology given in Etienne Gilson, *The Christian Philosophy of St. Thomas Aquinas* (New York, 1956), pp. 386 f., 392.

Now this in itself could have the effect on the exegesis of the Old Testament of releasing the exegete from the obligation to extract Christian doctrine from its words. Christian doctrine is, to be sure, everywhere prefigured in the Old Testament, but its *sensus historicus,* defined according to the intention of the human author,[34] means just what it says.

The advantage gained here in favor of historical exegesis is balanced by a loss in theological value: now there is no way to derive any "spiritual sense" from the Old Testament, since the first of the threefold spiritual senses, the allegorical, when applied to the Old Testament, refers to things done in the New Testament. The "*res*^{II}" that can bestow theological meaning on the Old Testament are all in the New Testament.[35] The Old Testament words themselves yield no spiritual sense. At the same time, this situation does not necessarily strip the Old Testament of all theological significance, since Thomas holds, with Augustine, that there is a normative-literal sense in the Bible (as well as the *sensus historicus*) — material which in its plain meaning teaches those things to which all Scripture is ordered, namely, "right faith and right action." [36] And the

34. Thomas' position in the *ST* is thus a departure from his earlier statement in the *Quodlib.* that the prophets, as "instrumental authors" of Scripture, intended several things in one word, because they "spoke concerning the present *facta* so that they also intended to signify the future (ita loquebantur de factis praesentibus, quod *etiam intenderunt futura significare*); and thus [answering the Philosopher] it is not impossible to understand several things at once, insofar as one thing is the figure of another" (*Quodlib.* VII q. 6 a. 1 ad 5 [IX, 563]). This opinion still harmonizes with the Augustinian idea that several humanly intended senses are contained under one letter — an idea abandoned in the *ST*. By then Thomas believed that multiple intention exists only in the *Divine* mind, as shall be seen. Perez of Valencia revived the older idea, as ch. VII shows.

35. *ST* I q. 1 a. 10 corp. (I, 10a): "Secundum ergo quod ea, quae sunt veteris legis, significant ea quae sunt novae legis, est sensus allegoricus."

36. *Quodlib.* VII q. 6 a. 2 corp. (IX, 564): "Veritas autem quam sacra Scriptura per figuras rerum tradit, ad duo ordinatur: scil. ad recte credendum, et ad recte operandum." Applied to the Old Testament, this statement *may* mean that the contents of the Old Testament can be "or-

possibility of this sort of material being also in the Old Testament has not been eliminated. All that has been denied theological validity is the historical part of the Old Testament. Nevertheless, as has been argued, the precision of Thomas' definition carved out an area of work for literal and historical exegesis.

A point that may have been even more important for the succeeding years is a kind of loophole in Thomas' theory, which tends to subvert the stringency of his definition of "literal." Whether this loophole is there because of Thomas' desire to "save" Augustine, or whether he would have included it anyway, is hard to decide. At any rate, Thomas is answering the Objection that multiple senses of words create confusion. Augustine had held the multiple-sense view, to which Thomas' reply, that words are univocal in meaning, runs counter. But before he takes the contrary position, Thomas allows this much: "Truly, the literal sense is that which the author intended; but the author of sacred Scripture is God, who comprehends in his *intellectus* all things at once. Therefore it is not inappropriate, as Augustine says . . . if even according to the literal sense there are several meanings in one letter of Scripture." [37]

---

dered" as follows: "in illo modo figurationis quo vetus testamentum figurat novum: et sic est *allegoricus*." (Italics mine.) But Thomas also quotes the Augustinian axiom: "nihil est quod occulte in aliquo loco sacrae Scripturae tradatur quod non alibi manifeste exponatur; unde spiritualis expositio semper debet habere fulcimentum ab aliqua litterali expositione" (*Quodlib*. VII q. 6 a. 1 ad 3 [IX, 563 f.]). In the next objection is a statement to which Aquinas himself holds: "nullus sensus preter litteralem habet robur ad aliquid confirmandum." The classic citation from Augustine is given in *ST* I q. 1 a. 10 ad 1 (I, 10b): "omnes sensus fundentur super unum, scilicet litteralem, ex quo solo potest trahi argumentum, non autem ex his quae secundum allegoriam dicuntur, ut dicit Aug. in epistola *Contra Vincentium*" (*Ep*. 93, c.8 [*PL* 33, 334]). This passage is part of Augustine's reply to a Donatist interpretation of Cant. 1:6, according to the mystical sense, supporting their exclusivistic notion of the Church.

37. *ST* I q. 1 a. 10 corp. (I, 10b): "Quia vero sensus litteralis est, quem auctor intendit; auctor autem Sacrae Scripturae Deus est, qui omnia

Perhaps Thomas did not see the implications of this statement. But alongside his definition of "literal sense," whereby the *human* intention is accounted for and the meaning of the words is found in the grammar, he provided an ultimate, *theological* definition. According to this definition, the *sensus litteralis* is that which the divine author intended. What is more, this divine-literal sense comprehends all the senses of Scripture — literal and spiritual, plain and hidden, present and future. What man comprehends only by stages, depending on what happens in history, God comprehends all at once, for the "intention" of the Divine Author embraces the whole course of redemptive history to its end. God, in his Providence, has seen fit to order the events of redemptive history in such a way that everything which happens in it — all the *res gestae* of Scripture — are capable of becoming signs of other things. To human beings, this significative character of things constitutes the threefold spiritual sense. But to God, these events (*res*^{I}, *res*^{II}, etc.) are stages in His "literal sense," his unfolding purpose in *Heilsgeschichte*.

The way is thus opened for a compelling new theological definition of *sensus litteralis* that can subvert Thomas' grammatical definition based on the human intention. Looking ahead in history, one can see how easy it will be to infer (if the *sensus litteralis* is simply what God intended) that the New Testament is the Old Testament's *literal* sense (not merely its spiritual or allegorical sense). For who could deny that the new dispensation is "what God intended" even in the Old Testament time? [38]

---

simul suo intellectu comprehendit; non est inconveniens, ut dicit Augustinus XII *Confess.* [c.31 (PL 32, 844)], si etiam secundum litteralem sensum in una littera Scripturae plures sint sensus."

38. I press this point because of what happened later (most clearly with Faber Stapulensis) and also because of its implications for the place of the Old Testament in the Church. When this point is reached, the Old Testament virtually disappears, for its whole meaning — literal, spiritual,

In summary, three important kinds of literal sense occur in Thomas' theory: the grammatical and historical, corresponding to the intention of the human author; the divine-literal, corresponding to the intention of the divine author and unfolded piecemeal to human beings; and the traditional normative-literal, to which the spiritual senses apparently are to conform. I say "apparently" because, as will be shown, the redemptive-historical schema of Thomas seem capable of overwhelming it.

The problem now concerns the relation between the second and third senses: are they contradictory, harmonious, or in tension with each other? They are significantly different, in any event, for the third is entirely available in the Bible, while the second is not there *in toto*.

The Spiritual Senses. — The spiritual senses of Scripture correspond to the unfolding of redemptive history. But how does one discern the theological meaning of the biblical history? The answer for Thomas, as for Hugh, is that this meaning can only be revealed — indeed, can only be constituted outside of God's mind — by later history. The spiritual meaning of the first *res,* which is going to be the sign of something else, can be revealed only upon the occurrence of a second *res,* which in turn points to a third one, and so on until the end of history. For all of biblical history, including those things that were done in Christ, is *signum*.[39]

---

and all — is outside and beyond itself, and there is no longer much reason for having it in the canon.

39. *ST* I q. 1 a. 10 corp. (I, 10a f.): "Secundum ergo quod ea, quae sunt veteris legis, significant ea quae sunt novae legis, est sensus allegoricus; secundum vero quod ea, quae in Christo sunt facta . . . sunt signa eorum, quae nos agere debemus, est sensus moralis; prout vero significant ea, quae sunt in aeterna gloria, est sensus anagogicus." Cf. *Quodlib.* VII q. 6 a. 2 ad 5 (IX, 564), in which the spiritual senses depend on the occurrence of later things: "ideo quandoque in sacra Scriptura secundum sensum litteralem dicitur aliquid de priori quod *potest spiritualiter de posterioribus exponi,* sed non convertitur." (Italics minc.)

The outcome of this theory seems to be that no *historical* event can be of unique significance, or have that once-for-all character which seemed to belong to the normative-literal sense. All historical material — even the Christ-events — is subject to further interpretation, because "things passing through their course signify something else: res cursum suum peragentes significant aliquid aliud." [40] This *aliquid aliud* which everything signifies is that which is to be believed and done, and Scripture is supposed to contain such material somewhere in its normative literal sense.

But a question arises here: is *everything* that is to be believed and loved found within Scripture? Can the Bible itself, which after all belongs to a past stage in God's unfolding intention, be said not only to contain but also to circumscribe the whole scope of *credenda, diligenda,* and *speranda*? How can the entire normative-literal sense of Scripture be held within the Bible itself, now that centuries have passed?

The answer depends upon which of two fundamental answers one gives to the question, Why is the Bible a unique book? One may answer that it is unique in virtue of the significative character of the biblical events, a quality that makes spiritual senses possible (so Thomas, following Hugh [41]); or

---

Thus, Scripture can be expounded in all four, three, two, or only one sense, depending upon what stage in *Heilsgeschichte* the *letter* refers to: "unde ea quae ad litteram de ipso Christo capite dicuntur possunt exponi et *allegorice,* referendo ad corpus ejus mysticum; et *moraliter,* referendo ad actus nostros, qui secundum ipsum debent reformari; et *anagogice,* inquantum in Christo est nobis iter gloriae demonstratum." (Italics mine.) What is said *de littera* of the Church can be explained also *moraliter* and *anagogice*; what is said *moraliter* in the letter can also be explained *anagogice*; finally, "illa vero quae secundum sensum litteralem pertinet ad statum gloriae, nullo alio sensu consueverunt exponi; eo quod ipsa non sunt figura aliorum, sed ab omnibus aliis figurata."

40. *Quodlib.* VII q. 6 a. 3 corp. (IX, 564 f.): "spiritualis sensus sacrae Scripturae accipitur ex hoc quod res cursum suum peragentes significant aliquid aliud, quod per spiritualem sensum accipitur."

41. See *Quodlib.* VII q. 6 a. 3 corp. (IX, 565), where Thomas observes that all human books have only *sensus litteralis.*

one may locate the Bible's uniqueness in the fact that its literal sense expresses clearly everything that is to be believed, loved, and hoped. If one now follows out the logic of the first of these, the sign-character of past events becomes transparent as history unfolds, and new *res* appear in history to fulfill the old *res*. Thus, the New Testament exegetes the Old Testament. The literal sense of the New Testament provides a normative guide for the spiritual meaning of the Old Testament history. What has happened is that the locus of the normative-literal sense has shifted from the Old to the New Testament, for a new stage in God's intention (God's literal sense) is now revealed to men.

A Question about the New Testament. — The next question is: by what warrant does one now proceed beyond the literal to arrive at the spiritual interpretation of the New Testament? There is no "third testament" (as book) which has been given to exegete it spiritually (that is, allegorically and tropologically, which means ecclesiologically and existentially for the present). But new *res have* appeared, presumably intended by God, of which the New Testament *res* must be the signs. So where now is to be found that authoritative, normative word which reveals the spiritual meaning of what has happened? The obvious answer is: the new *res significata*, of which Christ is the *res significans,* is his mystical body, the Church, endowed with the Spirit. The answer is obvious because the Church is the allegorical sense of the deeds of Christ, just as Christ is the allegorical sense of the deeds of the Old Testament. Would it not now be perfectly consistent to say that the locus of the *sensus litteralis* has shifted again, in the same way that it shifted from the Old to the New Testament? And to say that the new normative-literal word is the word not only about, but of, the Church?

It is true that the Bible contains so-called eternal truths — doctrine and law. But redemptive history did not end at the close of the Bible, and the manifold significative character of the New Testament events will never be exhausted until the end of the world. For only the anagogical sense can be the ultimately literal sense of the historical process itself, since God Himself is the *res ultima* toward which everything is intended and ordered.

The questions for the New Testament, then, are: does it definitively contain all *doctrina* and *lex* necessary for Christians until the end of history? Or, just as the literal sense of the New Testament determines the spiritual sense of the Old Testament, does the "literal sense of the Church" — what the Church teaches — now determine the spiritual sense of the New Testament?

The logic of this second alternative seems rather compelling, for one peculiarity of this hermeneutic is that the words of the text first get theological value when they describe what is already present (res^{II}) in the light of what is past (res^{I}). Theological, or spiritual, meaning lies in the special language that performs this function of describing the relationship between past and present events. Words do not have theological or spiritual meaning, according to this hermeneutic, in virtue of reference to the future. Thus, when the future comes to pass and becomes the present, new words have to be spoken to explain the theological connection, or relationship, between the past and the new present. In this way, that which the word of old only signified in a hidden way can now be revealed.

In this hermeneutical state of affairs lies the fundamental rationale for that which H. A. Oberman has called "Tradition II" and "Tradition III." [42] There is need for a new source of

42. See H. A. Oberman, *The Harvest of Medieval Theology* (Cambridge, 1963), pp. 365–375. Oberman's categories of Tradition I, II, and III are defined by the roles that Scripture and tradition (or Church) play in the designation of the sources and interpretation of revelation. Tradition I designates a single source of revelation (the Bible) and explicitly denies extrascriptural revelatory tradition; it "represents the sufficiency of Holy Scripture as understood by the Fathers and doctors of the church.

revelation, beyond the Scripture, which can take theological account of the ongoing *cursus rerum*. The need for this second, extrabiblical source arises because the events of the New Testament are *signa* whose *res* are found in the Church. The justification for this second source is more than merely logical, however. Appeal can be made at this point to a clear biblical promise, quoted repeatedly in medieval literature and used in precisely this connection by Henry Totting of Oyta: Christ's promise of the Spirit to lead his Church into all truth.

The thought-structure for later developments is now complete in its broad outlines: the promise of Christ to the Church can now emerge as the third dimension of a schema in which *doctrina, lex,* and *promissio* are three kinds of normative Biblical word that are not susceptible of further spiritual or figurative interpretation. The correlate of *promissio* — the response to it — is not so much hope and trust in the promise itself as faith (understood as assent) in the judgment of the Church. When the promise to the Church is made the primary one, the way is clear for the claim that all the other biblical promises (such as that of the Spirit or of eternal life) are subject to the Church's interpretation of them, since Christ has granted her the normative key to Scripture. As a consequence, the hermeneutical function of promise is transferred out of the sphere of biblical interpretation into ecclesiology. The

---

In the case of disagreement between these interpreters, Holy Scripture has the final authority" (p. 372). The validity of ecclesiastical traditions is not regarded as self-supporting. Tradition II, which allows for extrabiblical oral tradition, "refers to the written *and* unwritten part of the apostolic message as approved by the Church . . . The hierarchy is seen to have its 'own' oral tradition, to a certain undefined extent independent, not of the Apostles, but of what is recorded in the canonical books" (p. 373). In Tradition III (which Oberman describes in "Quo Vadis? Tradition from Irenaeus to Humani Generis," *Scottish Journal of Theology* 16 [1963], esp. 248 and 253 f.), the contemporary faith and teaching of the Church clearly stand over both Scripture and tradition as their *norma normans.*

question now is: who in the Church is authorized to expound the normative-literal sense of Scripture? The problem is removed from the Bible itself, and hence outside the sphere of this investigation.

IV. THE PROLOGUE LITERATURE: NICHOLAS OF LYRA

The primary focus from now on will be the hermeneutical theories of biblical commentators, as expounded in their own prefaces or prologues to scriptural commentaries. These writers will include Nicholas of Lyra (Franciscan, d. 1340), Paul of Burgos (Dominican, d. 1435), Matthias Doering (Franciscan, d. 1469), James Perez of Valencia (Augustinian Hermit, d. 1490), Jacobus Faber Stapulensis (secular, d. 1536), and Martin Luther (Augustinian Hermit, excommunicated 1520).

The interpretation of these writers is aided by inclusion of a few additional figures, who help fill in certain important gaps. Between Lyra and Burgos, whose prologues appear together in the late medieval *Glossenbibeln*, there is a gap of a full century, which is frequently ignored in the historiography of hermeneutics. I have attempted to fill in somewhat by considering two theologians not primarily known for their work on the Scriptures: the German Nominalist Henry Totting of Oyta (d. 1397), and the great French conciliarist of the Schism, Jean Gerson (d. 1429). In addition, after the investigation of Perez, the scene of systematic school-theology is revisited briefly, represented by Gabriel Biel and others, to see what changes have occurred since the thirteenth century which might bear on hermeneutics and the Old Testament. Alongside of Faber I examine a tractate written by another contemporary of Luther, and one of his first literary opponents, Sylvester Prierias (Dominican, d. 1523).

Nicholas of Lyra, perhaps the greatest Christian commentator of Scripture in the Middle Ages, is customarily described as one who, in his *Postilla* (written 1322-1330),[1] adopted the hermeneutical system of Thomas and applied it to his exegesis of the whole Bible. Lyra is admired for his protest against excessive allegorization and for his efforts at understanding the literal, historical sense of the Scriptures.[2] It is certainly correct that in his own prologues to the Bible, Lyra quotes certain of Thomas' principles almost verbatim.[3]

Contingentia *and* Prophetia

It must not be forgotten that Lyra was a Franciscan contemporary of William of Occam (d. 1349), and that between him and Thomas had come John Duns Scotus (d. 1308). Scotus had criticized Saint Thomas at several points, one of which was the question of whether theology is a science,[4] that is, whether it embodies knowledge in the strictest sense. Without discussing the whole question, I wish only to point out what the two great doctors say about *contingentia* — contingent, temporal events — in the theological enterprise.

1. Henri de Lubac, *Exégèse Médiévale*, II/2 (Paris, 1964), 344. For further detail, see Hailperin, *Rashi*, pp. 138 f.
2. Beryl Smalley, "The Bible in the Middle Ages," in D. E. Nineham, ed., *The Church's Use of the Bible, Past and Present* (London, 1963), p. 66; Hailperin, *Rashi*, pp. 143 f., 216, 252, etc. De Lubac's treatment of Lyra is devoted largely to an attempt to show Lyra's love for the spiritual senses, but he gets textual support mostly out of Lyra's exegesis of the Apocalypse and Canticles (*Exégèse*, II/2, 345-348).
3. Ebeling, *Evangelienauslegung*, p. 131, nn. 81, 82, quotes the relevant passages. Werbeck regards their hermeneutical presuppositions as "essentially identical" (*Perez*, p. 120).
4. The history of hermeneutics in the late medieval period, like late medieval theology itself, is more than a pale shadow of Saint Thomas. What I include of it in the present study no more than scratches the surface of the problems. Ebeling and others have observed that the genesis of Reformation theology implies and involves the appearance of a new hermeneutic; by the same token, developments in medieval theology involve (or at least appear to invite) changes in biblical hermeneutics. This has already been seen in the fact that Augustine's interpretation of letter

In the first question of his *Summa Theologiae,* "Whether sacred doctrine is knowledge," Thomas is faced with the following Objection (obj. 2): knowledge is not concerned with individuals (*singularia*), but sacred doctrine is; therefore, theology is not knowledge.[5] This is an important question, for at stake is the status of historical events as theological data. Thomas, who is arguing the affirmative of the question, answers the objection with ease: it is true, he says, that *singularia* are dealt with in sacred doctrine, but this is not because theology deals *principaliter* with such things. Rather, "they are introduced at times as examples of life, as in the moral sciences, and at other times in order to demonstrate the authority of the men through whom divine revelation proceeds, upon which [revelation] holy scripture or doctrine is founded."[6] This answer corresponds with Thomas' hermeneutical principles, whereby historical events function as *signa* and *figurae* in support of the real subject matter of theology: *lex* and *doctrina.*

Scotus, and the Nominalist tradition after him, emphasized more than did Thomas the integral role of "contingents" in theology. In the prologue of his *Ordinatio,* for example, Scotus asserts: "I say that theology contains not only *necessaria,* but *contingentia.* This is obvious, for all truths about God —

---

and spirit as law and grace resulted in hermeneutical transposition into Old Testament/New Testament terms. In Ch. IX I ask whether the resurgence of semi-Pelagianism in the late medieval period, which questions the absolute priority of grace in justification, has implications favorable to renewed theological interest in the Old Testament.

5. *ST* I q.1 a.2 obj.2 (I, 3a): "Scientia non est singularium. Sed sacra doctrina tractat de singularibus, puta de gestis Abrahae, Isaac et Iacob, et similibus. Ergo sacra doctrina non est scientia."

6. *ST* I q.1 a.2 ad 2 (I, 3b): "Dicendum quod singularia traduntur in sacra doctrina, non quia de eis principaliter tractetur; sed introducuntur tum in exemplum vitae, sicut in scientiis moralibus, tum etiam ad declarandum auctoritatem virorum per quos ad nos revelatio divina processit, super quam fundatur sacra scriptura seu doctrina."

whether as triune or as regards one of the divine persons — in which he is considered *ad extra*, are contingent [truths], as for instance that God creates, that the Son is incarnated, and so forth . . . Therefore the primary structural parts of theology are two, namely necessary and contingent truths." [7] This incorporation of contingents and particulars as part of the very subject matter of theology certainly leaves room for the development of an idea of historical events quite different from that of Thomas. So does the basic outlook of the Franciscan tradition regarding the nature of theology as a primarily "practical" rather than "speculative" enterprise, whose main purpose is to make clear the will rather than the mind of God.[8] I would further point to the different dualism applied here by Scotus and the Nominalists, as against that of Thomas. In the former, the primary attribute of God is his will, and it is theology's task to explicate what in fact God has freely willed and established (the *contingentia* of the *potentia ordinata*). Theology spells this out against the background of God's sovereign freedom (the *necessaria* of the *potentia absoluta*), which at least in theory may become actually operative in history,

7. John Duns Scotus, *Ordinatio,* prol. pars 3 q.3 par.150 (in *Opera Omnia,* I [Vatican City, 1950], 101): "dico quod theologia non tantum continet necessaria, sed contingentia. Quod patet, quia omnes veritates de Deo, sive ut trino sive de aliqua persona divina, in quibus comparatur ad extra, sunt contingentes, et quod Deus creat, quod Filius est incarnatus, et huiusmodi . . . igitur primae partes integrales theologiae sunt duae, scil. veritates necessariae et contingentes." Gabriel Biel follows and quotes Scotus on this point: "theologia habet tractare de quolibet ente in particulari, quia de deo creatore omnium et causa communissima" (*Collectorium in quattuor libros sententiarum,* Bk. I [Basel, 1512; cited hereafter as I *Sent.*], prol, q.9 concl.3 J. Scotus and Occam do not allow theology to be called, properly, "knowledge" (*scientia*); its only resemblance thereto is the certainty of its conclusions. But theology's involvement with *contingentia,* and its dependence on the testimony of others, disqualify it. See the succinct summary of Johannes Altenstaig, "Theologia," in *Vocabularius theologie* (Hagenau, 1517), fol.253va.

8. See Oberman, *Harvest,* p. 374 n.40.

breaking unpredictably into its order with a new order of things.

In Thomas, the dualism is between singulars and universals: theology's task is to transcend the particulars of history, breaking through to the universal, supernatural truths that are signified or exemplified in the history. In the Scotist-Nominalist tradition, then, one would expect greater emphasis on historical particulars as manifestations of the liberality and mercy of God, while for Thomas, as already shown, the *res gestae* of history serve as *signa* of dogmatic truths, as *exempla* for morals, and as pedigrees of authority for those through whom divine revelation is given to man.

With regard to the Franciscan Lyra, no obvious expression of these developments appears in his prologues to the Bible. As already noted, he adopts Thomas' basic hermeneutical notion of things (including historical events) as capable of serving as signs of other things. Nor does he raise the Scotistic point against Thomas. However, in his Preface to the *Postilla* on the Psalms, the Scotist-Nominalist interest in *contingentia* comes through sharply. Lyra argues, against Thomas, that David is a greater prophet than Moses, for even though it is true that Moses was momentarily granted the *visio dei,* a glimpse of the Divine Essence (the decisive argument in Moses' favor, according to Thomas), David spoke more clearly about the events of the Messiah.[9] And these events are among future contingents, knowledge of which is among the best evidence of truly extraordinary prophetic gifts.[10] More im-

9. Thomas had granted David's superior foresight, but valued the experience of Moses more highly. Lyra's comment: "david plenius et clarius expressit mysteria christi quam moyses. lex autem vetus et prophetie ordinabantur ad christum sicut ad finem . . . et ideo cum finis sit nobilior his quae sunt ad finem, prophetia david videtur sortiri quaedam excellentiam" (*Prefatio in postillam super Psalterium* [Basel, 1502], III, fol. 84[va] E).

10. Pref. (84[rb] D): "ille qui est de futuris contingentibus videtur perfectior, quia futura sunt magis remota a cognitione nostra quam praesentia vel preterita."

portant is Lyra's contention that the vision of the Divine Essence, on the one hand, and the prophetic mode, on the other, are by definition mutually exclusive, because in the *visio dei* one breaks through the status of *fides*, which the prophet, as a *viator*, does not transcend.[11]

Lyra, then, does not want to allow mystical categories to be determinative for his understanding of the prophecy,[12] which is concerned with the contingent and the historical. There is a connection between this understanding of prophecy and Lyra's interest in the historical-literal sense of Scripture, his urgent protest against the excesses of allegorical interpretation, together with the historical and linguistic orientation of his whole *Postilla* on the Old Testament.[13] His approach to Scripture is not merely owing to an accidental turn of mind, without theological relevance; he works with a sharpened

11. *Pref.* (84va E): "claritas cognitionis actum prophetandi excludens non potest constituere excellentiorem gradum prophetiae . . . visio autem divine essentie excludit actum prophetandi, sicut et actum fidei."

12. Oberman has established an important link between the study of mysticism and that of hermeneutics by isolating what he calls "exegetical mysticism," represented by James Perez of Valencia and others (" 'Simul Gemitus et Raptus': Luther und die Mystik," in Ivar Asheim, ed., *The Church, Mysticism, Sanctification and the Natural in Luther's Thought* [Philadelphia, 1967], pp. 45 ff.). In the light of this insight, it is interesting to notice that Thomas' definition of high prophecy is identical with his definition of mysticism: in both, the *definiens* is the *visio Dei*. Lyra, by contrast, flatly rejects such an identification, bringing forward rather the knowledge, or the *fides*, of future contingents as a decisive factor in prophecy. William of Occam, with his interest in the question whether contingency and freedom in history can be protected if God knows the future, allows the possibility that the prophets really knew future contingents by evident knowledge (*Quodlibeta Septem* IV q.4 ad 3 [Strasbourg, 1491]): "dico quod prophete habuerunt talem noticiam evidentem de futuris contingentibus. Vel potest dici quod deus revelavit eis tales veritates creando in eis solam fidem. Sed quid sit de facto nescio, quia non est mihi revelatum."

13. Gerhard Ebeling has observed that Lyra's Prologue does not yet reveal the unique attention that Lyra pays to historical and (in terms of his own time) critical problems of the Old Testament text, and the care with which he attempts to understand the Psalms in terms of their own context (*Evangelienauslegung*, p. 130; cf. Hailperin, *Rashi, passim*).

awareness that *res gestae contingentiae* are somehow an irreducible part of the subject matter of theology.

Irony of the Double Literal Sense

Lyra's theory of a "double literal sense" (*duplex sensus litteralis*) is well known in the secondary literature. But no one has pointed out the element of irony that appears when one knows what his intention was and then compares it to the results to which it led in later medieval hermeneutical theory.

As to his intention, Lyra is reminiscent of Hugh of Saint Victor: both have harsh words for contemporary allegorizers.[14] Lyra follows Saint Thomas fairly closely in defining the four senses of Scripture.[15] The fact that he reintroduces future hope in connection with the definition of the anagogical sense is certainly consistent with the nonmystical and future-oriented bent observed in his disagreement with Thomas on the Moses-David issue.[16] Lyra takes special pains to insist that all the senses presuppose the literal sense as their *fundamentum* and norm.[17]

14. Lyra complains that the literal sense has become much obscured because of the too common practice of ignoring it in favor of mystical exegesis: "Sciendum etiam quod sensus litteralis est multum obumbratus, propter modum exponendi communiter traditum ab aliis, qui . . . parum tetigerunt litteralem sensum, et sensus mysticos intantum multiplicaverunt, quod sensus litteralis inter tot expositiones mysticas interceptus partim suffocatur" (*Prologus secundus de intentione auctoris et modo procedendi* [cited hereafter as *II Prol.*], fol. 3vb G).

15. Ebeling gives the texts of both Thomas and Lyra in "Luthers Psalterdruck vom Jahre 1513" (*ZThK* 50 [1953], p. 92 n.1.

16. *Prologus primus de commendatione sacre scripture in generali* (cited hereafter as *I Prol.*), fol. 3va E: "si res significate per voces referantur . . . ad significandum ea, quae sunt speranda in beatitudine futura, sic est sensus anagogicus." Thomas writes merely: "prout vero significant ea quae sunt in aeterna gloria, est sensus anagogicus" (*ST* I q.1 a.10 corp. [I, 10b]).

17. *II Prol.* (fol. 3va F f.): "omnes tamen [sensus] presupponunt sensum litteralem tanquam fundamentum. Propter quod sicut edificium declinans a fundamento disponitur ad ruinam, sic expositio mystica dis-

So much for Lyra's clear intention. Now comes the innovation — his double-literal sense. This appears in his exposition of the Tyconian third rule. These rules (except the third) had to do with figurative interpretation of obscure texts. Strangely enough, Lyra does not tell how these rules — which he takes over from, and attributes to, Isidore of Seville (d. 636) — apply to the scriptural senses. Only in the explanation of the third rule is this problem dealt with.

After handing on the traditional explanation of the rule, Lyra advises that it can also be explained in a different way: "so that it ["letter"] can apply to a [second] literal sense which is just as literal as the first. In the light of this, one should consider that the same letter at times has a double literal sense." This can be shown by an illustration: "For example, in I Chron. 17, the Lord says of Solomon: 'I will be a father to him, and he will be like a son to me.' And this is understood as speaking of Solomon literally . . . Now this same authority, 'I will be as a father to him,' etc., is used by the Apostle, writing to the Hebrews, *as having been said literally of Christ.* This is evident for the following reason: the Apostle uses it to prove that Christ was greater than the angels. But such proof cannot be made through the mystical sense, as Augustine says." Lyra's conclusion is: "The aforesaid authority, then, was fulfilled literally in Solomon, yet less perfectly because he was a son of God by grace only; but in Christ [it is fulfilled] more perfectly, because he is son of God by nature. Now, although *each exposition is literal* simply speaking, still the second one, which concerns Christ, is [also] spiritual and mystical in a derived sense, in that Solomon was a figure of Christ." [18]

---

crepans a sensu litterali, reputanda est indecens et inepta." Lyra goes on, as did Thomas, to quote Augustine to the effect that only the literal sense is valid for argument, "vel declarationem alicuius dubii."

18. *II Prol.* (fol. 4ra B): "Potest etiam aliter exponi: ut referatur ad sensum litteralem tantum sicut et aliae. Circa quod considerandum, quod

It will no doubt come as a surprise to the modern reader that Paul was operating with Augustine's axiom, else he would not have appealed to an Old Testament passage for theological proof about Christ! Here is where the irony appears. For the first time in the literature, a New Testament reading of an Old Testament passage is dignified with the label "literal," and arguments are brought forward to defend it. Given Lyra's authority in the years that followed, it would now be easy for someone simply to dispense with the first of these literal senses (the historical) in favor of the more edifying second "literal" sense. The near-suffocation of the historical-literal meaning, about which Lyra complained, would now be able to proceed, armed with the apparent authority of Augustine, Thomas, and the foremost champion of historical exegesis in the late Middle Ages.

This step by Lyra is not really inconsistent with the thought of Saint Thomas, for Thomas had a comprehensive definition of "literal" as "that which God intends" — which could be brought to bear to defend Lyra's move. Furthermore, in harmony with Thomas' theory, Lyra makes no appeal to the intention of the Old Testament author to support the New Testament meaning. The whole weight of his argument is simply upon Saint Paul's use of the passage.

---

eadem littera aliquando habet *duplicem sensum litteralem.* verbi gratia: 1 Paral. 17 [:13; cf. 2 Sam. 7:14] dicit dominus de salomone: 'Ego ero illi in patrem et ipse erit mihi in filium.' Et intelligitur de salomone ad litteram . . . Predicta enim auctoritas: 'Ego ero . . .' inducitur ab apostolo ad Hebr. [1:5] tanquam dicta de christo ad litteram, quod patet ex hoc, quia apostolus inducit eam ad probandum quod christus fuit maior angelis. Talis autem probatio non potest fieri per sensum mysticum, ut dicit Aug . . . predicta enim auctoritas impleta fuit ad litteram in salomone, minus tamen perfecte, quia fuit dei filius per gratiam solum. In christo autem perfectius, qui est dei filius per naturam. Licet autem *utraque expositio sit litteralis simpliciter,* secunda tamen, que est de christo, spiritualis et mystica est secundum quid, inquantum salomon fuit figura christi." (Italics mine.) Lyra launches exactly the same argument in his christological exegesis of Ps. 2:1.

What does this mean in terms of the interpretation of spirit and letter, since after all the passage in question is a new explanation of the third rule of Tyconius-Augustine? It will be recalled that Augustine interpreted the rule in terms of law and grace, and that the transportation into Old Testament-New Testament terms followed naturally. In terms of this survey, then, it is enough to explain that Lyra is expressing in a different way that which was already held, namely, that the "spiritual" meaning of the Old Testament is clearly given in the *letter* of the New. The appropriateness of Lyra's thought to his time is further seen in the fact that the New Testament interpretation belongs to what has here been called the normative-literal sense: it is a clear item of *doctrina* that Christ is the natural son of God.

An unresolved conflict of interest appears in this aspect of Lyra's thought. On the one hand, he desires to exegete the Scriptures according to their historical meaning, as far as possible in harmony with the best Hebrew scholarship; on the other, he is a Christian who wishes to establish the legitimacy of the New Testament's, and the Church's, use of the Old Testament, and to find in the Old Testament some testimony to his own faith. This dual motivation comes forward clearly in places like the exegesis of Psalm 2, where he defends his exegesis "de christo ad litteram" in part by appeal to Rabbi Rashi himself, who admits that ancient Hebrew rabbis expounded the Psalm "de rege messia" — an interpretation that Rashi and later Hebrew doctors abandoned in face of Christian exegesis. Lyra has the best of both worlds at this point: "I therefore, wishing to follow the doctrine of the apostles *and* the sayings of the ancient Hebrew doctors, will explain this psalm as being literally about Christ." [19]

19. Fol. 88vb G: "Ego igitur volens sequi doctrinam apostolorum *et* dicta doctorum hebraicorum antiquorum exponam hunc psalmum de christo ad litteram." (Italics mine.)

Despite this tension in Lyra's mind, I would resist the conclusion that he intended to contribute to the hermeneutical trends that were endangering the place of the Old Testament in the Church. Testimony against this is the fact that he finds more in the letter of the Old Testament than just *historia,* which must be allegorized in order to gain theological significance. In spots, the Old Testament also has normative-literal material; Lyra has not transposed the letter-spirit duality completely into a hermeneutical divide between Old and New Testaments: "For at some places one has only the literal sense, as in Deut. 6: 'Hear O Israel, the Lord your God is one. You shall love the Lord your God with your whole heart . . .' For in these and similar passages no mystical sense is to be sought." [20]

The concept of promise plays no role whatever in Lyra's Bible- and Psalms-prologues. Although the text that Lyra uses as an example of the occurrence of the double-literal sense happens to be a promise of God to David, this fact is of no special significance for Lyra's argument.

20. *Prologus in moralitates biblie* (fol. 4va E): "Sciendum autem quod licet sacra scriptura habeat quadruplicem sensum predictum, hoc tamen non est in qualibet sui parte secundum quod dicitur in collationibus patrum coll. viii [Cassian, *Conlationes* VIII, c.3 (*CSEL* 13/2, 219)]. Nam alicubi habet tantum sensum litteralem, sic Deut. 6 [:4 f.] 'Audi israel . . .' In istis enim et consimilibus non est mysticus sensus requerendus."

V. TWO NOMINALIST THEOLOGIANS

In late medieval glossed Bibles, and up until the eighteenth century, the *Additiones* of the Spanish Dominican Paul of Burgos were printed alongside the *Postilla* of Lyra. In view of this textual juxtaposition, historians of medieval hermeneutics have found it convenient to move in their interpretation straight from Lyra to Burgos, even though a century separates them. But what happened in between cannot be ignored; Burgos' views are more than merely responses to Lyra (to whose commentary he continually refers) and can be understood and interpreted better if some account is taken of important developments in the intervening years.

In order to provide a better framework for understanding Burgos, and a better feeling for the late medieval hermeneutical situation, I include here a study of two writings, both of which fall within the period between Lyra and Burgos, and incidentally within the period of the momentous Great Schism. They are the *Quaestio de Sacra Scriptura et de veritatibus catholicis* by Henry Totting of Oyta, written about 1380,[1] and *De sensu litterali sacrae scripturae* by Jean Gerson, a brief tract written at Paris about 1414.[2] There is added interest in the fact that both of these writers belong to the Nominalist school of late medieval theology.

1. Ed. Albertus Lang, Münster, 1953; cited hereafter as *De sac. script.*). This writing is part of the Prologue of Totting's *Quaestiones super libros Sententiarum*; see Lang's Preface, p. 5.

2. In *Oevres Complètes*, ed. P. Glorieux, III (Paris, 1962), 333-40; cited hereafter as *De sens. litt.* The date is given in the editor's Introduction, p. xiv (albeit misprinted "1313-14").

Henry Totting of Oyta

Redefinition of the Normative-Literal Sense. — The first thing to be noticed about Totting's definition of the literal and spiritual senses is that he considers as fundamental that which in Saint Thomas served only as a "loophole" — the idea of the divine intention: "The *sensus literalis* is the primary sense intended by the Holy Spirit, the principal author of Scripture, and this sense can appear quite clearly from the form itself of Scripture, and from its circumstances [roughly, the context], or is more or less in conformity with the circumstances of Scripture, or can be proved from them." [3] The *sensus mysticus* is in like manner defined by the divine intention, but is less clear and poses a new problem. Although it is "intended by the Holy Spirit, it does *not* appear primarily from the form of Scripture and its circumstances, nor can it be proved from them except together with the authority of the one who expounds it." [4] Here, however subtly, a significant move has been made: for the first time in these texts, the criterion of authority has been formally introduced alongside the traditional criterion of the normative literal sense as a criterion and warrant for adducing the spirit-intended sense of Scripture. Theological proof can be adduced from some source other than clear passages of Scripture.

Totting's new criterion and *norma normans* — proper authority — is highlighted in his reaction to Lyra's argument for the double-literal sense, which Totting rejects, and in his in-

3. *De sac. script.*, p. 47, line 32 – p. 48, line 4 (cited hereafter as p. 47.32, etc.): "sensus literalis dicendus est sensus primarius a Spiritu S. seu auctore principali scripture intentus, qui ex ipsa forma scripture et circumstanciis eius clarius poterit apparere seu qui circumstanciis scripture exstat conformior aut ex eis probari potest."

4. *De sac. script.*, p. 48.4–7: "Misticus . . . est iste qui intentus a Spiritu S. *non* apparet primario ex forma scripture et circumstanciis eius nec ex eis probari potest *nisi una cum auctoritate exponentis.*" (Italics mine.)

sistence that not only the literal but also the spiritual senses are valid in theological argument, if expounded by proper authority. In Lyra's defense of a double-literal sense, it will be recalled, the weight of the argument rested on Paul's use of an Old Testament passage, and Lyra made the remarkable inference that even Paul was bound to exegete according to the Augustinian-Thomist axiom that theological proof could be made only from the *sensus literalis*. Totting makes two crucial adjustments. First, he shifts the weight of the argument to the apostolic authority of Paul (so that Paul did not have to operate according to the literal-only rule); second, and consequently, Totting rejects Lyra's label of "literal" for the christological interpretation of the Old Testament passage in question. Why? Because the authority-principle has been posited to supplement the literal sense of Scripture as sufficient authorization for theological doctrines among Christians.[5] Since Christians accept the authority of Saint Paul, the spiritual sense of Scripture has validity for proof on the basis of his personal authority as its interpreter; meanwhile, however, the literal sense of the Bible also retains its traditional honors.

It seems to me that here is witnessed the birth of a scientific

5. *De sac. script.*, p. 15.17–22: "Quamvis per solum literalem sensum assumi possit argumentum efficax . . . generaliter ad omnes [that is, including non-Christians], ex quolibet tamen vero sensu scripture apud fideles sufficiens haberi potest probacio *per auctoritatem ipsam scripturam allegantis.*" (Italics mine.) This states the general principle. Totting then explains what the consequence would be were this *not* the case: "si non, tunc neque Petrus neque Paulus *sufficienter probarent,* quorum unus [Paulus] accepit dictum de Christo . . . 'Ego ero ipsi in patrem' etc., Ad Ebreos primo et 2 Refum [= 2 Sam.] 7" (p. 52.1–5; italics mine). This sort of Old Testament exegesis in New Testament belongs to the *sensus misticus* (p. 52.9 f.). A little later, Lyra is mentioned by name and the same Old Testament passage is cited, with the comment: "Quid clarius dici potest, quam quod Deus hoc dixit [literaliter] de Salomone, uno filiorum David. Sensus autem *allegoricus sive spiritualis* est de Christo, quo *auctoritate Apostoli probatur* esse sensus istius scripture, non autem ex circumstanciis ipsius loci [that is, not on the basis of the historical and literal sense]. Aliter . . . Nicolaus de Lira" (p. 59.26–60.3; italics mine).

"Tradition II" theory in the midst of a carefully argued hermeneutical treatise. Totting has granted that proper authority can establish theological truth and validate theological argument on the basis of nonliteral exegesis; a second source of "catholic truth" has been opened up. Of paramount interest, furthermore, is the way in which Totting defends this position.

Role of the New Testament Promise. — Totting does not adduce his second source — "Tradition II" — out of thin air. He justifies the move by what seems to him to be clear biblical authority: the promise of Christ to the Church. As Totting moves to the question of the definition of "catholic truths," [6] Christ's promises to the Church are appealed to at least six times as support for the contention that there are binding *extra*scriptural truths (that is, Christian *credenda, diligenda,* and *speranda*).[7]

Two of these instances of the use of *promissio* are of special interest. The first deals with an Objection that appeals to Saint Augustine's *De doctrina christiana*. Augustine writes that whatever men teach that is harmful is condemned in Scripture, and whatever is useful is found there.[8] The objector claims, therefore, that outside Scripture no catholic truth is to be found.[9]

6. *De sac. script.,* pp. 61 ff. Lang points out the importance of this tract for just this combination, within one treatise, of hermeneutical and ecclesiastical concerns. Here, the category of ecclesiastical authority has been formally recognized and introduced as integral to scientific hermeneutics.

7. References to Christ's promise: *De sac. script.,* pp. 62.17 (Mt. 16:18); 64.8 (Jn. 16:12); 65.21 (Mt. 28:20); 66.20 (Lk. 22:32); 75.10 (no biblical reference, but "Christus promisit apostolis multas veritates catholicas revelandas pro futuro"); 75.29 (no biblical reference).

8. *De sac. script.,* p. 72.28 f., referring to *De doc. chr.* II, 42, 63 (CSEL 80, 78): "quidquid homo extra didicit, si noxium est ibi damnatur, si utile, ibi invenitur."

9. *De sac. script.,* p. 72.22 f.: "Extra istam scripturam nulla catholica veritas invenitur, in qua omnis veritas utilis ad salutem habetur."

In reply, Totting concedes, yet without yielding a thing, that no truth necessary for salvation is found outside Scripture, as long as "outside" (*extra*) means "neither expressed in it, nor following from it formally, nor being chiefly founded in it." [10] Totting had explained earlier that while not all catholic truth is explicitly *contained* in the Bible, nevertheless it is all "founded" therein.[11] But — and here is the clinching argument — propositions recognized as "catholic truths" are not the *only* thing that have their *fundamentum* in the Bible. "In the same way also, the authority of the church is sufficiently founded in it." [12]

How can this be so? Because among those very catholic truths that can be drawn directly from the Bible is Christ's *promissio* to the Church. Thus, the authority of the Church itself is *similiter fundata* in Scripture because, Totting concludes, "it is held that Christ promised to the apostles that many catholic truths were to be revealed in the future." [13] Thus *promissio,* itself a normative element of the Scripture text, justifies expansion of that norm so as to include an extrascriptural foundation on which valid theological arguments and conclusions can be erected — by proper authority.

10. *De sac. script.,* p. 75.1–5: "Conceditur conclusio . . . accipiendo sic extra, quod nec in ea exprimitur nec ex ea formaliter sequitur nec in ea principaliter fundatur." It is crucial from now on to notice the use of *fundo* and *fundamentum.* The bearing of Totting's train of thought on contemporary Catholic discussion is evident in the discussion of Johannes Brinktrine, "Beiträge zur katholischen und reformatorischen Lehre vom Wort Gottes," *Theologie und Glaube* 54 (1964), esp. p. 229.

11. *De sac. script.,* p. 69.27–31: "Licet omnes veritates catholice fundate sint in canone biblie non tamen omnes tales explicite continentur in biblia nec ex solis contentis in ea formaliter inferri possunt."

12. *De sac. script.,* p. 70.7–10: "tam veritates in biblia expresse quam formaliter ex eis inferibiles sufficienter in ea *fundate* sunt. Similiter et auctoritas ecclesie sufficienter *fundata* est in ipsa." (Italics mine.)

13. *De sac. script.,* p. 75.10 f.: "habetur quod Christus promisit apostolis multas veritates catholicas revelandas pro futuro." The statement of Augustine to which the objector appealed pertains chiefly *ad mores* that

An important piece of this study now falls into place. It will be recalled that in the interpretation of Thomas, I raised a question about the New Testament, wondering how it could maintain itself as authoritative or whether, just as the locus of the normative-literal sense had shifted from the Old Testament to the New, which it turned out to signify, so again that normative sense would have to shift from the New Testament to that which *it* signifies, that is, the Church. Precisely this shift has taken place with Totting: a way has been shown to warrant this new shift in order to provide an authoritative word for the time beyond the time of the New Testament. In Totting's solution, the normative *sensus literalis* of Scripture remains authoritative in itself, yet at the same time itself bestows on the Church the right to declare the spiritual (that is, the present) meaning of the text. The tension that might have arisen by setting a literalistic biblicism *against* the new determinations and decisions of the Church can now be relaxed; the two hermeneutical principles can now work in harmony, because an unimpeachable biblical word giving theological account for the future (as well as for present and past) has been discovered — the biblical word of promise. This word, *literally* addressed to the Church, can now function as the norm for interpreting everything else in the Bible (whose other meanings for the future remained ambiguous because addressed to their own time).

Another instance of the use of Christ's promise to be examined here reveals Totting's assessment of the religious situation in the *Old* Testament time. Totting faces a new Objection, which runs: "The New Testament, together with the Old, is no less [sufficient] for faithful Christians than was the Old Testament by itself for the Hebrews. But the whole faith to which the Hebrews were tied was expressed in the Old

---

are also found in other human spheres of knowledge, not to those special matters belonging to the Church cultus (p. 75.11–16).

Testament. Therefore the whole faith to which Christians are held is expressed in both; therefore *de necessitate salutis* someone is not held to believe that which is neither contained in the Bible nor able to be inferred from its contents alone as necessary and clear consequence."[14] This comes from a representative of Tradition I,[15] to whom Totting replies with the argument from promise. The Old Testament people could get along on very little, he argues; they were, after all, "sub umbra" and therefore "pauca sufficiebant eis." Now, everything is different: "the light has come, illuminating the *christifideles* for contemplation of divine things and the *mirabilia* of God, not only through those things which are contained in the written law, but also through various other modes . . . And this also Christ has promised."[16]

14. *De sac. script.*, p. 73.3–11: "Non minus pro fidelibus christianis est novum testamentum una cum veteri, quam fuit solummodo vetus testamentum pro Ebreis. Sed tota fides, ad quam stringebantur Ebrei, fuit expressa in testamento veteri. Igitur tota fides, ad quam tenentur christiani, expressa est in utroque; igitur de necessitate salutis non tenetur aliquis credere quod nec in biblia continetur nec ex solis contentis in ea potest consequencia necessaria et manifesta inferri."

15. Gregory of Rimini is one such Tradition I representative, and Totting singles him out for attack by name, accusing him of teaching *falsitas* (*De sac. script.*, p. 76.14–20). The view of Gregory to which Totting objects is given by Lang (p. 76 n.1): "Ceterarum autem veritatum scilicet, non sequentium ex dictis sacre scripture nullam dico esse conclusionem theologicam" (I *Sent.* prol. q.1 a.2 concl.3). Gregory here excludes, as Lang might have added from Gregory's preceding sentence, all other truths — "sive etiam sint determinate per ecclesiam sive non." J. W. O'Malley has challenged this biblicist interpretation of Gregory on the basis of other evidence, concluding that "for Gregory the *determinatio* was an unquestioned prerogative of the Church, and her *determinatio* was final and authoritative" ("A Note on Gregory of Rimini: Church, Scripture, Tradition," *Augustinianum* 5 [1965], 378). Gregory seems to contradict himself, and the strong assertions referred to by Totting remain to be explained.

16. *De sac. script.*, p. 75.24–29: "Nunc autem lux venit illuminans christifideles ad contemplacionem divinorum et mirabilium Dei non solum per ea que in scripta lege continentur, sed eciam per alios modos varios . . . Et hoc eciam Christus promisit etc."

The implication is that Christians should expect much more than a mere "written law," because Christ by his promise has led us to expect more. The people of the Old Covenant, by contrast, living "sub umbra," existed at a considerably lower level of spiritual awareness. For them, the book was enough. It does not occur to Totting that the Old Testament people also lived *sub promissione,* and that their existence could equally be described as fraught with expectation of "much more" from God! Thus, in Totting is seen the further precipitate of the systematic draining of theological value from the Old Testament, in conjunction with an apparent deafness to the word of promise and the expectation that at times sounds forth with such eloquence from it. For medieval theology, the Old Testament was submerged almost completely "sub umbra."

Jean Gerson

Beyond Totting. — If in Henry Totting there was an explicit step toward extending the *fundamentum* of Christian doctrine so that it stood on the two pillars of the literal sense of Scripture and the authoritative churchly interpretation of the *spiritual* sense of Scripture, so in the thought of Gerson (d. 1429) a further and more radical step is taken: the *fundamentum* rests in the Church *alone.* For to the Spirit-governed Church, Gerson argues, belongs the authority to judge and declare what the *literal* sense of Scripture is.[17] The occasion for this innovation by Gerson was a hermeneutical impasse, namely, the

17. *De sens. litt.*, propositio 3 (p. 335): "Sensus . . . litteralis judicandus est prout Ecclesia Spiritu Sancto inspirata et gubernata determinavit, et non ad cujuslibet arbitrium et interpretationem." Note that ecclesiastical *determinatio* is opposed to biblical *interpretatio* – according to Oberman, one of the hallmarks of Tradition II as against Tradition I (*Harvest*, pp. 372 f.; 403 f.). Cf. the decision of the Council of Trent, given in Henricus Denzinger, *Enchiridion Symbolorum*, 32nd ed. (Freiburg, 1963), no. 1507, for a remarkably similar statement.

heretical claim which was also held by the Church, that its doctrine was based on the literal sense of Scripture.[18] Totting's writing, which Gerson knew and used,[19] would be inadequate to this impasse, for as long as a sort of "public" literal sense of Scripture was acknowledged, to which anyone could appeal, the possibility of setting it against the spiritual interpretations of the Church remained open. A solution had to be found which would both preserve the time-honored axiom that "only the literal sense of Scripture is valid for proof" and at the same time prevent its being used against the teaching of the Church.

This is precisely what Gerson accomplishes, by carefully creating a new definition of the normative *sensus litteralis* itself. For him, it must mean nothing else than what may be called the "literal sense of the Church." Gerson is doing this at the expense of the traditional *sensus litteralis,* which is simply the plain sense, or grammar, of the Bible as it expresses the intention of its author. This problem is solved by Gerson when he insists that the Bible has "its own proper logic," different from that which the grammarians and logicians and dialecticians use (and incidentally different from Lyra and Thomas).[20] This solution undercuts the "public," grammatical-literal sense as theologically authoritative, and it opens the way for the derogatory definition of the grammatical sense whereby it will be linked with "carnal," Jewish, and heretical

18. *De sens. litt.* (p. 334): "seminatores haeresum . . . dicunt fundari dicta sua in Scriptura Sacra et ejus sensu vero litterali." Fritz Hahn gives a quotation from another treatise that succinctly sums up the situation: "Haec regula [namely, that scripture is the rule of faith] fundamentum est commune nobis et haereticis, quos impugnare conamur" ("Zur Hermeneutik Gersons," *ZThK* 51 [1954], 40, from Gerson, *Opera Omnia,* ed. L. E. du Pin [Antwerp, 1706], I, 457).

19. Totting and his *De sac. script.* are referred to approvingly by Gerson, *De sens. litt.,* p. 334 f.

20. *De sens. litt.,* prop. 2 (p. 334): "Sensus litteralis Sacrae Scripturae accipiendus est non secundum vim logicae seu dialecticae, sed potius juxta locutiones in rhetoricis sermonibus usitatas . . . Habet enim Scriptura . . . suam logicam propriam, quam rhetoricam appellamus." There follows an appeal to Augustine's *De doctrina christiana* as a whole.

usage. The proper literal sense has become the private property of the Spirit-endowed Church.

Gerson now has two literal senses to account for: the *sensus logicalis* and the *sensus theologicus*.[21] The contrast to Lyra's double-literal sense, however, could hardly be greater.[22] For Lyra, there were two true and proper literal senses. They were not two *kinds* of literal sense, for both were grammatically defined, their duality arising quite simply from the literal contents of the two testaments. Were he to have used Gerson's terms, Lyra would have said that the theological-literal is simply a part — the normative part — of the logical-literal. He would have allowed no disjunction between theological and grammatical, for the grammatical-literal sense is the *fundamentum* for any theological argument, as well as for all spiritual interpretation. By contrast, Gerson has removed any claim of the logical-literal sense when the question of theological interpretation arises. The "proper" literal sense is now unequivocally founded in the determination and judgment of the Church. This is the only literal sense to which appeal can now be made in theological debate.

In the last analysis, the Bible itself has no theologically authoritative literal meaning. The possibility of argument from Scripture against the *magisterium* is for the first time, in the material covered here, programmatically and theoretically eliminated.

Gerson thus pushed beyond Totting. According to Totting, the Church could decide what the spiritual interpretation should be, but as yet claimed no special privileges in determining what the literal sense should be. This he left intact.[23]

---

21. *De sens. litt.*, prop. 5 (p. 335).

22. I fail to see, therefore, how Werbeck can maintain that Gerson was "strongly influenced" by Thomas and Lyra (*Perez,* p. 122). He refers to Hahn, "Zur Hermeneutik Gersons," p. 41 f., where no such suggestion is made.

23. Perhaps just this difference can serve as a refinement of Oberman's distinction between Tradition II and III, although Oberman dates Tradi-

Indeed, the logic of his argumentation suggests that the legitimation of the Church's authority is itself dependent on the grammatical — and normative — literal sense of Scripture, that is, Christ's promise to the Church, and is therefore always a derived, dependent authority. Gerson has changed that. For instance, suppose a conflict arises between a conclusion reached on the basis of grammatical exegesis and a determination of the Church — between, in Gerson's terms, the logical- and the theological-literal senses of Scripture. Gerson's solution can only be as follows: "In a theological assertion, a true *logical* sense does not excuse the one who asserts it from the duty to retract, if it is false in the theological-literal sense." [24]

Following Totting, Gerson makes a statement that also seems to be directed against Gregory of Rimini (although his name is not mentioned). Gregory had used the word *theologia* (short for *conclusio theologica*) in the sense of "normative doctrine," or "dogma." Gerson, in his eighth thesis, declares, "The literal sense . . . once decided and determined in decrees and decretals and conciliar books, must be regarded

---

tion III much later. Totting represents Tradition II in that Scripture's *sensus litteralis* still stands in its own right alongside the Church's spiritual interpretations. But Gerson, by absorbing the literal sense into the Church's *determinatio*, has all but emptied the traditional literal sense of theological authority. In "Quo Vadis," Oberman refers to the observation that Irenaeus would have regarded appeal to extrascriptural tradition as Gnostic (p. 227). In the same vein, I suspect that Augustine may have regarded Gerson's position as Donatistic, for Gerson's heretics seem to be making the same appeal against him as Augustine was making against his Donatist opponents: an appeal to the plain and open sense of Scripture.

24. *De sens. litt.*, prop. 5 (p. 335): "Senus *logicalis* verus in assertione theologica, non excusat asserentem quin talem assertionem debeat revocare si falsa sit in sensu theologico litterali." (Italics mine.) From now on, it can never simply be assumed that "literal sense" has an ordinary meaning; as often as not, the ordinary meaning would designate to medieval authors the bad, or improper, literal sense. My conclusions regarding Gerson are in agreement with those of G.H.M. Posthumus Meyjes, *Jean Gerson: zijn Kerkpolitiek en Ecclesiologie* (The Hague, 1963), pp. 262–264.

as *theologia* and as belonging to Holy Scripture no less than the Apostolic Symbol." [25]

The Fate of the Old Testament. — Perhaps just as significant in Gerson's theory is the admission that the Old Testament never has had any proper literal sense. Gerson's sixth proposition is the place where this is made clear: "The literal sense . . . was *first revealed* through Christ and the apostles and elucidated by miracles, then confirmed by the blood of martyrs; afterwards holy doctors searched this literal sense out against heretics . . . Then followed the determination of holy councils, so that what had been *doctrinaliter* discussed by the doctors might become defined *sententialiter* by the Church. Finally, punishments were added . . . against those who with wanton rashness refused to subject themselves to the determination of the church." [26] The passage admirably illustrates the ever-advancing *loci* of the *sensus* (*theologicus* and *normans*) *litteralis,* as it keeps pace with the unfolding revelation of God's intention in redemptive history.

This hermeneutical situation, as it affects Scripture, is also reflected in Gerson's discussion elsewhere of the fourfold sense: he calls the first sense not "litteralis" but "historicus."[27] It will be recalled that this is only *part* of the grammatical-

25. *De sens. litt.,* prop. 8, p. 336; "Sensus litteralis . . . si reperitur determinatus et decisus in decretis et decretalibus et codicibus conciliorum, judicandus est ad theologiam et sacram scripturam non minus pertinere quam symbolum apostolorum."

26. *De sens. litt.,* prop. 6 (p. 335): "Sensus litteralis . . . fuit *primo* per christum et apostolos revelatus et miraculis elucidatus, deinde fuit per sanguinem martyrum confirmatus; postmodum sacri doctores . . . contra haereticos diffudius elicuerunt praedictum sensum litteralem . . . postea successit determinatio sacrorum conciliorum ut quod erat doctrinaliter discussum per doctores fieret per Ecclesiam sententialiter definitum. Appositae sunt tandem poenae . . . contra eos qui proterva temeritate nollent ecclesiasticae determinationi subjacere." (Italics mine.)

27. Here I depend on a quotation given by Altenstaig, who reports Gerson's four senses as *historia, allegoria, tropologia,* and *anagoge* "Historia est significatio vocum ad res, videlicet quando res qualibet quomodo

literal sense; moreover, that it is the part which is inevitably subject to figurative interpretation, since all *res gestae* are *figurae* and *signa*; and finally, that the norm for such interpretation was traditionally the *other* part of the literal sense of Scripture, the normative-literal sense. This is precisely the sense that Gerson has eliminated from Scripture and put in the Church, where the Spirit is. For the Old Testament, the upshot will be (as James Perez will show) that the entire Old Testament is allegory.

A Late Medieval Antithesis. — In Gerson and Lyra appears a late medieval antithesis. For Lyra, the grammatical and historical sense of the Bible is the *fundamentum* for all theological interpretation; for Gerson, it is theoretically irrelevant for such interpretation. Lyra accepts it as an irreducible and unavoidable task to attain an understanding of the Old Testament based on its historical and philological meaning, arrived at in company with the best Hebrew scholarship. Gerson needs only the New Testament and the Church to find out the "literal" meaning of the Old Testament

Ironically, Lyra perhaps contributed to the Gersonian line by being the first to allow the New Testament interpretation of an Old Testament passage to be called "sensus litteralis" (rather than *allegoricus,* or *spiritualis*). But he would have been surprised at the outcome. Perhaps it would not be too far wrong to suggest that Lyra's work represents a search for some middle way between the Scylla of Marcionism and the Charybdis of Total Allegory, that is, between the view that the Old Testament, understood literally, is offensive to Christian faith, and the alternative view that it is really only a New Testament in disguise.[28] Lyra did not give theological expres-

---

secundum litteram gesta sit plano sermone refertur, ut quomodo populus israeliticus ex egypto salvatus, tabernaculum domino fecessi narratur." ("Sacra Scriptura," in *Vocabularius,* fol. 230rb).

28. This "alternative," as suggested in my Introduction, is more ap-

sion to his convictions on this point, and his method was not accepted intact by those who followed him. Yet one may fairly attribute the utmost theological importance to what he attempted.[29] For Lyra's irreducible double-literal sense — based on what was plainly written in the Old Testament, on the one hand, and in the New, on the other — corresponds to reality. That is, it corresponds to the irreducible double-literal sense, so to speak, of the actual people of God, which arises from the continued presence together in history of both the Christian Church and Israel — not Israel as a mere *figura* and *umbra* of the Church, not as something outmoded and embarrassing that should disappear, but as the elect community of hope and expectation, awaiting with Christians God's next move.

---

parent than real, since it accepts the Marcionite premise that the Old Testament, read historically, is for the most part irrelevant, and at worst scandalous to Christians.

29. Beryl Smalley sharply posed to theologians the problem of honoring the historical integrity of medieval exegetes such as Lyra, on the one hand, while on the other, giving a theological account of the place of the Old Testament in the canon. ("The Bible," pp. 61, 71.)

VI. PAUL OF BURGOS

In the *Additiones* that the Spanish Dominican Paul of Burgos appended to Lyra's *Postilla,* one meets what appears to be a resounding call to return to Lyra, a repeated and passionate insistence on the primacy and hegemony of the *sensus litteralis.*[1] Augustine's axiom (in Thomistic form) that only from the literal sense can argument be made is the single central point of his whole prologue *Additio* and is repeated time and again. The total dependence of the spiritual senses upon the literal is shown more clearly, and argued more urgently, than in any of the previous texts. But the question is: *what* literal sense? In the light of what has happened since Lyra, nothing can be taken for granted regarding the meaning of "literal."

If Burgos' prologue is read immediately in light of Lyra, it seems as though they are saying about the same thing.[2] Lyra is for the most part commended for his analysis, and criticized by Burgos only on peripheral issues.[3] But the special

1. The *Additiones* were published about 1429, according to de Lubac, *Exégèse* II/2, 355. Unless otherwise noted, citations are from Burgos' *Additiones super utrumque prologum* (of Lyra; cited hereafter as *Add. prol.*). According to Hailperin, Burgos was a convert from Judaism (Lyra was not). Hailperin, however, has misread Burgos as a "most characteristic exponent" of the opposition to Lyra's historical method (*Rashi,* p. 259). Failing to recognize that the structure of Burgos' prologue is that of a scholastic *quaestio,* done in good Thomistic form, Hailperin cites as Burgos' own position the objections that Burgos will refute (p. 358 n.21). Hailperin is not the first to make this mistake: de Lubac lists others, and in reply has even been able to find a place where Burgos defends a literal reading against Lyra (*Exégèse* II/2, 357 f.).

2. Thus, Ebeling lists Burgos as holding the double-literal sense along with Lyra ("Luthers Psalterdruck," p. 93 n.2). In this Ebeling is followed by Werbeck, *Perez,* p. 122. Their view is correct but needs further comment in light of Burgos' important revisions in Lyra's thought.

3. Ebeling, *Evangelienauslegung,* p. 133 n. 88, lists Burgos' objections

significance of Burgos appears more clearly in light of what has happened in the intervening century, as epitomized in the writings of Totting and Gerson: Burgos represents a revolt against the direction that they have taken. Much more than a mere repristination of Lyra, Burgos represents a return to Tradition I, based on a reinstatement of the grammatical sense of Scripture as theologically normative.

Simply by contrasting the way in which Burgos uses Christ's promise to the Church, the difference can be seen. In Totting it was used to provide the foundation for a second source of Catholic truth. In Burgos' long prologue, the word "promise" occurs only once, but significantly, it is used to argue that the Church's interpretation of Scripture is more reliable than that of the Jews and non-Christians, since Christ has promised the *spiritus veritatis* to those who belong to the Church.[4]

Sensus Litteralis *and Church*

To establish my thesis about Burgos, I can best begin with the problem of Lyra's double-literal sense.[5] Although Burgos uses that term in the body of his commentary, he never uses or explains it in his prologue. This fact should give one pause

---

to Lyra. De Lubac aptly characterizes Burgos' criticisms as sometimes "un peu mesquine" (*Exégèse* II/2, p. 357).

4. *Add. prol.* (fol. 6ʳᵃ B): "magis presumendum est quod illi qui in gremio ecclesie sunt, cui christus promisit spiritum veritatis, *verum intellectum sacre scripture* habeant quam infideles qui veritati fidei cummuniter adversantur, tum ne ad hoc detur infidelibus occasio credendi quod ipsi melius sacram scripturam exponant quam catholici." (Italics mine.) I see in the words italicized here an indication of Oberman's thesis that Tradition I exponents apply Christ's promise to scriptural interpretation. Notice also that the opponents are not Christian deviants but the *infideles*.

5. For an outline of the whole *Add. prol.*, which cannot be treated in full here, see Ebeling, *Evangelienauslegung*, p. 133 f., n. 89. He characterizes the tract as a good compendium of the main problems of medieval hermeneutics but does not go into detailed interpretation.

before identifying the position of Burgos too quickly with that of Lyra.

Burgos is willing to agree that part of the Old Testament is literally about Christ. He compliments Lyra on his use of the New Testament to establish this fact with certain texts.[6] Nevertheless, an explicit refusal to accept the strained line of argument by which Lyra posited his double-literal theory occurs in Burgos' comments on Psalm 2. There, in exactly the same fashion as in his own prologue, Lyra argued that this Psalm is literally about Christ because Paul quotes it as *probatio* in theological argument.[7] Burgos wants to read the Psalm christologically too, but he rejects Lyra's way of arriving at that conclusion: "In order to show that this psalm necessarily is understood literally of Christ, and consequently to show that the allegations of the apostles against their opponents concerning this psalm are valid arguments, it seems that something else has to be said."[8]

Totting, it will be recalled, had also rejected Lyra's argumentation and had instead located the legitimation of a christological reading in the apostolic authority of Paul: as an heir of Christ's promise, he has the authority to judge and determine the right sense. Whatever Saint Paul says is authoritative, and that settles it. But Burgos does not take this herteronomous tack either.[9] He tries to keep the argument founded

6. *Add. prol.* (fol. 7vb H): "Unde et magister Nicolas hoc recte considerans in tota postilla sua veteris testamenti, ubi occurrit aliquis textus allegatus in novo a christo vel a discipulis, semper exponit eum secundum sensum litteralem."

7. *Postilla* Ps. 2:1 (fol. 88vb G).

8. *Add.* Ps. 2:1 (fol. 89va F): "ad ostendendum quod hic ps. ex necessitate litere de christo intelligatur, et per consequens quod allegationes apostolorum contra adversarios de hoc ps. sint efficaces, aliter videtur dicendum."

9. I have no evidence that Burgos had read Totting or Gerson. But even supposing he had read neither of them, he was certainly aware of the ecclesiastical thinking that had emerged during the period of the

within the Scripture itself. He apparently understands how far-fetched Lyra's assumption is, namely, that Saint Paul was operating with the Augustinian-Thomist axiom regarding prooftexts. And perhaps also he feels dissatisfied with the positivist tendency of Totting's authority-argument.

At any rate, he proceeds as follows: it is not Paul's interpretive use of the Psalm passage that gives the required "necessity" to the claim of a literal-christological reading; rather, it is the fact that in the Old Testament passage itself God addresses the "son" in the singular: "You are my son." Further, as Saint Augustine maintains,[10] only Jesus can call God *"my Father"*; the rest of us must say "our," speaking *communiter*. And "only him [Christ] does God beget; us he creates . . . Thus it is evident that the apostle was arguing most cogently in Hebrews 1, out of the necessity of the letter."[11] Burgos' attention, then, has shifted to Christ himself in determining the "true" literal sense of the Old Testament passage. The importance of this shift to a christological argument will shortly become more apparent.

Burgos' understanding of the formal meaning the *sensus litteralis* deserves further examination. First, he rejects the definition that covers only historical narration, recognizing that the historical material of Scripture is only that part of the literal sense which is susceptible to figurative interpretation. One must also, he argues, include under the literal sense "doc-

---

Schism, ended only about fifteen years earlier, and in reaction to the Hussite affair.

10. See Augustine, *Enarrationes in Psalmos*, Ps. 2, par. 6 (*CChr* 38, 5).

11. *Add.* Ps. 2:1 (fol. 89ʳᵇ H): "illum [christum] enim solum genuit; nos autem creavit. Hec Aug. Patet ergo quod apostolus efficacissime ex necessitate littere arguebat ad Heb. 1[:5]." For the most part, I shall bypass the comments of Matthias Doering, the eager defender of Lyra, whose *Replica* follows the *Additiones* of Burgos. My reason is seen in this typical contribution of Doering to the issue at hand: "Bur. irrationaliter movetur contra rationem postille."

trinal or prophetic material" — material that does not narrate history.[12] It is more proper to begin with the definition of Saint Thomas, whereby the literal sense is "that which is gotten through what the letter signifies, by which words signify things." [13] But this is not finally adequate either, Burgos argues, since falsehoods would then appear in what is called the literal sense. One must go further: in order that a sense of Scripture may be designated literal, "it is required that it is intended by the author of Sacred Scripture, who is God." This is true in the interpretation of any writing, Burgos observes; the author's intention is always the final criterion of what is meant in the words. Thus, in dealing with Scripture, one must account for the intention of God.[14] This intention is marked out (*signatur*) "through the words contained in the letter" [15] — a signal that Burgos has not taken Thomas' "loophole" as a way out of the grammar in the way Gerson had.

But then Burgos abruptly states a conclusion: "from this it follows that the literal sense of Holy Scripture ought not to be called that sense which in any way opposes the authority or the decision of the church." What goes against the Church's determination cannot be the *sensus litteralis,* for "it would be

12. *Add. prol.* (fol. 5[rb] D): "doctrinalia seu prophetica et huiusmodi, cum in talibus non videtur narrari aliqua historia."
13. *Add. prol.* (fol. 5[rb] D): "Unde aliter et magis proprie dicitur sensus litteralis, scilicet ille qui habetur per significationem littere, qua voces significant res . . . prout patet in prima parte [of Thomas' *ST*]." Burgos is an enthusiastic student of Thomas: see fol. 6[va] E, where he reprimands Lyra for occasionally criticizing Thomas, "cuius sancti doctoris eloquia firmiter credo esse igne charitatis examinata, et naturalis rationis dictamine multipliciter purgata, a quo etiam sancto doctore ipse postillator [Lyra] multa frequenter accipit."
14. *Add. prol.* (fol. 5[rb] D): "Unde addendum . . . quod sensus . . . scripture ad hoc, quod litteralis dicatur, requiritur quod sit intentus ab auctore sacre scripture . . . sed constat quod auctor sacre scripture est deus, et sic patet quod sensus litteralis de quo agitur est ille qui a deo intenditur." Here is Thomas' "loophole," by which one could enlarge on a grammatical definition of "literal."
15. *Add. prol.* (col. 5[rb] D): "et per voces in littera contentas signatur."

contrary to that which has been revealed by the Holy Spirit." [16] How can this be Tradition I? Rather, the Totting-Gerson position seems to be suggested: the intention of the divine author is known by the Church because the *Spirit* of the divine author has been granted to the Church, leading her into all truth.

Yet it would be a mistake to stop here. First of all, this is one of only two statements of this type in Burgos' whole prologue. In the other statement he contends that the determination of the Church and right reason are two norms to which interpretation should not be "repugnant." [17] Thus, for Burgos the Church is acting only as a negative check on what the literal sense may be; the Church does not, as in Gerson, preempt the very articulation of the *sensus litteralis* by attributing to Scripture a unique grammar which only the Church can understand. Rather, Burgos makes a rigorous attempt to get the "true literal" [18] sense out of Scripture itself; the literal sense "conforms to the letter." Furthermore, he flatly denies that there are truths outside Scripture which are necessary to salvation. Instead, he insists on the sufficiency of the Bible, in its literal sense: "It holds good therefore that all things that are handed down as necessary for salvation, to be believed or done, are found in Holy Scripture in its literal sense." [19] He gives

16. *Add. prol.* (fol. 5rb D): "Ex quibus sequitur quod sensus litteralis . . . non debet dici ille sensus qui in aliquo repugnat ecclesie auctoritati seu determinationi . . . talis enim sensus . . . est hereticus . . . quod contrariatur ei quod per spiritum sanctum revelatum est."

17. *Add. prol.* (fol. 5vb H). Here Burgos is explaining that several senses of Scripture can be allowed, under the divine intention, but the criterion by which their propriety is judged is as follows: "quod . . . tales sensus sint littere conformes, et quod determinationi ecclesie seu recte rationi non repugnent."

18. It will be recalled that this qualifier "true" first appeared in Gerson, having been made necessary by the negative connotation now attached to the grammatical sense.

19. *Add. prol.* (fol. 7va F f.): "Constat . . . quod *omnia* que de necessitate salutis traduntur credenda seu agenda in sacra scriptura sub sensu litterali reperiuntur." (Italics mine.) The only "loophole" that Bur-

examples, and then demands: "Who therefore of sound mind would dare to say that there is no spiritual life in the literal sense, since in it *all* things which belong to the spiritual life are delivered, which must be believed and done?"[20] To the objection that the spiritual senses are also directed toward that which must be believed and done, Burgos answers: "To this it has to be said that *nothing* is contained under the spiritual sense necessary to faith and morals which Scripture does not plainly (*manifeste*) give elsewhere through the literal sense."[21]

But the following assertion, I think, is the one that decisively identifies Burgos with Tradition I. Here he stands with Gregory of Rimini, and against Totting (who had charged Gregory with teaching "falsitas") and Gerson. The statement is decisive because it spells out the relation of the literal sense of Scripture to valid theological conclusions: "The study of Holy Scripture, rightly ordered, begins from the articles of faith divinely revealed in Holy Scripture, which are founded in the literal sense of Holy Scripture. Of these articles, one — found together with others in Scripture, or discovered by true and right reason — is advanced in order to prove another, just as the Apostle argues, in 1 Cor. 15, from the resurrection of Christ to a general resurrection. Through this process, one ar-

---

gos leaves appears a few lines later: "Manifestum est quod omnia circa hoc de necessitate salutis credenda, in sensu litterali *principaliter* traduntur." The context shows that the "chiefly" leaves room for the classic Christian dogmas: Trinity, Incarnation, Creation, along with the Law and the institution of the Christian sacraments (of which only baptism, eucharist, and penance are mentioned); they are in Scripture, but room is left for their elaboration in the tradition.

20. *Add. prol.* (fol. 7vb H): "Quis ergo sane mentis audeat dicere, quod in sensu litterali non est spiritus vite, cum in eo *omnia* credenda et agenda ad vitam spiritualem pertinentia tradantur?" (Italics mine.)

21. *Add. prol.* (fol. 7vb H): "Ad quod dicendum quod *nihil* sub sensu spirituali continetur fidei vel moribus necessarium, quod scriptura alicui [=*alicubi,* or *alibi*] per litteralem sensum non manifeste tradat." The "nihil" (italics mine) is stronger than Augustine's "nihil fere," referred to in Ch. I.

rives at all things which are legitimately handed down in sacred theology, all of which are led back to the literal sense of Holy Scripture itself." [22] As far as possible, then, Burgos intends to conform dogma to the literal meaning of Scripture — and not the other way around, as Gerson had done.

But if Burgos really wants to ground the true literal sense back in Scripture itself, the question now arises: what are the criteria of interpretation? Does Burgos firm up his position by serious attention to this hermeneutical issue, so important for a Tradition I position?

Christological Interpretation

In Burgos, more than in any commentator so far encountered, Christ himself is the center and axis of interpretation. Some evidence of this has already appeared in the discussion of Psalm 2. The most compelling evidence, however, is Burgos' insistence that as Christ is, and remains, the *fundamentum* of the Church, so the literal sense remains the *fundamentum* of all the others. Christ and the *sensus litteralis* are primary; the Church and the spiritual senses are secondary and dependent.

This assertion comes in Burgos' development of the thesis that the literal sense is "dignior" than the spiritual senses. An objection is raised that the spiritual senses are of greater value because the literal sense is given for their sake.[23] Burgos' an-

22. *Add. prol.* (fol. 7ra A): "studium sacre scripture recte ordinatum incipit ab articulis fidei divinitus in sacra scriptura revelatis, qui fundantur in sensu litterali sacre scripture. Ex quibus articulis una cum aliis in sacra scriptura traditis seu per veram et rectam rationem inventis [note the conspicuous absence of *determinatio ecclesie*] proceditur ad aliqua alia probanda, sicut Apostolus 1 Cor. 15 ex resurrectione christi arguit resurrectionem communem, et per istum processum devenitur ad omnia quae in sacra theologia veraciter traduntur, que omnia reducuntur ad sensum litteralem ipsius sacre scripture."

23. *Add. prol.* (fol. 5ra B): "Secundum philosophum [Aristotle] . . .

swer first shows how the analogy of foundation and building applies in spiritual things: "It must be said that in spiritual things the *fundamentum* is often said to be more noble or of more value than the *edificium*. For Christ, who remains incomparably more worthy, given the other supports of the church, is called a *fundamentum*; hence 1 Cor. 3: 'No one can lay a foundation besides that which has been laid, which is Christ Jesus.' This is said by way of metaphor, for just as a foundation in physical things sustains the building and is prior to it, so that when it fails, the building falls to ruin, so in the spiritual building, Christ sustains the whole body of the church, and is prior to it in dignity and causality, without whom the ecclesiastical building would be done away with." [24]

Although one could thus allow that in a sense Christ is there "for the sake of" the Church, one may not go on to infer that the Church is more worthy than Christ. Burgos' analysis is now applied to the relation of the literal to the spiritual senses of Scripture: "One must speak in the same way about the literal sense, which is the *fundamentum,* that is, of the other senses, according to a certain likeness . . . [to a physical building]. So also the whole spiritual sense of Holy Scripture would tumble down were the literal sense completely taken away,

---

Propter Quod unumquidque et illud magis. Sed sensus litteralis est propter sensum spiritualem. Igitur sensus spiritualis est dignior. Consequentia tenet, et antecedens pro secunda parte probatur, nam sensus litteralis se habet ad spirituales sicut fundamentum ad edificium, prout ponit postillator in secondo prologo. Constat autem quod fundamentum est propter edificium, et non econtra."

24. *Add. prol.* (fol. 6vb H): "Dicendum quod fundamentum in spiritualibus sepe dicitur esse nobilius seu dignius quam edificium. Christus enim, qui ceteris suppositis ecclesie incomparabiliter dignior existit, fundamentum dicitur, unde 1 Cor. 3 [:11]: 'Fundamentum aliud nemo potest ponere . . .' quod dicitur secundum similitudinem. Nam sicut fundamentum in corporalibus sustinet edificium et est prius eo, et ipso deficiente edificium tendit in ruinam, sic in edificio spirituali christus sustinet totum corpus ecclesie, et est prior eo dignitate et causalitate sine quo edificium ecclesiasticum evacuaretur."

since the spiritual sense, in those things which pertain to salvation, has to be founded in the literal sense, as has been said." [25] Burgos goes on to insist that "the whole *certitudo* of the other senses of Scripture depends on the certitude of the literal sense." As Augustine maintains, spiritual explanation must have its *fulcimentum* ("prop") in some literal exposition.[26]

Further, it is denied that sanctifying grace is needed to apprehend Scripture's spiritual sense. For if such were the case — if the certitude of interpretation depended upon experience, the affects, or the inspiration and testimony of the Spirit [27] — "it would follow that no one would have certitude of any mystical or spiritual sense . . . since no one knows . . . whether he is worthy of love or hate, it follows that no one would know that he had such certitude of the aforesaid *sensus mysticus*." [28] Here, Burgos is in revolt against an *indi-*

25. *Add. prol.* (fol. 6vb H): "Similiter suo modo dicendum est de sensu litterali, scilicet quod est fundamentum, scilicet respectu aliorum sensuum secundum quandam similitudinem. Nam sicut in edificio . . . Sic totus sensus spiritualis sacre scripture rueret sensu litterali totaliter sublato, cum sensum spiritualis de his que ad salutem pertinet fundari habeat in sensu litterali, ut dictum est."

26. *Add. prol.* (fol. 6rb D): "Tota enim certitudo aliorum sensuum sacre scripture a certitudine sensus litteralis dependet, unde Aug. de doc. christiana: Nihil est quod occulte in aliquo loco sacre scripture traditur quod non alibi manifeste exponatur. Cuius ratio est, nam spiritualis expositio semper debet habere fulcimentum ab aliqua litterali expositione."

27. In this section Burgos is answering the first *Replica* of Matthias Doering, a heated protest against Burgos' arguments for the superiority of the *sensus litteralis*. Doering was apparently not acute enough to realize that on this issue, when he swung at Burgos, he was hitting his own mentor, Lyra. Burgos accurately reproduces Doering's position *Add. prol.* (fol. 8va E): "quod certitudo spiritualis intelligentie non est speculationis sicut litteralis intelligentia, sed est certitudo experientie et secundum affectum et per modum gustus, per inspirationem et testimonium spiritu sancti." As will be shown, this corresponds almost exactly to Luther's earliest sentiments in his Psalms lectures. Werbeck incorrectly characterizes Doering as a "faithful shadow" of Lyra (*Perez*, p. 122).

28. *Add. prol.* (fol. 8va F): "Ex hoc dicto tuo . . . sequeretur quod

vidualistic modification of the line of thought established by Gerson, by way of which the hermeneutical problem would be shifted to the qualifications of the exegete, with a correlative downgrading of the theological status of exegetical science. Burgos' firm reply is that one cannot set the Spirit against the literal sense of Scripture.[29]

To go back to the role of christological thought in the definition of the *sensus litteralis,* in Totting it was observed how the *fundamentum* (via Christ's promise) had shifted partially to the Church, even though the literal sense was still something to be found in Scripture. Then in Gerson, the church was finally given constitutive, articulative authority over the literal sense itself. In Burgos, however, none of this takes place. For him, it is Christ who alone establishes the *sensus litteralis.* This appears especially in answer to an objection of Doering's based on John 5:39: did not Christ here mean that the Jews should search the *spiritual* sense of Scripture? Not at all, answers Burgos: "I dare to say to you, brother [Matthias]: search all the holy Gospels of God, and you will not find that Christ appealed to any authority of the Holy Scriptures — either when he was instructing his disciples, or when he was contradicting the Jews, or even when the devil was tempting him — except as understood under the literal sense." [30]

---

nullus haberet certitudinem alicuius sensus mystici seu spiritualis sacre scripture nisi existens in gratia. Et cum nemo sciat de lege communi utrum sit dignus amore vel odio, sequitur quod nullus sciret se habere talem certitudinem predicti sensus mystici de lege communi, quod esset valde inconsonum rationi."

29. The position represented by Doering (and later by Faber and for a time by Luther) is a sort of Tradition II (or III) in the *individualistic* sense: rather than being located in the Church, the Spirit is in the individual. Although Gerson, like Doering, puts great weight on the qualifications of the exegete, he keeps the Holy Spirit reserved to the Church when it comes to establishing the sense of Scripture (see Altenstaig, "Sacra Scriptura," in *Vocabularius,* fol. 230rb).

30. *Add. prol.* (fol. 7vb H): "Audeo tibi dicere frater: Scrutare omnia

There follows a compliment of Lyra for establishing the literal sense even of Old Testament passages on the basis of the New Testament. But, as already noted, the basis is different, for with Burgos the emphasis is more on who Christ is and what Christ himself says: "From which the case is decided against you: Christ was commanding that those senses be searched out which he himself was daily speaking, preaching and arguing, which are only the literal senses." The blindness of the Jews was not that they could not discern the spiritual senses; rather, Jesus reproved them for their "false understanding of the literal sense." [31] The literal sense, then, is celebrated by Burgos as the proper sense of Scripture, upon which all other senses depend just as the words and person of Christ are the reality on which the Church depends.

On the following grounds, then, it can be concluded that Burgos represents a late-medieval, orthodox Tradition I position: the promise of Christ is applied to proper interpretation of Scripture, rather than to the very constitution of Scripture; all valid theological conclusions are derived from the literal sense of Scripture; no extra-Scriptural catholic truths are necessary for salvation; the literal sense is the living, spiritual *fundamentum* of all the other senses, just as Christ is the *fundamentum*; sanctifying grace and the testimony of the Spirit (the individual analogue to the Spirit-filled Church) are not requirements for spiritual exegesis (and thus the hermeneutical problem is not shifted, as it were, from the Bible's contents to the exegete's qualifications, or to questions of ecclesiology); there is no subversion (as in Gerson) of the gram-

---

sacra euangelica dei, et non reperies christum allegasse auctoritatem aliquam sacre scripture vel discipulis erudiendis, aut iudeis contradicentibus, seu etiam diabolo tentanti nisi sub sensu litterali intellectam."

31. *Add. prol.* (fol. 8ra A f.): "Ex quo concluditur contra te. Ipsos enim sensus mandabat christus scrutari de quibus ipse quotidie dicebat, predicabat seu disputabat, qui sunt tantummodo litterales ut dictum est . . . Unde cecitas iudaica quam christus reprobat circa falsum intellectum sensus litteralis consistit."

matical definition of "literal sense"; and finally, aside from the brief references noted, preoccupation with the criterion of authority is singularly lacking.

Results for the Old Testament

But this literal sense so celebrated by Burgos — the literal sense that even Jesus exclusively uses — is not, in fact, the literal sense of the *Old* Testament. Nor is his theory conducive to new, closer attention to the Old Testament as a theologically relevant source. True, there remains with Burgos, as with Lyra, the still valid moral precepts and the doctrine of one God in the Old Testament, and these are not subject to figurative interpretation.[32] But when it comes to the Old Testament *historia,* Burgos is evidently very close to the Gersonian idea that the true literal sense of Scripture was first revealed in the time of Christ, for he believes that Christ's use of Scripture decisively defines and establishes the literal sense of the whole Bible, Old Testament included.[33] The Old Testament "literal sense" for which Burgos has been arguing always depends on Christ's actual presence in Israel among the Jews. Therefore, the problem of a pre-Christ understanding, and hence of the faith of the Old Testament people, remains below Burgos' horizon of interpretation.

Added confirmation of Burgos' blurring of the distinctions

32. *Add. prol.* (fol. 5ᵛᵃ E): "Sunt . . . multa in libris canonicis tam veteris testamenti quam novi quae non habent nisi sensum litteralem, quod patet in multis, et specialiter in duobus preceptis charitatis, in quibus tota lex pendet et prophete." Cf. 6ᵛᵇ G: "per sensum litteralem non solum habetur historia tantum, sc. rerum gestarum, sed etiam que sunt *agenda,* ut patet ex preceptis charitatis, in quibus secundum doctrinam Christi tota lex pendet. Similiter per sensum litteralem habentur que sunt *credenda,* ut de unitate dei, Dt. 6 [:4]: 'Audi israel . . .' " (Italics mine.)

33. Notice, for example, in the preceding note, how the *doctrina Christi* confirms the validity of the Old Testament *lex* and *doctrina.* The Old Testament *promissio* does not function anywhere in the prologue of Burgos.

between literal and spiritual is his characterization of the Rules of Tyconius: the seven keys that Isidore handed down are, Burgos believes, "nothing but species of the *literal* sense, as is evident to one who understands." [34] The tradition has thus come a long way from Augustine, who had recognized Tyconius' rules as pertaining to the figurative senses of Scripture (with the exception of the third rule).[35]

Furthermore — and here Burgos is in accord with the Augustinian interpretation of letter and spirit as law and grace — spirit belongs wholly to the New Testament, for it is the new law to which Paul refers in 2 Cor. 3:6.[36] Thus, despite Burgos' protest that the *sensus litteralis* is full of spirit and life, he has so placed the hermeneutical divide between letter and spirit at the division between the two testaments that the remnant of normative-literal sense which he allows to the Old Testament — which alone gives it theological status — seems about to be overpowered by the strong christological motif.

The Tension Between Historia *and* Doctrina

A tension remains — the same tension that was found in Saint Thomas — between the authority of certain events and the authority of eternal, trans-historical verities. Burgos (quoting Thomas frequently) sees all historical events as subject to figurative interpretation,[37] including the Christ events. The

34. *Add. prol.* (fol. 8ᵛᵃ E): "et septem claves seu regulae quas Isid. tradit . . . non sunt nisi quedam species sensus *litteralis,* ut patet intelligenti." (Italics mine.) It is difficult to avoid concluding that here Burgos has deceived himself.

35. Burgos has no extended comment on the rules; there are only two passing comments on them, one of which is given in the preceding note.

36. *Add. prol.* (fol. 6ᵛᵇ G): "[Paulus] intendit distinguere . . . inter legem veterem que fuerat data a litteris scriptis . . . et inter legem novam que data fuit in spiritusancto in cordibus, prout fuit prophetatum Hiere. 31 [:33]. Unde lex vetus dicitur lex littere, et lex nova lex spiritus."

37. The New Testament warrant for this is I Cor. 10:11: "Omnia in

New Testament events, like those of the Old Testament, can be the basis of fourfold interpretation.[38] *Historia* can be contrasted to *revelata* and *precepta*.[39] How then is it possible for Burgos to maintain that the historical Christ constitutes the definitive normative-literal sense of Scripture? How can that which has occurred in Christ function in a decisive, definitive way for later times, if it shares the significative character of all the other moments of biblical history? As a matter of fact, it cannot. Given the thomistic, significative view of the event of Christ, therefore, it is not surprising, when one asks what is the ultimate literal sense of the New Testament, that the answer seems to be: not Christ himself, but his *doctrina* and *lex*: "In the Gospels, many things are handed down to which it is not necessary to assign a mystical sense, but only the literal sense, as for example in those things which are delivered as precepts, e.g., John 13: 'Believe in God, and believe in me,' and similar passages. Likewise in those things which are given as counsels, as it says in Matthew 19: 'If you want to be perfect, go and sell all that you have . . .' These are received on the basis of things designated by the words; in them and

---

figuris contingebant illis." Burgos points out (arguing against Doering and the notion of the Old Testament as total allegory): "non dicitur quod omnia *dicebantur* illis in figura [thus leaving room for *lex* and *doctrina*], sed *contingebat*, in quo manifeste ostendit quod loquitur de *gestis contingentibus*, non autem *revelatis aut preceptis* eisdem." (Italics mine; *Add. prol.,* fol. 8rb D.)

38. Burgos here (*Add. prol.,* fol. 5va F) refers to Thomas, *Quodlib.* VII, to explain the use of the fourfold sense. The Old Testament events can be interpreted according to all four senses; "similiter ea quae ad litteram de christo capite dicuntur possunt exponi litteraliter de christi gestis, et allegorice referendo ea ad corpus eius mysticum." It seems to me that Burgos, with his emphatically christological understanding of the Bible's total meaning, has already virtually done what Ebeling sees Luther as having first done, namely, to designate Christ as the "true" *sensus* of the Old Testament, and then to make Christ the basis of fourfold interpretation (see "Die Anfänge," p. 222).

39. See n. 37 above.

similar passages no spiritual sense is to be sought, but only the literal sense." [40]

A systematic comparison between Totting-Gerson and Burgos suggests itself here. Totting resolved the tension between the ongoing redemptive *historia* and the biblical *doctrina* in favor of the former. He appealed to Christ's promise to the Church, by which authority was bestowed on the Church to become the new locus of Scripture's normative spiritual meaning — which in Gerson's usage became the normative *literal* meaning. Thus, the move was made from Tradition II to Tradition III. But Burgos, consistent with his Tradition I position, rests instead with the self-witness of Christ in his "precept": "Believe in me!" So Christ himself, and his word in the New Testament rather than the Church, can remain the locus of the normative-literal sense, even for the future.

40. *Add. prol.* (fol. 5va E f.): "In euangeliis etiam multa traduntur quibus non oportet assignare sensum mysticum sed tantum litteralem, sicut in his que traduntur ut precepta, ut cum Jn. 14 [:1] dicit: 'Credite in deum et in me credite,' et similibus. Similiter in his que dantur ut consilia, sicut cum dicit Mt. 19 [:21]: 'Si vis perfectus esse, vade et vende omnia que habes et da pauperibus':in quibus et similibus non est querendus sensus spiritualis, qui ex rebus signatis per voces accipiatur, sed tantum sensus litteralis qui ex significatione vocum accipitur ut est manifestum."

VII. JAMES PEREZ OF VALENCIA

James Perez of Valencia (d. 1490) has excited interest among Reformation scholars because of the theological richness of his commentary on the Psalms, and because of the possible — but as yet undemonstrated — relationship between him and Luther.[1] Whether or not Luther read him, he belonged to the same order as Luther, the Augustinian hermits, and was an influential representative of that order's theology in later years.[2] Further, he may have influenced Faber Stapulensis,[3] who did at first affect Luther. Finally, with Perez the concept of *promissio* plays a significant and potentially explosive role in light of this study.

If Paul of Burgos was a devoted disciple of Thomas Aquinas, and if his favorite axiom was that "only the *sensus litteralis* is valid for theological proof," then Perez seems at first glance diametrically opposed. He is an enthusiastic student of Augustine; his favorite axiom is that "the Old Testament was not given *gratia sui,* for its own sake"; he argues that the spiritual

---

1. Werbeck's monograph on Perez is a valuable contribution in the little-explored field of late medieval hermeneutics. Werbeck shows (*Perez*, pp. 27–33) that Perez' commentary represents about twenty years' labor, having been finished and first published at Valencia in 1484. The edition used here is *Centum ac quinquaginta psalmi Davidici* (Lyon, 1514). Werbeck examines the evidence regarding Luther's possible use of this commentary (pp. 47 ff.). The external evidence is disappointing, and the internal evidence includes the fact that Perez' name is never mentioned by Luther in the whole first Psalms lectures.

2. Werbeck has found that in the compendious *Vocabularius theologie* of Johannes Altenstaig, Perez is the single exegete represented among a host of systematic theologians. For his discussion of the subject "Sacra Scriptura," Altenstaig depends wholly on Perez, whom he had studied in detail, and on Gerson (Werbeck, *Perez*, pp. 45 f.).

3. Again, it has not been shown whether Faber actually used Perez. But Perez' Psalms commentary was published at Paris in 1506 (Werbeck,

senses are valid for theological proof [4] and that "non est sistendum in littera; one must not stay with the letter." Furthermore, if Burgos' prologue was structured as a scholastic *quaestio*, that of Perez is in large part an extended discussion of the rules — he calls them "keys" — of Tyconius-Augustine, of which Perez gives ten rather than the traditional seven.[5]

The fact that the work under discussion is the introduction to an Old Testament book, rather than to the whole Bible, does not prevent it from posing the broadest hermeneutical issues. Moreover, the central focus of this long prologue (24 folio pages) is the interpretation of the Old Testament. For Perez, that means: how are evangelical mysteries to be extracted from the Old Testament? [6]

Although Perez and Burgos seem at first to stand in direct opposition to each other, their position regarding the Old Testament is rather close. The difference is that Perez discards the normative-literal remnant retained by Burgos, which allows his christological interpretation of the Old Testament to be still more thoroughgoing.

According to Perez, the whole of the Old Testament is

Perez, p. 47), in time for Faber to use it for his own Psalms commentary of 1509. The two works are fairly congenial in thought structure, and Perez' work is illuminating for an understanding of Faber.

4. Perez, *Centum ac quinquaginta psalmi Davidici*, Prologus, tractatus 3, capitulum 2, clavis 10 (cited hereafter as *prol.* tr.3 c.2 cl.10; fol. 17ra f. The "claves" appear only in this one chapter; they are the 10 "keys" of Tyconius-Augustine as Perez adapts them): "Ex quibus [that is, the whole series of arguments already made] patet qualiter argumentum factum per discursum et processum allegoricum, a figura ad figuratum aut a signo ad signatum, et a parabola veteris testamenti ad suam veritatem euangelicam sibi correspondentem, licet non sit efficax contra cecos iudeos, tamen est efficax inter catholicos fideles." This statement recalls the position of Totting.

5. Werbeck argues for Perez' direct dependence on Augustine in the discussion of the rules (*Perez*, p. 92).

6. *Prol.* tr.3 c.2 (fol. 11va): "ex quibus [propositiones veteris testamenti] eliciuntur et inferuntur conclusiones euangelice."

parable, *allegoria, propositio*,⁷ and written *ad figurandum*.⁸ These statements are predicated on the assumption that the entire theological content of the Old Testament is its *mysteria euangelica*, and that these do not have *esse reale* in the Old Testament.⁹ So pervasive are these statements that I suspect Perez is ready to scrap the traditional schema and deny that the Old Testament has at least those fragments of normative *lex* and *doctrina* that are granted to it by others, and which gave the Old Testament a theological toehold in the canon.¹⁰ Even so, Perez has not altogether emptied the Old Testament of meaning, as will be shown.

Nowhere in his prologue does Perez give a technical definition of the *sensus litteralis*. It is possible that he has simply

7. *Prol.* tr.3 c.2 cl.10 (fol. 16ᵛᵇ): "tota scriptura veteris testamenti est allegorica, quia non ponitur gratia sui, sed gratia novi testamenti . . . Omnia gesta veteris testamenti non erant gratia sui, sed erant quaedam figure et picture et signa et exemplaria et parabole respectu novi testamenti, inquantum figurabant et significabant . . . alia futura mysteria in novo testamento." The term propositio is used in the Aristotelian sense, whereby it requires a *conclusio*, which for the Old Testament is the New. See Werbeck's explanation, where he describes Perez' view as "heilsgeschichtliche" (*Perez*, pp. 74 ff.).

8. *Prol.* tr.1 c.2 (fol. 3ʳᵃ): "nihil scribitur nec ponitur nec fuit gestum in veteri testamento gratia sui, sed ad figurandum . . . mysteria euangelica."

9. *Prol.* tr.1 c.2 (fol. 3ʳᵃ): "veritates et mysteria novi testamenti non habent esse reale in veteri testamento, sed tantum esse figurativum et representativum."

10. To the "nihil" which is given above, note 8, can be added an "omnia" and a "non nisi" (the first Platonic, the second Aristotelian in pedigree). The first: "Sicut nostra humana cognitio procedit a sensibilibus, nobis magis notis, ad intelligibilia, ita deus voluit procedere in lege. Nam omnia que precipiuntur in lege veteri sunt sensibilia et corporalia, ut per illa manu duceremur in spiritualia et intelligibilia mysteria euangelica, quia sic apti nati sumus scire." The second: "Nam scriptura veteris testamenti non adducitur nisi tanquam propositiones et parabole ex quibus prophetice inferuntur conclusiones et mysteria euangelica de christo et ecclesia." *Prol.* tr.1 c.2; fol. 3ʳᵃ.

given up the task of defining nomenclature. "Literal" and "spiritual" have become so confused (especially since Gerson) that it makes little difference what labels are used. A chaos of terminology prevails in Perez. In a quotation given by Werbeck, Perez holds, in effect, that the *spiritual* understanding of the Old Testament is to see that it is *literally* about Christ.[11] This confusion of language, already in evidence in the prologue,[12] is testimony to the loss of a meaningful distinction between literal and spiritual interpretation. Perez does not completely give up the grammatical sense as legitimate; he is too appreciative of Lyra and the Hebrew exegetical tradition. But the literal sense has very nearly become for him a "bad," "carnal" letter.[13]

The only obstacle in the way of this total discrediting of the literal sense, in the material so far examined, is application to the Old Testament of the honored axiom of the Thomas-

11. At Ps. 100:8, Perez writes: "Allegorice . . . exponitur de Christo, immo verius dicam litteraliter." Even more remarkable, at Ps. 104:5 ff.: "Iste psalmus . . . solum exponendus litteraliter, sed principaliter est exponendus allegorice et litteraliter de Christo et ecclesia." Werbeck, *Perez*, p. 129.

12. *Prol.* tr.3 c.2 cl.5 (fol. 13vb), in a discussion of Cyrus as the "Christ": "illa prophetia est intelligenda materialiter de cyro rege persarum, sed *litteraliter* et finaliter . . . de Christo figurato per cyrum." A few lines later, the same type of interpretation involves seeing in these Old Testament events a "sensum spiritualem *ultra litteralem* . . . [that is,] mysteria futura de Christo et ecclesia." (Italics mine.) Thus, "literal" is used within a few lines to mean both the historical and the figurative senses of the Old Testament words.

13. Werbeck cites examples that for Perez, the Jewish-literal sense is not false, and that he always begins with it as part of his method (*Perez*, p. 130 n.1). But in these passages Perez grants no more than that these events actually occurred. No one in the medieval tradition would have denied that. The problem (as with the whole tradition) is that Perez has no answer to the question of contemporary theological relevance; these things are all signs, and therefore a point of departure only, to be gotten beyond as quickly as possible. Smalley's judgment, though harsh, is correct on this particular point: "He was a well-meaning cheat" ("The Bible," p. 71).

Lyra-Burgos tradition, which insisted on the grammatical basis of the normative theological contents of Scripture. This axiom located valid theological truth in the letter of the Old Testament text, and thus saved at least part of it. But Perez sweeps this axiom away. Along with it, he denies the axiom that only the literal sense is valid for proof. It is the spiritual sense that must be sought; it is the spiritual sense that Jesus and Paul used, for proof, against the Jews. In cutting the last connection between the grammatical sense of the Old Testament and the normative sense of the Bible, Perez is able to proceed to a christological reading of the Old Testament which is more complete than that of Burgos, because no longer encumbered and qualified by the competing notion that *lex* and *doctrina* are normative and are contained also in the Old Testament. In holding on to *lex* and *doctrina,* Burgos retained a notion that was in competition with his strong inclination to make Christ the literal sense of the Old Testament. Thus, he was able to retain a remnant of the Old Testament, in its grammatical meaning, as theologically normative in the Church. Perez eliminates this remnant when he remarks, without qualification, "the whole Old Testament is allegory."

Perez can now proceed to an interpretation of 2 Cor. 3:6 which is diametrically opposed to that of Burgos, making possible the equation of grammatical-literal with "carnal," a common term of opprobrium among exegetes. As long as the theologically normative senses were viewed as being grounded in grammar, this could never be done. But now, grammar loses its high status; spiritual exegesis is set free of dependence on what the words say. "Spiritual" is understood now as an existential category, so that the decisive question about any interpretation is whether or not the interpreter has the "spiritual ears" to hear the real intention of the words. On this point, then, Perez has joined forces with Matthias Doering. One may now set the spirit (however defined) against the letter of Scripture.

To explicate his position, Perez proposes a distinction between understanding a word 'or passage "ad sensum quem facit" and understanding it "ad sensum in quo fit," that is, between the grammatical meaning of the words and the hidden sense which corresponds to the real intention of the one who spoke them — and which requires that one has the Spirit. Jesus' own words illustrate the distinction when he says, "Let him who has ears to hear, hear." Perez glosses these words: "ears for hearing, that is, for understanding, namely spiritually and not carnally; that is, let him understand the spiritual sense toward which and in which the spiritual words were said." [14]

This is the same point reached in the discussion of Gerson: the bridge between literal and theological or spiritual interpretation cannot be built any further with hermeneutical axioms, since the living Spirit is required for such interpretation, and the Spirit is apparently not "located" in, or available through, the words of Scripture, but is in the Church (Gerson), or in the exegete (Doering, Perez). In any case, the Spirit is presupposed, and the discussion ceases to concern the Bible.

The Prophet's Duplex Spiritus

Perez has here set up the possibility of a new kind of "double sense" — one grammatically discernible, the other resting in the hidden intention of the speaker. Lyra and Burgos would have disagreed with this separation of the intention of the human speaker from what the words plainly convey.[15]

14. *Prol.* tr.3 c.2 cl.6 (fol. 15ra): the greatest part of the Scripture, in both testaments, is to be understood according to the sense in which it is intended, not according to the sense it makes: "ad sensum in quo fit, et non quem facit." "For the spiritual ears of the mind," Perez explains, "receive the spiritual and secret sense: Nam aures spirituales mentis suscipiunt sensum spiritualem et secretum." Reference is then made to the words of Jesus (Mt. 13:9): "Qui habet aures audiendi, i.e. intelligendi, audiat, scil. spiritualiter et non carnaliter, i.e. intelligat sensum spiritualem *ad quem et in quo verba spiritualia fiunt.*" (Italics mine.)

15. In his prologue, Burgos shows awareness of the difference between

Perez, by contrast, proceeds to construct a sense based on the "duplex spiritus" of the prophets.

For my purpose, Perez's way of introducing this notion is of paramount importance, for it again introduces the duality of the use of *promissio* that was originally found in Augustine.[16] Perez introduces the notion in his discussion of the third rule of Tyconius-Augustine, on the spirit and the letter. At first, Perez appears to have accepted the transposition of this idea into strictly Old Testament-New Testament terms, for he argues that all "gesta et facta" of the Old Testament are to be understood as signs and figures which were to be verified in Christ; therefore, it is the "spiritual" (that is, the *New* Testament) senses that are chiefly to be sought.[17]

But then, rather abruptly, Perez observes that the Old Testament promises and prophecies are of a different order from the "gesta et facta"; "All the promises of the patriarchs, and all the predictions and prophecies of the prophets are to be understood literally of Christ and the Church, since all of

---

the human intention and God's intention, the latter being capable of comprehending more than the apparent meanings of the words, covering, as it does, the future, spiritual (for us) senses. "But since," Burgos writes, "it is impossible for two literal senses at once to be attributed to any sacred author, it is necessary to say that only one of them is literal" (*Add. prol.*, fol. 5vb H).

16. It will be recalled, on the one hand, that the Old Testament promises and their fulfillment are seen as *figurae* of the New Testament promises, so that the Old Testament promises are fit into the overall schema of *signum-res* by which the relation between the testaments is described; on the other hand, the Old Testament actually promises Messiah, or the New Covenant grace, opening the way to a quite different relationship between the testaments, whereby the Old Testament history is not mere sign and allegory, utterly opaque in its own time, but is rather a time of expectation and living under God's promises, and therefore in some way analogous with the situation in our own time. Perez, as will be shown, is the first of the sources here studied to be really aware of the difference this makes in the interpretation of the Old Testament.

17. *Prol.* tr.3 c.2 cl.5 (fol. 13rb): "omnia gesta veteris testamenti non erant gratia sui, sed gratia christi et ecclesie, inquantum erant omnia verificanda de christo propter quem gerebantur."

them were literally fulfilled in him. For that promise to Abraham, 'In your seed shall all nations be blessed' (Gen. 22) was fulfilled *litteraliter* in Christ; and that promise made to Judah himself (Gen. 49): 'The sceptre will not be taken away from Judah,' etc. Likewise that prophecy in Isa. 7: 'Behold, a virgin will conceive' . . . And thus it is evident that all the promises and predictions of the prophets are to be understood *litteraliter* of Christ and the church." [18] This passage is startling, for it seems to indicate the discovery of the Old Testament as a book of promise. *Promissio* seems — for the first time since Augustine — to have recovered its place alongside *lex* and *doctrina* as one element of the Old Testament that is to be understood simply *litteraliter, not figurative*.[19]

But how can this be? Perez has described the Old Testament as nothing but sign and allegory. How is it possible now to assert that an important element of the Old Testament is to be read literally? At this juncture, Perez does not carry through his idea. Rather, he carefully tailors it to make it conform to the basic *signum-res* schema: "But it must be carefully noted that just as the patriarchs had a *double spirit* in their promises, and the prophets spoke in a *double spirit* in

18. *Prol.* tr.3 c.2 cl.5 (fol. 13ʳᵃ): "Licet omnia gesta et facta veteris testamenti sint intelligenda ad duplicem sensum [that is, both *historice* and *allegorice*] . . . tamen omnes promissiones patriarcharum et omnia vaticinia et prophetie prophetarum sunt intelligende litteraliter de christo et ecclesia, eo quod omnia litteraliter fuerunt in eo impleta. Nam litteraliter fuit impleta in christo illa promissio abrae, 'In semine tuo benedicentur omnes gentes,' Gen. 22[:18], et illa promissio facta ipsi iude, Gen. 49 [:10], 'Non auferetur sceptrum de iuda,' etc. Item illa prophetia Esa. 7[:14], 'Ecce virgo concipiet' . . . et sic patet quod omnia promissa patriarcharum et vaticinia prophetarum sunt intelligenda litteraliter de christo et ecclesia."

19. The appearance of *promissio* in the context of discussion of the Third Rule raises the question of whether Perez had read Tyconius, since Tyconius' concern was to show the uniqueness of the people of the promise. Apparently Perez had not read him, for he speaks of Augustine's criticisms and revisions of Tyconius as if they were much more serious than they were.

their predictions, so those promises and predictions were doubly fulfilled *ad litteram,* and consequently are to be understood *dupliciter ad litteram.*" [20] After giving four examples,[21] Perez observes: "And this occurred as Isaiah and the other prophets were foreseeing in simple spirit future *temporal* events of that people and temple and city, but after that, more elevated in a double prophetic spirit, they saw how those material and temporal events were future *figures* of Christ and the church. And then, having the spiritual sense of those material events, they prophesied *litteraliter* and predicted the future mysteries of Christ and the church." [22]

Perez then turns to the Davidic prophecy in the Psalms. David contemplates Israel's entire history as it has unfolded, with its promises and his own difficulties and successes, "and then, *in duplici spiritu et lumine prophetico,* he perceives in those things their spiritual meaning beyond the letter, and thus foresees the future mysteries of Christ and the church." [23]

20. *Prol.* tr.3 c.2 cl.5 (fol. 13[va]): "Sed est valde advertendum quod sicut patriarche habuerunt *duplicem spiritum* in suis promissionibus et prophete locuti sunt in *duplici spiritu* in suis vaticiniis, ita illa promissa et vaticinia fuerunt dupliciter impleta ad litteram, et per consequens sunt *dupliciter ad litteram* intelligenda." (Italics mine.) The idea of prophetic "duplicity" is lacking in Lyra.

21. *Prol.* tr.3 c.2 cl.5 (fol. 13[va]): The Old Testament texts concerned are Gen. 12:3 and 49:8-10; 2 Sam. 7:12 ff.; Isa. 45:1 ff. In each case it is shown how an initial fulfillment in the Old Testament time was followed by a "perfect" fulfillment in Christ and the Church.

22. *Prol.* tr.3 c.2 cl.5 (fol. 13[vb]): "Et hoc accidit, nam Esayas et ceteri prophete in simplici spiritu previdebant futuros eventus materiales et temporales illius populi et templi et civitatis, sed postea magis elevati *in duplici spiritu prophetico* previdebant qualiter illa gesta temporalia et materialia futura erant *figura* christi et ecclesie. Et tunc, habentes sensum spiritualem ex illis gestis materialibus, litteraliter prophetabant et predicebant futura mysteria de christo et ecclesia." (Italics mine.)

23. *Prol.* tr.3 c.2 cl.5 (fol. 13[vb]): "tunc in duplici spiritu et lumine prophetico, percipiebat in illis sensum spiritualem ultra litteralem, et sic previdebat mysteria futura de christo et ecclesia." It is not clear in these passages how important for Perez was the question whether the prophet only "sees," secretly, the christological meaning, or whether he also forthrightly proclaims it to Israel. For if the first of these possibilities is empha-

Two Ways of Interpreting the Old Testament

However unlikely this theory of prophecy may seem, Perez has introduced a notion of the Old Testament word that tries to account for the future — for the promising word in which the intention and commitment of God are made known. This word has no present referent that can be a secret sign of some distant thing; this word literally reaches and points beyond the immediate *res* of the prophet's milieu and directs the expectation of the hearers to the future.

Thus, Perez is giving some immediate theological validity to the promising, prophetic word *per se*. This is difficult to do in the Thomistic framework, where the theological sense of the words can only be revealed, because it is first constituted, by later events in history (every res^I needs a res^{II}). The occurrence of the second event alone gives the theological meaning of the word; once the New Testament events have occurred, the Old Testament words are theologically empty.[24]

But here Perez has momentarily opened a fresh avenue of interpretation by introducing the promises of the Old Testament as both belonging to its literal sense and calling attention openly to the Messiah who is also the object of Christian faith. Is this only a momentary, passing thought that Perez quickly drops? No. It is more, for he repeats the idea later and gives it precise hermeneutical formulation. In the context of

---

sized (which seems to be the case), one can hardly avoid being uneasy about the deception perpetrated on the Old Testament hearers, who do not discern the duplicity of meaning. If, however, the second possibility is developed, the word that Israel hears is an authentic word of God, in which God's intention is declared, and expectation and hope in the coming Messiah are awakened.

24. For Thomas the Old Testament time was one of unequivocal not-having; having the promise was unfavorably compared to having the *res* in the present. The Old Testament people were thus divided in two: the ordinary folk who were just a *signum*, and the elite minority who already belonged to the new age before its time and already participated in its unique gifts.

a lengthy discussion of allegory, Perez reminds his readers: "But again we must be aware that a faithful understanding [or interpretation] runs from the Old to the New Testament *in two ways*: one way is allegorically, from the *figura* to the *figuratum* in the way we have explained it. The second way is literally, through the expressed promises, by calling attention to the promises expressly made in the Old Testament, and to the prophecies of the prophets, just as the evangelists frequently do." [25]

At this important juncture, it is clearly seen that the distinction between two ways of relating the Old and New Testaments, a distinction which I developed and discussed earlier, is appropriate to the medieval material. Perez is clearly aware of the difference between a *figura* and a *promissio,* and of the propriety of carefully observing the distinction when interpreting the Old Testament. This idea of promise could, if developed, significantly alter the predominant notions of the Old Testament's theological value, open it up to fresh theological interpretation, and call into question the merely figurative value usually given to its *res gestae.*

Although it can be shown that Perez is aware of these two quite different lines of interpretation, he seems in the end to prefer the allegorical mode. "The whole Old Testament is allegory" seems to be his last word — a statement in harmony with Gerson's, whereby the ("true") literal sense of the Old Testament was first revealed in the time of Christ. However, isolated cases demonstrate his awareness of the other mode of thinking about the Old Testament-New Testament relationship, and since their implications are worth noting, I shall deal with some specific cases in point.

25. *Prol.* tr.3 c.2 cl.10 (fol. 17[rb]): "Sed est iterum advertendum quod intellectus fidelis *dupliciter* discurrit a scriptura veteris testamenti ad novum. Uno modo allegorice a figura ad figuratum eo modo quo dictum est. Secundo modo *per expressa promissa* litteraliter allegando promissiones expresse factas in veteri testamento et prophetias prophetarum, sicut frequenter faciunt euangeliste." (Italics mine.)

The Old Testament Fathers. — If the reality of their existence under the promise of Christ is emphasized, as well as their hope, expectation, and petition for the fulfillment of the promises, these figures emerge as subjects of real theological interest, living in hope and expectation of the future, rather than appearing merely as carnal (the victims of the prophet's duplicity). They can also serve the interpreter as models and examples for Christians: the exegete can move directly from literal explication to tropological (or moral) application.

If, however, the *figurative* character of the Old Testament fathers is the focus of attention, the results are quite different: not the fathers' expectation and hope, but the figurative or typological similarity of their words and actions to Christ's words and actions is brought out; and they serve the interpreter as figures of Christ (whatever else they were then becomes irrelevant to the interpretation). The exegete in this case moves from literal (now meaning "unedifying") to allegorical exposition, that is, from Old Testament events to those of the New. The next natural step is tropology, in terms of *imitatio Christi.*

Both of these lines of interpretation can be found in Perez' prologue. Within the scope of the first mode is the idea that the Psalms were written as petition: "David made all the psalms for the most part *per modum petitionis.*" [26] This notion, although it occurs frequently, is not developed by Perez in an historical way; David, he explains, is usually speaking not for himself, or "in his own person," but in the person of the whole *genus humanum.*[27] Nevertheless, there are passages in the prologue in which Perez refers to the concrete people of Israel living under the promise. For example: "All the fathers and faithful of the Old Testament were stretching toward

26. *Prol.* tr.1 c.3 (fol. 4va): "David fecit omnes psalmos pro maiori parte per modum petitionis."
27. Werbeck has dealt thoroughly with this notion of the Psalm word as the generalized word of Adam, the "homo mysticus," the viator on his way toward Christ's coming (*Perez,* pp. 134–37).

Christ, in order that they might receive the promises in him, and consequently, they were saved more through faith in Christ than through works of the law. For they were not carrying out the works of the law except in professing faith in the future Christ." This description of life under promise is next given immediate application to Christian life: "Second, one must notice that just as God handed Adam and all the faithful of the Old Testament over to Christ, in order that they might be redeemed by him in the first advent, so also Christ hands his own people over to the second advent, that they might be glorified by him. For just as through the first advent redemption is promised to the faithful through Christ, so to us, now redeemed, glory and beatification are promised through the same Christ in his second advent." This immediate tropological, or moral, application to Christians is then expanded: "For already redeemed, we stretch toward Christ in order to be glorified, for we expect him to return to the marriage feast, as is plain in the whole Gospel story." [28] In this line of interpretation is seen the possibility for further development of an historical exegesis in which the actual religious situation of the Old Testament fathers becomes relevant for Christian faith. The structure of this mode of interpretation is built on two promised advents of the Messiah.

28. *Prol.* tr.3 c.1 (fol. 11rb): "omnes patres et fideles veteris testamenti tendebant in christum, ut in eo acciperent repromissiones, et per consequens magis salvati sunt per fidem christi quam per opera legis, quia non exercebant opera legis nisi protestando fidem Christi futuri. Secundo est notandum quod sicut deus remisit adam et omnes fideles veteris testamenti ad christum ut ab eo redimerentur in primo adventu, ita christus remisit suos ad secundum adventum ut ab eodem glorificarentur. Nam sicut per primum adventum promissa est fidelibus per christum redemptio, ita nobis iam redemptis promissa est per eundem christum in II adventum gloria et beatificatio. iam enim redempti, tendimus in christum ut glorificemur, expectamus enim eum a nuptiis reversurum ut patet per totum discursum euangelicum." Note that the exegesis moves directly from literal to tropological application.

Turn now to the second, allegorical mode of moving from the Old Testament text — the mode that predominates for Perez, under the overall rubric of the Old Testament as wholly allegory. Here, Perez sees all the fathers as figures of Christ: "It must be said that Christ was the true Adam, the true Abel, the true Noah, and Abraham, Isaac, Jacob, Moses, Joshua, David, Solomon, etc., because all of them were allotted such names insofar as they were figures of Christ according to the interpretation of the name. And thus it is said that these names are analogically spoken of Christ and of them, just as the picture of a man is not a true man, but the sign and figure of a true man." [29]

It appears, then, that as the first mode of interpretation held the Old Testament fathers to be living in the *expectatio* and *petitio* of the promise of Christ, so by contrast the second, allegorical mode considers them to be "pictures," early models, of Christ himself. The results are accordingly quite different when one proceeds to the *applicatio* — to a tropological or moral interpretation. For via the first route, there is continuity in the history of the people of God, which allows the Old Testament fathers to serve as models for Christian faith and hope of the future. Via the second interpretation, however, the faith of the Old Testament people is ignored; the point of departure becomes the words and deeds of Christ, and he becomes the model and exemplar for Christians.

29. *Prol.* tr.3 c.2 cl.5 (fol. 13rb): "est dicendum quod christus fuit verus adam et verus abel et verus noe; et abraham, et ysaac, et iacob, et moyses et iosue, et david et salomon &c., quia omnes illi sortiti sunt talia nomina inquantum fuerunt figure christi iuxta nominis interpretatione. et ideo talia nomina analogice dicuntur de christo et illis, sicut homo pictus non est verus homo sed signum et figura veri hominis." The *analogice* recalls Augustine's own designation of the spiritual senses. Perez' point is that all Old Testament *gesta* are *principaliter* to be understood of Christ, whose *figurae* they are. The actual outcome is that without (before) Christ, these figures are without meaning, and after Christ, they are unnecessary for our edification.

One result of the second mode is that when Christ is the focus, tropological exegesis will always concentrate on the virtues of *caritas*, humility and obedience, rather than on faith or hope. The reason is that Christ, according to unanimous medieval doctrine, had neither faith nor hope, for he was a *comprehensor,* not a pure *viator.*[30]

Christological Exegesis of the Old Testament. —As in his view of the Old Testament fathers, Perez also operated with two different methods of interpreting the Old Testament christologically. It is well known that Perez' interpretation of the Old Testament is emphatically Christ-centered.[31] What has not been noticed before is that this Christocentrism can be exegetically arrived at in both of Perez's two ways: via *promissio* (working in a "two-advent" schema), or via allegory (working within the traditional fourfold structure). Again, one finds Perez expressing both modes, although they are not sharply and explicitly distinguished.[32]

Examples have already been shown of the second way, whereby Christ is understood as the allegorical "truth" of everything the patriarchs said, did, and were. The way of *promissio,* however, will bring to expression the idea that the faith of the Old Testament fathers was the same as ours: "for

30. See *ST* III q.7 a.3 and 4 (IV, 2467a ff.).

31. For example, *Prol.* tr.3 c.l (fol. 11rb): "utraque lex est de christo . . . christus ut christus est obiectum et subiectum totius nostre theologie et sacre scripture . . . Unde . . . qui in tota sacra scriptura et in qualibet eius parte non intelligit christum, nihil intelligit." Cassiodorus, Hugh, and Augustine are named as authorities for this opinion.

32. Warning that something different is afoot is given in his first description of the three spiritual senses. The first, which pertains to *credenda,* is usually labeled *allegoria.* Perez frequently calls it "prophetic"; for example, "tria genera conclusionum possunt inferri . . . ex scripturis veteris testamenti . . . scil. conclusiones propheticae quae pertinent ad fidem" (*Prol.* tr.1 c.2; fol. 3rb). Here also is the specific linking of *spes* to the anagogical sense. *Spes* is based on *promissio*: "Anagogice procedimus ab euangelio in cognitionem futurorum bonorum glorie nobis promissorum" (fol. 3va).

even though Christ had not yet been incarnated, yet he was already believed . . . for all those fathers of the Old Testament accepted no promises except with us . . . For the same faith in Christ which saves us saved them also, since they were believing and expecting as future that same Christ whom we believe has now come, and whom we receive. And in such faith they were being saved." [33] Thus, Christ is the *terminus spei* of both old and new laws; in both, he is the "finis intentus et speratus." [34] In this small phrase is planted the potential for undermining the fourfold hermeneutic, as understood by Thomas: the "intentus" is also "speratus"; that is, what God intends has been declared, and so has become the foundation of hope for the future. In Thomas' schema, the *intentio Dei* tends to remain hidden under the figure until it comes to pass.

These two ways of interpreting Christ in the Old Testament — the Christ-figured and the Christ-promised, the allegorical and the literal — are not sharply differentiated by Perez, even though one can sift out a few quotations like those above. He does not seem to have had any particular reason to *contrast* one with the other.[35]

The Gesta Christi as Sacraments

It has been shown that the predominant medieval schema, in terms of which the Old Testament is mostly allegory, ulti-

---

33. *Prol.* tr.3 c.2 cl.7 (fol. 15ra f.): "Nam licet christus nondum esset incarnatus, tamen iam erat christus creditus . . . Quia omnes illi patres veteris testamenti non acceperunt repromissiones nisi nobiscum . . . Nam eadem fides christi quae salvat nos salvavit et illos, quia quem nos credimus iam venisse, et quem recepimus, illum et eundem christum, ipsi credebant et expectabant futurum. Et in tali fide salvabantur."
34. *Prol.* tr.3 c.2 cl.7 (fol. 15va).
35. Frequently the two ways are mixed in one statement. Thus, the time of the old law can be compared to the new in that the old is the time of "signifying, figuring, and desiring"; the new is the time of "fulfilling, verifying and receiving the promises" (*Prol.* tr.3 c.2 cl.7; fol. 16ra).

mately predominates also in Perez. The basis for this conclusion is precisely the repeated assertion that the *res gestae* of both the Old and New Testaments acquire theological significance for the future only when they are seen as *figurae* of something else.

But in Perez a distinction is drawn that reveals the unique significance of the *res gestae christi* — a significance lacking in the theory of Saint Thomas and Paul of Burgos. Perez makes a distinction regarding the efficacy of the Christ events that brings the hermeneutical theory into conformity with the traditional scholastic distinction regarding the respective value of the Old and New Testament sacraments.[36] The old dispensation, it is said, only promised salvation; the new gives it. Circumcision only *signifies* grace; baptism and the other Christian sacraments *contain* it.

Perez applies this distinction explicitly to an interpretation of the events recorded in the two testaments. In all *gesta et facta Christi,* he explains, one ought to look for the *sacramentum* that is hidden (*latet*) under the letter. For Christ's acts are *sacramenta* much more than the deeds of the old law were. The latter "were only a sign of a sacred thing insofar as they were signifying the future mysteries of Christ and the church. But they did not contain in the present that sacred thing which they signified for the future. Now all the *gesta et facta Christi* were not only signifying invisible grace, nay rather they were containing and making actual (*efficiebant*) in the present that grace which they signified." [37]

Therefore, although the spiritual sense is *principaliter* to be sought in the exegesis of both testaments, it has to be sought

---

36. I doubt that this is the invention of Perez. Rather, it only unveils the "sacramental" character of the fourfold schema as a whole.

37. *Prol.* tr.3 c.2 cl.5 (fol. 14^(ra)): "nam illa erant tantum sacre rei signum inquantum significabant futura mysteria christi et ecclesie. Sed non continebant de presenti illam rem sacram quam significabant de futuro, sed omnia gesta et facta christi non solum significabant gratiam invisibilem, immo in praesenti continebant et efficiebant gratiam quam significabant."

more (*magis*) in the Old Testament than in the New.[38] For the letter of the Old Testament only signifies, while that of the New already — somehow — contains the grace of redemption. The letter of the New Testament, of course, also has a spiritual sense which *signifies,* but does not yet contain, man's future glorification.[39]

This line of thought, whereby the Old Testament is emphatically *signum tantum,* makes unlikely a full development of the notion that what is chiefly to be noticed in the Old Testament is its "literal" thrust to the future via the promises, and that this promise is of abiding theological interest. For all grace, spirit, and life are in the words and deeds of Christ. On this particular issue, the hermeneutical divide is emphatically between the testaments.

The Unity of the Testaments

But Perez has also been seen to isolate *promissio* as an Old Testament idea of real theological significance. One must now go further into his understanding of the relation of the testaments, in order to see how he holds them together. His comment on Jer. 31:31 ff. is instructive. It will be recalled that Augustine had used this passage as an example of an Old Testament promise which is not a *figura* of some other New Testament promise, but a word to be understood in its literal sense. As such, it gave warrant for joining *promissio* to *doctrina* and *lex* as portions of the Old Testament not subject to figurative, spiritual exegesis.

38. *Prol.* tr.3 c.2 cl.5 (fol. 14rb): "ultra sensum litteralem magis est querendus sensus spiritualis in istis [gestis veteris testamenti] quam in illis [gestis n.t.]."

39. *Prol.* tr.3 c.2 cl.5 (fol. 14rb): "sub littera euangelica continetur gratia nostre redemptionis in presenti, et significatur glorificatio nostra futura." Therefore, one has also to get beyond the letter of the New Testament, for "omnia gesta et facta christi sunt quaedam profunda sacramenta in quibus preter sensum litteralem sit querendus sensus spiritualis de rebus occultis" (fol. 14ra).

In light of the two distinct tendencies noted in Perez, it would be difficult to anticipate how he actually interprets the Jeremiah text. Perez introduces this text as part of an objection to his contention that the Old Testament fathers, like Christians, are saved by faith in Christ. Jer. 31, says the objector, makes it clear that the New Covenant is different from the Old; its way of salvation must therefore differ.

Not so, answers Perez. The "accidents" of the two laws are different, but in *essence* they are the same. "For God did not intend, through Jeremiah, to give another law according to *essentialia*, but only according to *accidentalia* and offices, and according to rites and ceremonies, insofar as all those things would have to cease." [40] The essential unity of the two laws, Perez explains, consists in the single object of faith in both: "just as there was always one faith in Christ, so there was and always is one *lex* in both testaments, since the unity of the law is adduced from the unity of the faith." [41] The one *lex* is *fides Christi*. Christians, argues Perez, thus keep the law of Moses better than the Jews, "because we hold and preserve the essential *veritas legis*," [42] which is Christ and faith. For although times change, faith does not; justification "was, is and will be given *per fidem Jesu Christi*." [43] Therefore, although the two laws differ, or seem to differ, according to the letter, they are the same according to the spirit.[44]

40. *Prol.* tr.3 c.2 cl.7 (fol. 15va): "Nam deus per hieremiam non intendebat dare alteram legem secundum essentialia, sed secundum accidentalia et officialia et secundum ritus et cerimonias, inquantum omnia illa debebant cessare."

41. *Prol.* tr.3 c.2 cl.7 (fol. 15ra): "sicut fuit semper una fides christi, ita fuit et semper est una lex in utroque testamentis, quia unitas legis sumitur ab unitate fidei."

42. *Prol.* tr.3 c.2 cl.7 (fol. 15vb): "nos melius servamus legem moysi quam iudei, quia tenemus et servamus veritatem essentialem legis."

43. *Prol.* tr.3 c.2 cl.7 (fol. 15va): "tempora itaque mutata sunt; non fides. iustificatio igitur per fidem iesu christi data est, datur, et dabitur."

44. *Prol.* tr.3 c.2 cl.7 (fol. 15vb): "Item una secundum spiritum, sed altera secundum litteram."

Here again appears — but in altered form — the medieval axiom that the law, spiritually understood, is the same as the Gospel. According to *essentialia*, observes Perez, the old and new laws are one.[45] But the difference between Perez and Lombard is significant. Comparing Perez' way of arriving at this conclusion with Lombard's way, one sees them agreeing that the letter of the two testaments is different, but the spirit the same. What, then, is that unity of spirit which binds them together? With Lombard, the unity lies in the moral law, spiritually understood. With Perez, the unity is founded upon Christ and faith. With Lombard and those who followed him, such as Bonaventura and Thomas, justification could not occur until the time of Christ, because that is the time of the appearance of grace and *caritas* (which makes the moral law work spiritually); with Perez, the suggestion is that justification could already occur for the Old Testament fathers on the basis of the future, promised Christ.

But there is a problem. It is not at all clear from Perez' prologue whether he really means to say this — really understands this as the concrete situation of particular Old Testament men — or whether, finally, this is only a different form of spiritual exegesis in which the Old Testament people are merely *signa tantum* of the timeless "homo mysticus," the *heilsgeschichtliche* Everyman who appears everywhere in Perez' exegesis but nowhere in particular in history. Were actual Old Testament people being justified by faith in Christ, or is this the spiritual "meaning" of the Old Testament history as a whole, dehistoricized in terms of the universal Adam?[46] In the latter case, *all*

---

45. *Prol.* tr.3 c.2 cl.7 (fol. 15ᵛᵃ): "utraque lex est una secundum essentialia."

46. A typical quotation is: "iste mysticus peregrinatus est per fidem in primo testamento usquequo pervenit adeptionem in quo et a quo accepit nobiscum repromissiones, ut ait apostolus ad Heb.11 [:39 f.]. Quia omnes illi patres veteris testamenti non acceperunt repromissiones nisi nobiscum" (*Prol.* tr.3 c.2 cl.7; 15ʳᵃ f.).

history is an allegory in which concrete persons and events are signs of the "pilgrim's progress" toward Christ.[47]

Whatever is the case with Perez, it is still significant that by momentarily shifting the *definiens* of justification from grace and *caritas* to faith in Christ — from present *res* to faith in the future — Perez has hit on a way to see people as "justified" before the establishment of the Church and the implementation of her justifying ordinances, the sacraments. And this step makes possible as well as appropriate the "new tropology" already sketched in. At the same time, however, it poses a threat to the medieval doctrine of justification *sola gratia* as found in Saint Thomas. Developed further, Perez' idea would define justification in terms of promise and faith, rather than in the customary medieval terms of sacraments and grace.

47. Werbeck's discussion of the *homo mysticus* is not too helpful on this question (pp. 134-137). He rightly points out that Perez' extensive use of the *homo mysticus* as the speaker in twenty-three Psalms shows his awareness of the "heilsgeschichtlichen Aspekt" of the Bible. It enables Perez to call attention to various stages of development and eras of time, giving proper integrity to the notion of historical succession. But does it give integrity to the actual history itself? Or does it rather imply an ideal metahistory, which is not really history at all – in fact, not anything at all?

VIII. LATE SCHOLASTIC DEVELOPMENTS

It is time to revisit the field of medieval systematic theology, in order to bring developments in that field up to date with those traced in the biblical field. Attention must be given to issues that were raised earlier with reference to Lombard, Bonaventura, and Thomas. An appropriate focal point is Gabriel Biel, a contemporary of Perez. Through the theology of Biel one can gauge the continuity of late medieval thinking with that of the so-called "high" Middle Ages, and also discern new trends of thought that bear on the central issues of this book.

The continuity is most clear in Biel's discussion at the end of Book III of the *Collectorium,* his commentary on Lombard's *Sentences.*[1] There he quotes extensively from Bonaventura and Duns Scotus as he contrasts, in traditional fashion, the Old and New Testaments in terms of their respective promises. Biel's point, in agreement with his authorities, is that the New Testament is more excellent and perfect than the Old, especially because its promises contribute to the God-intended fulfillment of the law by exciting spiritual love. As observed in Bonaventura, the promises are in service of that spiritual love which is the fulfillment of the law, rather than in service of hope.[2] Biel summarizes his discussion with a quotation from

---

1. Gabriel Biel, *Collectorium in quattuor libros sententiarum* (Basel, 1512; cited hereafter as *Sent.*).
2. III *Sent.* d.40 a.3 dub.2 E (quoting Bonaventura): "In lege autem tria attenduntur, scil. moventia, sicut promissiones; dirigentia, sicut praecepta; adiuventia, sicut sacramenta. In lege nova ista sunt spiritualia, quia promissa aeterna, mandata ad viam morum intus animum dirigentia, sacra-

"Dionysius": "The New Law is a median between the heavenly church and the status of the Old Law. And thus, the eternal goods which will be openly and plenteously exhibited in heaven are manifestly promised in the New Law. But in the Old Law they were not being promised, except under certain figures." [3]

Here, then, can be found nothing that has not already been found elsewhere. The stage is set for the forthcoming discussion of the Christian sacraments by way of the traditional comparative description, whereby the Old Testament sacraments, laws, and promises serve as imperfect and incomplete figures of those of the New Testament. No historical connection between the testaments is envisaged in this mode of comparison, and nothing new seems to be happening.

However, in two thought contexts outside this hermeneutical sphere things have been happening since Saint Thomas — things that invite a new approach to the Old Testament, and in which the motif of *promissio* (along with *pactum*) plays a suggestive role. A full treatment of these areas must be reserved for a later study, but I shall at least indicate what they are, and how they can be related to hermeneutical problems. The two areas are the situation of the viator *prior* to justifica-

---

menta sacrificantia, quae omnia ad spiritum pertinet. Ideo legi novae convenit vivificare tripliciter: formaliter ratione gratiae sacramentalis; affectu ratione *amoris spiritualis, ad quem excitant promissa* . . . in lege autem veteri promissa erant temporalia . . . et sic promissa non excitabant ad amorem spiritualem." (Italics mine.) Quoting Scotus, III *Sent.* d.40 q.un. a.2 par.7 (in *Opera Omnia* [Paris, 1891–1895] XV, 1094), Biel writes: "Et est adiutorium valde notabile, quia nobis pro observatione legis christianae promittitur explicite vita aeterna; illis autem raro vel nunquam explicite nisi bona temporalia. Hec omnia Sco." (III *Sent.* d.40 a.1 not.1 B).

3. III *Sent.* d.40 a.2 concl. un. C: "Nam secundum beatum Dionysium . . . Lex nova media est inter ecclesiam celestem et statum veteris legis. Et ideo eterna bona que in celesti palam et copiose exhibentur in nova lege manifeste promittuntur. In veteri autem lege non promittebantur nisi sub quibusdam figuris." Thomas had also quoted Dionysius to this effect (*ST* I q.1 a.10 corp.; I, 10a); the editors give as reference *De Ecclesiastica Hierarchia* c.5 n.2 (PG 3, 501).

tion, and the comparison of the sacraments of the old and new laws.

The "Old Man" and the Old Testament

The first of these areas concerns *meritum de congruo,* or what man can do to dispose himself so as to incline God to grant him justifying (infused) grace. The man involved can be either a baptized Christian who has fallen into mortal sin and prepares himself for "second justification" through the sacrament of penance, or man in his natural fallen state.[4] Of interest here is the fact that the discussion of this problem was at times specifically integrated into the hermeneutical question of the theological status of the Old Testament people. This integration of the two separate problems now opened the way for a cross-fertilization of ideas that could enlarge and enrich the usual scope of Old Testament interpretation.

The focus here is the treatment of the "killing letter" question in the last (40th) distinction of Book III in the *Sentence* commentaries. In Bonaventura the intention, and therefore the spiritual sense, of the old law was not to kill but *principaliter,* with the help of grace, to become the way of salvation. According to the mere letter, it *occasionaliter* killed, but as a result not of the law's intention but of its misunderstanding by man. Understood spiritually, the law conforms to the Gospel. On this point also, Biel agrees with Bonaventura.[5]

---

4. These two situations are distinguished by Biel, *Canonis Misse Expositio,* Lectio 59 P (Wiesbaden, 1963 ff.; cited hereafter as *Expos.*), II, 443. In a quotation from the *Summa Theologica* of Alexander of Hales, a description has been given of the natural man doing his best, knowing that God is to be adored and seeking his aid: "et hoc est facere quod in se est generaliter in quolibet homine. Plus autem est in fideli existenti in peccato mortali." The text of the edition cited wrongly reads "est infideli existenti."

5. III *Sent.* d.40 a.3 dub. 2 E: "lex illa [that is, vetus] sccundum sensum litteralem erat occidens, non secundum spiritualem; secundum hunc enim concordabat cum euangelio."

In the theology of Scotus and his successors, a vigorous discussion arose over the definition, value, and function of merit and *caritas* in the justification and beatification of the viator.[6] It had been forcefully argued — especially by Scotus and William Occam — that no necessary connection could be established between the possession of *caritas* (New Testament grace) and the eternal reward awaiting the pilgrim at the end of life's journey.[7] *Caritas* was necessary only because God had so ordained and decreed to accept it ("de potentia ordinata"). Justification and beatitude could, *de potentia absoluta,* be carried through without it. But God's intention, revealed in Holy Scripture and the teaching of the doctors of the Church, was that man should reach his goal with the gift of *caritas,* not without it. This intention and decree of God alone was the sole ground upon which one could speak of the "necessity" of *caritas.*

The interesting thing here is the analogy between the *hermeneutical* statement of the relation between the Old and New Testaments and the *anthropological,* existential statement of the relation of man without grace to justification and salvation. In the discussion of both relations, one could say that God's intention in the first state was to lead to the second.

Thus, in the hermeneutical context, the resulting distinction is between the literal and the spiritual senses of the law. "Spirit," or sometimes "true" literal, corresponds to God's ultimate intention, and this is determinative in defining the normative sense of Scripture. In the anthropological context this distinction became, in Nominalist theology, the difference between the "substance of the deed" and the "intention of the

6. See Paul Vignaux, *Justification et Prédestination au XIVe siècle* (Paris, 1934), treating in detail Scotus, Auriol, Occam, and Gregory of Rimini; Oberman, *Harvest,* Chs. V and VI.

7. They showed that only God's *acceptatio* had of necessity to be presupposed for man to be saved. Auriol had made an elaborate argument, against Scotus, for the absolute necessity of caritas. Occam's devastating

lawgiver." [8] However much it may be true, the Nominalists argued, that man can *de facto* "love God above all things," and thus even without grace fulfill the letter of the law (the substance of the deed), such fulfillment is *de jure* insufficient. For God does not intend that the law be sufficient for justification when fulfilled in its literal sense. God intends that the law be fulfilled with *caritas*. This is the law's spiritual meaning. Biel, for example, writes that "one ought not to consider the words, but the will and intention, for the intention should not serve the words, but the words the intention." [9]

By their emphasis upon the *facere quod in se est,* upon the ability of man to work his way into the sphere of God's grace, these theologians had focused attention sharply on man *prior to,* or *outside,* justifying grace. Their question was: what is the nature and capability of man, when the grace of God is not yet a part of his religious situation? And my question is: what are the implications for the exegesis of the Old Testament, especially for the view of the Old Testament people, who are the precise exegetical *analogue* to "man prior to, or outside of, justifying grace"?

My answer is that the late medieval concentration on the "old man" prior to justifying grace brought into the scholastic discussion a new anthropological dimension, which held within

---

rebuttal is succinctly given in his III *Sent.* q.5 L. See Vignaux, *Justification,* Chs. II and III.

8. See Biel, II *Sent.* d.27 q.un. a.3 dub.2 prop.5 R, where he quotes Pierre D'Ailly and concludes that man "non implet preceptum ad intentionem precipientis nisi sit in gratia."

9. III *Sent.* d.37 q.un. a.3 dub.1 P (at issue is whether the law must be observed "ex charitate"): "Quod sic ... non debet quis considerare verba, sed voluntatem et intentionem, quia non debet intentio verbis deservire, sed verba intentioni. Sicut et deus plus respicit intentionem et voluntatem quam actus." Quoting Mt. 19:17 ("If you wish to enter life, keep the commandments"), Biel glosses as follows: "si quis voluerit ingredi ad vitam eternam, necesse est ut servet mandata ex charitate, quia necesse est ut servet mandata meritorie, et per consequens ex charitate."

it an invitation to closer exegetical and theological scrutiny of the situation of the Old Testament man. The new possibilities latent in this kind of question become clearer in light of the situation as reflected in Thomas' understanding of the Old Testament. He saw only those "carnal" ones who lived *sub figura* and who were simply outside the scope of theological interest, and those "special persons" who did not really belong to the old age at all but who already had *caritas* and Spirit ahead of time. Thomas' doctrine of justification *sola gratia* prevented his giving much attention to the Old Testament man, whom he had rendered theologically and spiritually irrelevant. Ironically, insofar as Nominalist theology tended to subvert the Thomistic doctrine of grace, it contributed to the opening up of the Old Testament to serious theological consideration.

Thomas, then, envisioned two types of "Old Testament man." Perez of Valencia gave yet a third such man, the man under the promise. This man can really belong to the old age, but he is much more than a mere shadow of the new; he is one who expectantly awaits Christ and grace, under the promise. Further, Perez at one point links justification with simple "faith in Christ," so that justification is in a sense already present in the promise and faith of the Old Testament.

In Nominalist theology, yet a fourth "Old Testament man" emerges — in the moment that the *facere quod in se est* problem is integrated into the hermeneutical discussion which always appears at the end of Book III of the *Sentence* commentaries. Such a combination appears early in the fourteenth century, with the Dominican proto-Nominalist, Durandus of St.-Pourçain (d. 1332), discussing the traditional "killing letter" question. Reflecting a new interest in the situation of man prior to grace, he injects a strictly historical note into the discussion: it certainly cannot be said that in its own time, prior to Christ's advent, the law was killing. On the contrary, it was life-giving, because it was rightly ordering man to God and to his neighbor. One can even say that it justified *meritorie,* even though not yet *effective*.¹⁰ And justifying grace was being merited *de congruo,* although not *de condigno.* Durandus then moves from a general axiom to a specific application to the Old Testament man: "He who uses well the acts of free will in these things which concern God and his neighbor merits at least *de congruo* divine aid necessary for salvation, for he does what is in him (facit enim quod in se est), and God does not fail such people. But *the good observers of the* [old] *law were people of this sort,* and therefore they were meriting, *de congruo,* the conferral of grace upon them by God, without which there is no salvation." ¹¹

In another Dominican Nominalist, the Englishman Robert Holcot (d. 1349), the *facere quod* is linked specifically to a *promissio* or *pactum* — an infallible covenant commitment of God — to grant grace to the one who does his best.¹² Biel does

10. Guillaume Durand, *Commentaria in IV Libros Sententiarum,* Bk. III d.40 q.3 n.8 (Lyon, 1562; fol. 247ᵛᵇ).

11. III *Sent.* d.40 q.3 n.8 (fol. 247ᵛᵇ): "non quidem de condigno quia sic nullus potest mereri gratiam ex operibus . . . sed de congruo patet sic. qui bene utitur actibus liberi arbitrii in his quae sunt ad Deum et ad proximum meretur saltem de congruo divinum adiutorium sibi necessarium ad salutem, facit enim quod in se est, et Deus talibus non deficit; *sed boni observatores legis erant huiusmodi,* ergo merebantur de congruo conferri sibi gratiam a Deo sine qua non est salus." (Italics mine.)

12. Here I depend upon Oberman (" 'Facientibus quod in se est Deus non denegat gratiam.' Robert Holcot O.P. and the Beginnings of Luther's Theology," *HTR* 55 [1962], 327, n. 49), who gives the following passage from Holcot's commentary on the Wisdom of Solomon (*Super Libros Sapientiae* [Hagenau, 1494], Lectio 145 B): "Necessitas coactionis nullo modo cadit in deo, necessitas vero infallibilities cadit in deo *ex promisso suo et pacto sive lege statuta* . . . Sed statuta lege necessario dat gratiam necessitate consequentie." (Italics mine.) In examining the context of this statement, I was unable to determine whether Holcot got the idea of linking the *pactum* with the *facere quod* directly from the Old Testament, which would further indicate awareness that the situation of the man is analogous to that of the Christian penitent, thus arousing new theological interest in the Old Testament, and even use of it as a theological authority.

not develop this idea in the sphere of prejustification merit, but the notions of *pactum, promissio,* and *conventio* come into full bloom in his discussion of *meritum de condigno,* that merit whereby justified man attains to eternal glory.[13]

This account, though by itself incomplete, serves to suggest what further research may be able to show: a renewal of interest, on the part of late medieval theologians, in the historical or existential situation of the Old Testament *viator,* a renewal that may have influenced the revival of interest in and study of the Old Testament in the Reformation period. In Holcot, at least, the question arises as to whether his idea of attaching the notion of promise/covenant to the problem of merit came from his own study of the Old Testament itself.

The Sacraments of the Old Law

The second broad area which bears on hermeneutical problems, besides that of *meritum de congruo,* is that of sacraments. If Gabriel Biel is typical, the trend of late medieval theology was to minimize the difference between the sacraments of the old and new laws in such a way that the Old Testament rite of circumcision became more than a mere *figura* of Christian baptism.

Here, a contrast may be drawn between Bonaventura and Biel, omitting any comment on the intervening period. According to Bonaventura, the decisive difference between the sacraments of the old and new laws is that the old sacraments came with no covenant attached — no promise from God that grace would infallibly be given through them: "no *pactio* was attached to those sacraments through which there might be an

13. For Biel, the *pactum* functions as a balance to the threat of arbitrariness and uncertainty that hangs over any theology which takes seriously the sovereignty of God. Biel wants to make clear that God's covenant with the Church and with the *viator* is reliable, stable, and infallible, despite the freedom and power of God.

efficacious and infallible *ordinatio* to grace such as there is in the sacraments of the new law, as is evident in the institution of Baptism, where it says, 'He who believes and is baptized, shall be saved.' " [14] For Bonaventura, the Old Testament sacraments are "figurae tantum ad significandum," while those of the New Testament are "figurae ad significandum et sanctificandum." [15] The New Testament sacraments "cause" what the Old Testament sacraments only signified.

This view was destined for quite radical change. Later defenders (with Bonaventura) of the *pactio* theory of sacramental causality,[16] instead of making the *pactio* the distinctive characteristic of the New Testament sacraments, defend their theory precisely on the basis of its Old Testament precedent. Here I quote Biel (although he is not the first to make the statement), in the context of his argument that Christ's *pactum* with his bride, the Church, is the sole and sufficient ground of the conversion of the eucharistic elements: "Let it not seem bad-sounding and fictitious to anyone that God in the New Law has celebrated this sort of *pacta* with the faithful, since you can read that *he did the same thing in the Old Law*. For He says: 'This is my *pactum* which you shall observe: every male of yours shall be circumcised.' And further on: 'Any man the flesh of whose foreskin has not been circumcised, his soul shall be wiped out from the people.' Where, in the converse sense, it can be argued: if he *has* been circum-

14. III *Sent.* d.40 a.un. q.3 dub.3 (III, 895): "Et differunt in hoc a sacramentis Legis Veteris, praecique quantum ad ipsam efficacem ordinationem, quia *non interveniebat ibi pactio* in illis sacramentis, per quam efficax et infallibilis fieret ordinatio ad gratiam, secundum quod in sacramentis novae Legis, ut patet in institutione Baptismi, ubi dixit, 'Qui crediderit . . .' [Mk. 16:16]." (Italics mine.)

15. IV *Sent.* d.2 a.1 q.1 arg.3 ad 3 (IV, 50).

16. According to this theory, God, honoring his convenant promise, confers grace directly upon the soul of the participant in the sacraments while the rite is being performed, and not (as Thomas taught) through the physical elements themselves as (meta-)physical instruments.

cised, *he shall be saved*. And on the basis of the establishment of this *pactum* God assists this circumcision by remitting original sin, and he causes grace, which is the means of leading man to salvation."[17] This is a significant analogue to the theological value that Perez of Valencia began to see in the literal understanding of the Old Testament promises. The literal sense of the Old Testament functions here as an authority for theological proof. The *pactum dei* is now more than mere *figura*; it has the status of the normative-literal sense of Scripture.[18] It is perfectly appropriate *now*, Biel is arguing, for God to deal in this way with his Church, for this is the way he dealt with his people before the advent of Christ.

Here, in a surprising way, the law *literally* understood has been discovered to conform to the Gospel — a significant departure from the traditional axiom that the law spiritually understood conforms to it. Biel has found the basis of a real continuity between the Old and New Testaments in the *pactum*, the covenant, understood historically; this contrasts with the usual, nonhistorical relationship envisioned in the notion of the moral law and the ordinances of the Old Testament understood spiritually.

17. *Expos.* Lect.47 X (II, 228): "Nec cuiquam absonum videatur et fictum deum in nova lege cum fidelibus huiusmodi pacta celebrasse, cum etiam in lege veteri similia fecisse legatur, unde ait [Gen. 17:10]: 'Hoc est pactum meum quod observabitis: Circumcidetur omne masculinum ex vobis.' Et infra [vs.14]: 'Masculus cuius caro prepucii circumcisa non fuerit, delebitur anima eius de populo.' Ubi a contrario sensu arguitur: *Si circumcisa fuerit, salvabitur*. Et ex hoc pacto statuto, deus huic circumcisioni assistit remittendo originale peccatum, *et causat gratiam,* que medium est hominem perducendi ad salutem." (Italics mine.) Biel also uses the term *promissio* in this context, although *pactum* or *pactio* are most frequent in this tradition.

18. The hermeneutical application is mine, not Biel's. Oberman has observed that as a proponent of Tradition II, Biel does not find hermeneutical issues to be of much interest (*Harvest*, p. 404).

IX. THREE LATE MEDIEVAL CONTEMPORARIES

Sylvester Prierias

Prierias (O.P., d. 1523) for the most part echoes the tradition of Saint Thomas, Lyra, and Burgos. He reveals little that is new in his tractate on Scripture, the first part of the *Aurea Rosa* (1503). But Prierias was one of the first literary opponents of Martin Luther, and a sixteenth-century representative of the Dominican hermeneutical tradition; as such, he is worth attention.

Most revealing here is Prierias' attempt to clarify that much-abused technical term, *sensus litteralis*, in face of the disagreement and confusion to which it had been subjected, and which Prierias recognizes.[1] He begins his painstaking definition-building with Burgos, with whom he rejects the narrow definition whereby the *sensus litteralis* is only the *sensus historicus*. He moves to the definition of Thomas, whereby the literal sense is "that according to which words immediately signify things."[2] But because this definition cannot handle certain metaphorical or figurative expressions, one must add that the literal sense is "that which the author intended, which author . . . is God."[3]

  1. Prierias, *Aurea Rosa super evangelia totius anni* (Venice, 1582), *Tractatus primus: de regulis exponendi sacram scripturam* (cited hereafter as *Tr.*1), 9 chs. The fourth chapter is entitled "Quis sensus sit literalis." Prierias begins it (fol. 3vb) by observing that "est in hoc non mediocris inter peritos concertatio."
  2. *Tr.*1 c.4 (fol. 3vb): "alii dicunt, quod sensus quidem literalis est secundum quem voces significant res immediate."
  3. *Tr.*1 c.4 (fol. 3vb): "ideo dicunt isti, quod oportet superaddere et dicere, quod sensus literalis est ille quem autor intendit, qui autor, inquiunt, Deus est." So Thomas and Burgos.

Then comes perhaps the most interesting insight in the tractate. Prierias argues that this opinion, despite its impressive pedigree, cannot stand. His argument runs: "If the literal sense is that which God intended, it is either that which he intended immediately through the words, or it is that which he intended by the mediation of things." [4] Prierias continues: "If you say [that the literal sense is] the former, then the opinion you have already rejected is true, namely, that the whole literal sense is that which is received immediately through the words.[5] But if you say that it is the second, then it follows that *every spiritual sense is literal,* since each of these is constituted by the mediation of things intended by God. Therefore, this opinion is not true." [6] Prierias has here exposed the crucial soft spot in the hermeneutical theory of his mentor, Thomas Aquinas: he has detected the "loophole" whereby one could appeal to the intention of the divine author in proposing some spiritual interpretation, both avoiding the strict literal sense and dignifying his own interpretation with the label "literal." Using this "divine-literal" definition of Thomas has the effect of destroying any meaningful distinction between the literal and spiritual sense.[7]

---

4. *Tr.*1 c.4 (fol. 3vb): "Sed ista opinio quamvis sit cuiusdam magni viri, et tam latinae quam hebraicae docti, tamen stare non potest. Et arguo sic: Si sensus literalis est quem intendit Deus, aut est ille quem intendit immediate per voces, aut quem intendit mediantibus rebus."

5. This first definition was rejected because it could not account for figures of speech intended as such by the author. Thomas had already worked out this problem, showing that what the human author intended must determine the literal sense of such passages: *ST* I q.1 a.10 ad 3 (I, 10b f.).

6. *Tr.*1 c.4 (fol. 3vb f.): "Si dicas primum, sic vera est opinio quam negasti, scilicet quod omnis sensus literalis est, qui immediate per voces accipitur. Si vero dicas secundum, sic sequitur quod *omnis sensus spiritualis sit literalis,* cum omnis talis fit mediantibus rebus intentis a deo. Non ergo est ista opinio vera neque motivum eius est efficax." (Italics mine.)

7. This objection of Prierias is not merely academic. Faber Stapulensis will use the divine-literal definition to do exactly what Prierias is disturbed about.

Two elements of Prierias' rather intricate solution should be noticed. First, the problem of the hearer (or reader) comes momentarily into focus: [8] in his first, tentative solution to the problem, Prierias seems eager to supplement the exclusively intention-based definition of "literal." The literal sense, he writes, is that which the human author immediately intended through the words, as well as that which "the prudent intellect immediately conceives from the heard words when they are set forth, or from the words that are seen when the writings are read." [9]

But this apprehension of meaning involves more on the part of the man of "prudent intellect" than merely recognizing a metaphor when he sees it. For there are some things reported in Scripture that really occur just as stated (as opposed, for example, to apocalyptic narration), but whose *sensus litteralis* is still not the immediately apprehended one. As an example, Prierias refers to Jesus' cursing of the fig tree. How, he asks, can one account for the fact that "all the saints — and the non-saints — explain this passage literally of the Jewish synagogue"? Prierias answers that although things of this sort were really done, they were not done to be ends in themselves ("ad proprios fines"), but only in order to signify something else.[10] In a proper definition of "literal sense," one needs to take account of this sort of material. Here, then, is the definition that

8. My interest in this aspect of the discussion arises from the question as to what the hearers or first readers of the Old Testament words thought, or were supposed to think, the words meant — a question that rarely comes up in these discussions.
9. *Tr*.1 c.4 (fol. 4ra): "Dico ergo, quod sensus literalis est ille, quem autor scripturae intendit immediate per voces, et quem intellectus prudentis ut sic immediate concipit auditis vocibus dum proferuntur, aut visis dum scriptae leguntur."
10. *Tr*.1 c.4 (fol. 4va): "sensus literalis non sumitur hic secundum propria vocum significata, sed secundum secundaria. Nam omnes sancti et non sancti hunc passum literaliter exponunt de synagoga Iudeorum . . . Licet enim ista fuerint vere res, non tamen fuerunt ad proprios fines factae, sed solum ad significandum." In the example given, Jesus' act was done only "ad significandum desiderium Christi pro salute Iudaeorum" (fol. 4vb).

Prierias finally proposes: "We do not say that the literal sense is that which is had from the proper signification of the words in all real events, but in all events that are both real and produced for their own end. And this is not the case in fictitious things, or in things that are true but nevertheless done only for the sake of signifying something else." [11]

Recalling the thought of Perez, one may now move to the second problem to be dealt with here: does Prierias include the whole Old Testament as something given "solum ad significandum"? [12] It is clear that he did not wish to go down this road. The Old Testament history seems, for him, to have its "own proper end," as one example taken from the Old Testament shows.[13] Further, Prierias is following Burgos very closely throughout the treatise. His arguments for the superior dignity of the literal sense are practically identical; he gives the same objections and the same answers, and goes beyond the strict grammatical sense at the same point as does Burgos. But the special problem of Old Testament interpretation does not seem to have occupied Prierias, so one is left without a final answer to the question.

There is nothing new in the tractate regarding the other issues concerned here. The word "promise" occurs once, in a passage that Prierias takes directly from Burgos, to the effect that the interpretation of Scripture which is done in the

11. *Tr.*1 c.4 (fol. 4vb): "Non autem diximus nos in ombnibus veris rebus literalem sensum esse secundum propria vocum significata, sed in omnibus veris et ad proprium finem productis. Secus in rebus fictis, aut in veris, sed tamen solum ad significandum factis."

12. This terminology is very close to the "gratia sui" of Perez. An identical expression from Biel refers to the Old Testament: "Nam lex instituta ad significandum gratiam novi testamenti quae per christum facta est" (IV *Sent.* d.1 q.4 a.4 dub.4 Q; given in Altenstaig, "Cessatio Legalium," in *Vocabularius,* fol. 36va).

13. *Tr.*1 c.4 (fol. 4rb): "Quaedam enim sunt vere res, seu fuerunt, et productae sunt ad suos fines proprios, ut Ismael et Isaac filii vere fuerunt Abrae."

Church is more reliable than that of outsiders, because of Christ's promise of the spirit of truth.[14]

Faber Stapulensis

Like his contemporary Prierias, the French humanist Jacobus Faber Stapulensis (d. 1536) is troubled about the confusion of definition surrounding the *sensus litteralis* of Scripture. And like Prierias, he proposes a solution of his own, which is laid out in the Preface of his *Quincuplex Psalterium* (1509). The solution is formulated in response to the dilemma of his friends in Paris monasteries who have become so confused that they can scarcely read the Psalter with profit. It is as though they have been duped by the various definitions of "literal." [15]

Faber's solution of the problem is quite the contrary to that of Prierias, and almost breathtaking in its simplicity: the proper literal sense of Scripture is that which corresponds "to the intention of the prophet and of the Holy Spirit speaking in him." [16] Gone is the involved discussion of traditional problems. There is no treatment of the grammatical issue, no direct dealing with the fourfold senses — except the assertion that his own "literal sense" is not what others call allegory or tropology.[17] There is no reference to the relation of Scripture to

14. *Tr.*1 c.9 (fol. 9ʳᵃ). The text is practically verbatim from Burgos. The new study by Heiko Oberman, *Forerunners of the Reformation* (New York, 1966), in a penetrating survey of the hermeneutical tradition (ch. 6), shows that Prierias agrees with Gerson regarding the Church's authority vis à vis Scripture (pp. 291 f).

15. Faber, *Quincuplex Psalterium* (Paris, 1513), Pref. fol. Aiiʳ: "Tunc caepi mecum ipse cogitare ne forte ille non verus litteralis sit sensus, sed (quod mali Pharmacapolae de herbis facere solent) sit res pro re, et sensus pro sensu inductus."

16. *Pref.* (fol. Aiiʳ): "et videor michi alium videre sensum, qui scilicet est intentionis prophetae et spiritussancti in eo loquentis. et hunc litteralem appello, sed qui cum spiritu coincidit."

17. *Pref.* (fol. Aiiᵛ f.): "Sensus igitur litteralis et spiritualis coinci-

theological proof or to tradition, no discussion of the relation of Old and New Testaments. There is one controlling idea, and one only: the divine author's intention, the human author's intention, and the right interpretation all coincide and are the literal sense. Everything else is subordinate to that.[18]

This single valid sense of Scripture is radically opposed to the traditional *sensus historicus,* which is condemned as an improper literal sense.[19] The actual situation of the psalmist (that is, David throughout), and the "autobiographical" confession arising out of that situation, have nothing to do with the proper interpretation of the Psalms. In fact, Faber *opposes* to that history David's claim of having been a mouthpiece of the spirit.[20] One could scarcely remove himself more decisively from the sphere of historical exegesis.

Although there is no explicit rejection of the grammatical foundation of interpretation, Faber's clear rejection of the historical sense has practically the same effect. For the historical sense, in the language and thought of the tradition, has always

---

dunt, non quem allegoricum aut tropologicum vocant, sed quem spiritus sanctus in propheta loquens intendit."

18. This is contrary to Prierias, who had correctly rejected an intention-based definition on grounds that it destroys the distinction between the spiritual and literal senses.

19. *Pref.* (fol. Aii^v): "Absit igitur nobis credere hunc litteralem sensum, quem littere sensum appellant [the Hebrei], et David historicum potius facere quam prophetam." Faber makes this specific point against historical exegesis also at an earlier point (fol. Aii^r): he complains of "certain Rabbis," "qui divinos David hymnos maxima ex parte deipsomet exponunt de pressuris eius in persecutione Saulis et aliis bellis que gessit, non facientes eum in psalmis prophetam, sed per eum visa et facta narrantem et quasi propriam texentem historiam."

20. *Pref.* (fol. Aii^r f.): "tamen ipse de se dicat: 'Spiritus domini locutus est per me, et sermo eius per linguam meam' [2 Sam. 23:2], et scriptura divina eum appellet virum cui constitutum est de Christo dei Iacob, egregium psaltem Israel [2 Sam. 23:1]. Et ubi illi constitutum est de Christo dei Iacob et vero Messiah, nisi in psalmis?" Faber apparently takes the "constitutum" to mean "revelatum." The Douai translation is not helpful: "the man to whom it was appointed concerning the Christ."

been regarded as part of the grammatical sense, the other part consisting of that normative literal sense in which *doctrina* and *lex* are found.[21]

But for Faber, the literal sense — that sense alone which the interpreter has to unveil — is "that which the Holy Spirit shows."[22] It depends, then, on the illumination of the Spirit to arrive at correct literal interpretation; any other "letter" is simply false.[23] It is "another letter" which is opposed to the Spirit, and kills (2 Cor. 3:6);[24] it is a *"figmentum* and a *mendacium."*[25]

In spite of the fact that Faber uses the term "double literal sense" coined by Lyra and redefined by Perez, Faber has gone beyond both of them, especially in his outright rejection of the historical sense, which for Lyra was not only proper but the *fundamentum* of all interpretation, and which for Perez was at least the springboard for the more proper spiritual interpretation. The antithesis to Lyra is especially striking: Lyra's *fundamentum* is Faber's *mendacium!*

Faber seems especially eager to close up any interpretive gap between what the original author intended and what the

21. There is no reference to this traditional normative-literal sense anywhere in the preface. It seems to have been eliminated, as it was in Gerson and Perez: "We know (as *diviniloquus Paulus* says) that the law is spiritual. And if it is spiritual, how will the literal sense, if it is the sense of the law, not be spiritual?" (*Pref.* fol. Aii^v).

22. *Pref.* (fol. Aii^v): "Sed eum sensum litterae vocemus qui cum Spiritu concordat et quem spiritus sanctus monstrat."

23. *Pref.* (fol. Aii^v): "duplicem crediderim sensum litteralem, hunc improprium caecutientium et non videntium, qui divina solum carnaliter passibiliterque intelligunt; illum vero *proprium, videntium et illuminatorum;* hunc humano sensu fictum; illum *divino spiritu infusum."* (Italics mine.) One is reminded of Doering and Perez. As Oberman observes, "the most necessary exegetical tool of all" is the Spirit who authored Scripture (*Forerunners,* p. 288).

24. *Pref.* (fol. Aii^r): "non videntibus autem, qui se nichilominus videre arbitrantur, alia littera surgit quae (ut inquit apostolus) occidit, et que spiritui adversatur, quam et iudei nunc sequuntur."

25. *Pref.* (fol. Aii^v).

exegete apprehends in the text; he seems to be trying to eliminate not only the duality of literal senses in Lyra's system but also Perez' duplicity of intention in the prophetic spirit, and even the multiplicity of God's intention which, in the theory of Saint Thomas, covers all four senses. All these distinctions have been swept away, and everything is narrowed to the one point: the divine author meant one thing, the Old Testament writer meant the same thing, the New Testament authors discerned that thing, and the interpreter must discover it.[26]

But where is that single meaning revealed? Faber does not leave one with a bare abstraction here. His own clue to the proper literal sense was, in fact, identical to that used by Lyra to support his double-literal sense: the New Testament use of the Old Testament. It is the apostles, he writes, who first opened Scripture to man's understanding.[27] But in contrast to Lyra, the literal sense given by the New Testament authors now excludes the obvious *sensus litteralis,* which is a mere fiction. The outcome is identical to Gerson's thesis: the literal

26. This radically reductionist tendency comes through in the whole preface. Two passages add to what has already been expressed. In the first, Faber contrasts himself to former commentators: "illos diffuse tractasse, nos succincte; illos non unum sensum, nos *unum* praecique, et eum qui spiritus sancti et mentis esset prophetae quaesisse" (*Pref.* [fol. Aiii^r]; italics mine). In the second, Faber writes: "hunc litteralem appello, sed qui cum spiritu coincidit; neque prophetis neque videntibus alium littera praetendit (non quod alios sensus: allegoricum, tropologicum et anagogicum, praesertim ubi res exposcit, negare velim); non videntibus, autem, qui se . . . videre arbitrantur, alia littera surgit" (Aii^r). I would read the "neque" clause: "this letter [which I am defining] does not provide [one sense] to the prophets and another to those who see [=those who are illumined by the Spirit]." Faber's intention here is to deny that the interpreter first has to determine the sense intended by the prophet and then go on to a second, "spiritual" sense. He is arguing for complete unity of intention and meaning, and calling it "literal sense." There is no distinction between "what it meant" and "what it means" here.

27. *Pref.* (fol. Aii^r): "me contuli ad primos duces nostros apostolos, dico euangelistas et prophetas qui primi animarum nostrarum sulcis divina mandarunt semina et litteralem sacrarum scripturarum aperuerunt ianuam."

sense of Scripture was first revealed at the time of Christ and the apostles. The Old Testament has no usable literal sense. Burgos, it will be recalled, managed to retain a remnant of the Old Testament literal sense via the old principle of *doctrina* and *lex,* and Perez abandoned that position, but intimated a new direction via the notion of *promissio.* In Faber, neither of these options remains.

In terms of content, the Psalter is about Christ and at times by Christ, for it is literally to Him that the apostles apply or attribute the Psalm words. Faber gives Psalms 1, 2, 17, 18, and 20 as examples: "Paulus litteram CHRISTO domino tribuit." [28] "Christ the Lord," Faber announces at the end of the Preface, "is the *principium et finis* of this whole psalmody." [29]

It is difficult to give a proper assessment of Faber, owing to the brevity of his remarks in this preface. But it is important not to be misled, as some scholars have been, because he was a "humanist," because he claimed to discern the true literal sense, and because he was a textual critic who could read Hebrew and was interested in establishing the correct text. Despite these credentials, in terms of modern exegetical presuppositions Faber can only be characterized as a reactionary. His Old Testament exegesis is if anything a flight from the *sensus litteralis,* an abandonment of the Old Testament *historia* as a proper subject of study. Faber has in effect solved the medieval problem of the *sensus litteralis* by eliminating it. The figure to whom he bears the most striking resemblance, of those studied here, is Jean Gerson. The principal difference is that Faber does not locate the Spirit so unequivocally in the Church. He leaves the way open for the independent, Spirit-endowed individual.

Faber is a striking example of a late medieval impatience

28. *Pref.* (fol. Aii^v).
29. *Pref.* (fol. Aiii^v): "Christus dominus . . . principium est et finis universae huius psalmodiae."

with fine distinctions and of the growing passion for simplicity and spiritual edification that characterizes late medieval piety.[30] Further, he has taken what seems to be the shortest, least arduous route to an altogether christological exegesis of the Psalms. However, the cost has been high: *doctrina* and *lex,* the *historia* and the traditional *sensus litteralis,* have all been given up in the process. It scarcely needs to be added that the notion of *promissio* — especially the Old Testament promise — is not mentioned by him at all, for in this setting there is no way it can be heard.

Martin Luther

The end of late-medieval prologue literature is marked by the brief introductory remarks to the Psalter made by Luther in the summer and autumn of 1513, when he prepared and opened his first course as professor of Bible at the University of Wittenberg.[31] In dealing with this material, I do not as-

30. Oberman suggests the influence on Faber of the piety of the *Devotio moderna,* citing the following from *De Imitatione Christi,* I,5, as an example: "The whole of Holy Scripture has to be read in the Spirit by which it was written. We had better look at Scripture for what is edifying than for precision of language" (*Forerunners,* p. 305 n.4). My assessment of Faber is more severe than that of Oberman. I do not find that Faber established any fruitful connection between his humanistic concern for a purified biblical text and his spiritual concern for a purified religious community.

31. I shall treat three brief documents here: the text on the verso of the title page (*WA* 55/1.2.1 ff.), the "Praefatio Ihesu Christi" (*WA* 55/1.6.1 ff.), and a second Preface (*WA* 55/2.25.1 ff.). The first of these is preserved in Luther's own hand as a gloss on the title of the whole work; the second is printed at the beginning of Luther's own Wittenberg edition of the Psalms, the Wolfenbüttler Psalter (1513), in which are contained the interlinear and marginal glosses; the third stands near the beginning of the Dresdener Psalter, the manuscript of Luther's Scholia. The new Weimar edition (*WA* 55, Weimar, 1963 ff.) of this first Psalms course (commonly referred to as the *Dictata super Psalterium*) is complete only through Ps. 15; for the rest, I use the earlier volumes, *WA* 3 and 4

sume, as do some scholars in the frequently hagiographic tradition of Luther interpretation, that one stands here in the presence of something radically new and different from what has been said by others in earlier times. Obvious continuity with his past and his times is immediately evident in what Luther says here, even though one must be alert for changes.

First of all, the christological, understood as the literal sense of the Psalms is radicalized by Luther to a degree anticipated but perhaps not equaled in the tradition.[32] The Old Testament, he argues, simply cannot be understood without the New; otherwise the New would have been given in vain. This assertion is traditional enough, but it proceeds from an appeal to Paul's understanding of Christ and the law: if the law had been sufficient, then Christ would have died in vain.[33] The difference here is that Luther's statement is a gloss on John

---

(Weimar, 1885 f.). Here and there, I incorporate material from Luther's earlier writings, particularly his marginals on Lombard's *Sentences*, 1510 f. Unfortunately, Luther made no comment on Bk. III, d.40, or on Bk. IV, nor do we have any other general hermeneutical treatise from this period. Therefore, I have presented no separate treatment of these earlier writings. According to Erich Vogelsang, the Psalms course began August 16, 1513, and ran until October 20, 1515 (*Der junge Luther* [*Luthers Werke in Auswahl*, ed. Otto Clemen, Bonn & Berlin, 1925 ff., vol. V], p. 40). I have used none of the material that scholars agree comes from 1516, that is, parts of the Scholia on Psalms 1 and 4 (the exact location of these passages is given in *WA* 55/1, p. 16*).

32. For full treatment, see Ebeling, "Luthers Psalterdruck," pp. 80 ff. Ebeling points especially to Luther's idea, in the "Praefatio Ihesu Christi," of having Christ himself step forward to identify himself, via his New Testament self-witness, as the speaker of the Psalms (p. 82). Ebeling also emphasizes the reduction of the discussion of the nature of prophecy to the one essential point that Christ is the subject of all prophecy (p. 89); he detects an unconcern as to how one labels the various senses, so long as it is understood that the *sensus Christi* is decisive (p. 91; the term is used at *WA* 55/1.8.6 with reference to 1 Cor. 2:16).

33. *WA* 55/1.6.26–28: "Si vetus testamentum per humanum sensum potest exponi sine novo testamento, dicam Quod novum testamentum gratis datum sit. Sicut arguit Apostolus, Quod 'Christus gratis sit mortuus', si lex sufficeret" [Gal. 2:21].

10:9 ("I am the door"). The gloss suggests that in Luther's mind the death of Christ is the place where the *sensus* of the Old Testament is opened up and revealed.[34]

Luther does not apply the term "spiritual" to the christological sense; in fact, he avoids the terms "literal" and "spiritual" when dealing with the description of the several scriptural senses. Letter-and-spirit are seen by him as a different problem. The terms Luther uses, in somewhat peculiar fashion, are *historicus* and *propheticus*.[35]

Luther uses *historicus* in a double and confusing way, which suggests the influence, on the one hand, of that part of the tradition which insisted on the literal sense as both the *fundamentum* and the norm of all the others, and on the other, of those who used the term *historicus* in a derogatory sense, as did Faber. In this mode, Luther opposes historic to "prophetic."

In the first, positive sense, Luther writes: "In the Scriptures no allegory, tropology or anagoge is valid unless the same thing is expressly said *hystorice*. Otherwise, Scripture would be a mockery. But it is absolutely necessary to take that alone for allegory [that is, for valid allegorical interpretation], etc.,

34. With Perez, it is argued the other way around, albeit with the same result (*Tr.*1 c.2; fol. 3ra): "nihil scribitur, nec ponitur, nec fuit gestum in veteri testamento gratia sui, sed ad figurandum et pronunciandum mysteria euangelica." Faber also made an appeal to Paul, but a different one: Paul says that the law is spiritual; therefore how can its literal sense be anything but spiritual?

35. I have already noted the medieval discussions of the relation of the historical and literal senses, such as in Burgos' and Prierias' objection to the reduction of the literal sense to the historical only. Perez combined *prophetia* and *promissio* in those passages that excited my interest because at times they seemed to combine a historical with a theologically meaningful Old Testament exegesis. Faber — who is closest to Luther's usage here — objects to the Jews' making David more a historian than a prophet ("historicum potius facere quam prophetam," *Pref.*; fol. Aii^{v}). Ebeling notes places where the term "propheticus" occurs in the tradition ("Luthers Psalterdruck," p. 93 n. 2, p. 94 n.1). Paul of Burgos uses it as Ps. 21 ("propheticus et vaticanaticus").

which is elsewhere said *hystorice*." [36] Luther apparently wants to avoid using "literal/spiritual" in the context of this problem, so he uses "historical" instead of "literal" even though it is out of place in the axiom he is stating.

Turning to the derogatory meaning of *historicus*, one finds it appearing twice in the sense of "carnal and Jewish." [37] Luther is here casting his vote for Faber and giving Lyra the back of his hand. Meanwhile, the "prophetic" sense is understood most emphatically as the christological one: "every prophecy and every prophet ought to be understood as *de Christo domino*, except where it is apparent by clear words that they are speaking about something else." [38] Every text is christological until proven otherwise. Jesus has said (John 5:39) that the Scriptures give *testimonium* of him, and this, among all interpretive rules, is *certissimum*.[39]

Luther illustrates his meaning in three examples which

36. WA 55/1.4.20–23: "In Scripturis itaque nulla valet allegoria, tropologia, anagoge, nisi alibi hystorice idem expresse dicatur. Alioquin ludibrium fieret Scriptura. Sed omnino oportet illud solum pro allegoria etc. accipi, quod alibi hystorice dicitur." The editors here quote Thomas on the *sensus litteralis* as the foundation on which alone argument can be based. Perhaps this is appropriate, but one must remember that Thomas, Burgos, Lyra, or Prierias would never use *hystorice* in this context, since the literal sense Thomas has in mind is really exclusive of the historical narrative; he refers rather to the normative literal sense from which the historical *res gestae* are excluded.

37. WA 55/1.2.10 f., against the "Iudei applicantes semper Psalmos ad veteres Hystorias extra Christum," indicating that for Luther, the pre-Christian history is without theological value. On the other side comes a thinly veiled attack on Lyra: "quidam nimis multos psalmos exponunt non prophetice sed hystorice, secuti quosdam Rabim hebraeos falsigraphos . . . Nec mirum. quia alieni sunt a Christo . . . Nos autem sensum Christi habemus" (WA 55/1.8.3–7).

38. WA 55/1.6.25 f.: "Omnis prophetia et omnis propheta de Christo domino debet intelligi, nisi ubi manifestis verbis appareat de alio loqui."

39. WA 55/1.8.1–3. By contrast, Burgos gave the same argument for the literal (grammatical) sense, namely, that it alone gives certainty of interpretation.

show how Christ is *litteraliter* the subject matter of the text; in this instance Luther uses the traditional terms *litera, allegoria,* and *tropologia*:

[Ps. 1] The letter is that the Lord Jesus did not yield to the favorite pursuits of the Jews and of the perverse and adulterous generation which were current in his time.

[Ps. 2] The letter concerns the fury of the Jews and Gentiles against Christ in his passion.

[Ps. 3] 'Lord, how they [my enemies] are multiplied' is *ad literam* a complaint of Christ about his enemies the Jews.[40]

This emphatically christological orientation is reinforced further in the references which Luther makes to the psalmist David. David was unique among the prophets, Luther notes, since he alone claimed that the Spirit spoke through him.[41]

40. *WA* 55/1.8.12–10.2; 55/1.10.6 f.; 55/1.10.10 f. On the significance of Luther's omission of the anagogical sense here, Ebeling incorrectly supposes it "without parallel" in the tradition ("Luthers Psalterdruck," p. 95). I have already shown how Hugh of Saint Victor had made *anagoge* a part of *allegoria*. In an earlier discussion, Ebeling sought to reduce anagogy to an existential category, a dimension of Luther's tropology: "Wenn . . . die eigentliche intentio des Wortes ist, nicht etwas über die Zukunft mitzuteilen, sondern auf die Zukunft auszurichten, und zwar so, dass man sich von den futura her versteht, dann kommt der eigentliche scopus des sensus anagogicus nur im sensus tropologicus zur Geltung" ("Die Anfänge," p. 227). In the medieval tradition, however, anagogy was frequently understood not at all in futuristic terms but rather in mystical terms. Gerson refers to the mystical theology as "motio anagogica" (*De mystica theologia,* Tr.1, consideratio 28 [ed. André Combes, Lugano, 1957, p. 72]). An analysis of Luther's well-known connections with the mystical tradition would, I think, yield a better explanation of his early tendency to ignore the eschatological dimension.

41. *WA* 55/2.27.8–10: "Alii prophete *sese* locutus fatentur, hic [David] autem *non se,* Sed per se locutum esse spiritum singulari modo pronunciat. Quamvis enim per omnes prophetas locutus sit, ut canimus [in the Nicene creed], tamen de nullo ita dicitur." (Italics mine.) Luther

As the three examples just given show, David is so much the Spirit's mouthpiece that as a plain human speaker-writer he has simply vanished. The events being described are totally removed from any relation to David's own time and situation; in the third Psalm Christ himself is speaking. As a result, the Old Testament situation is patently not within the scope of Luther's interpretation, nor is the word spoken by David of any relevance to that situation.

Insofar as the human author is noticed at all, he is assumed to be describing, as though totally out of his own time, future events.[42] In comparison to the actual grammatical sense of the Psalm words, this mode of interpretation is plainly what Augustine calls figurative, whereby "one thing is said, another is understood." That Luther, by contrast, accepts it as the prophetic-literal sense is testimony to the fact that his hermeneutical theory, as presented here, is merely bypassing the Old Testament text in its grammatical, historical sense. The Old Testament history is utterly devoid of theological relevance in the interpretation, as it was also for Faber Stapulensis.

But is there no place left open for historical interpretation? Yes — just one: "I frequently understand the Psalms *de Iudeis,* because 'We know that whatever the law says, it says to those who are in the law' [Rom. 3:19]."[43] In view of later developments, this is a pregnant statement, although Luther probably does not know it at this point. For here alone in the prefaces he has left the door open for attention to the situation

---

is probably dependent on Faber here: against rabbinic exegetes who turn David into an "historian," he points out that "ipse de se dicat, spiritus domini locutus est per me" (*Pref.;* fol. Aiiʳ).

42. Thus, Luther's David does just what Ebeling disapproves of in the "traditional" *anagoge*: he imparts information about the future that does not impinge on his own existence in the present (Ebeling, "Die Anfänge," p. 227).

43. WA 55/1.4.33 f.: "Ideo Psalmos frequenter de Iudcis intelligo, quia 'Scimus, quoniam quecunque lex loquitur, hiis qui in lege sunt loquitur' [Rom. 3:19]."

of the historical Israel *before* Christ, as well as for Israel outside Christ, as Luther knew it in his own day. And it is in contemplation of what Israel was before Christ that Luther is to discover existence "in promissione," as well as "in lege," in a unique way.

A word is necessary about letter and spirit. Ebeling has devoted considerable attention to a profound analysis of the problem, much of which falls outside the scope of this study.[44] However, one notable strand of continuity with the tradition seems to be present in Luther's explanation of "spirit" as the proper way of understanding the Scriptures: he writes that spirit refers to the understanding of Scripture given to the Church and revealed by the Holy Spirit, which no one was able to know "ante spiritus revelationem."[45] This position appears to be in full accord with that argued by Gerson: the true literal sense (which for Gerson means the Spirit-revealed sense) of Scripture was first known only in the time of Christ and the apostles, and is now known only where the Holy Spirit is — in the Church.[46]

As for the notion of *promissio,* it does not appear in these three prefatory pieces, nor is there any clue that it may be expected to hold special interest for Luther. On the contrary, the tendency to suppress the anagogical sense, on the one hand, and the irrelevance of the Old Testament history, on the other, seems to leave scarcely any room for the notion of promise.

44. Ebeling's most extensive discussion is in "Die Anfänge," pp. 185 ff.
45. WA 55/1.4.25–29: "Item in Scripturis Sanctis optimum est Spiritum a litera discernere, hoc enim facit vero theologum. Et a spiritu sancto hoc tantum habet Ecclesia, et non ex humano sensu." Luther then gives an example of an interpretation of the Psalm text which "nemo potuit scire ante spiritus revelationem."
46. Luther mentions Gerson by name in the *Dictata* (WA 3.151.5), but I have no internal evidence in favor of Luther's having read the *De sens. litt.* The ecclesial context of Luther's exegesis appears frequently in his castigation of the *singulares,* the "proprietors of their own opinions" who proudly insist on *sensus suus.*

Luther had read Augustine's *De doctrina christiana* by this time,[47] and had made a few glosses on it, but there is no reference to the rules of Tyconius in the prefaces.[48]

47. Luther briefly glossed this writing, along with others of Augustine, in 1509–1510; see *WA* 9.11.10–12.5. Most of his comments on *De doc. chr.*, too brief to be of much use, concern the fourth book.

48. Luther is well aware of the rules, however. Ebeling ("Die Anfänge," p. 217 n.4) cites five places in the *Dictata* where individual rules are referred to. None of these, however, concerns the third rule; Luther's reference to it at *WA* 3.612.29 f. is mistaken; he means the second. I have not found any reference to Tyconius by name in the *Dictata*.

PART TWO: LUTHER'S FIRST PSALMS COURSE, 1513–1515

X. A MEDIEVAL LUTHER

From now on, the focus will be on Luther himself, and the process whereby he ceased to be merely an imaginative late-medieval theologian and began to emerge as the reformer. I shall trace what I believe is significant development in his thinking on problems of Old Testament interpretation and use, with special attention to the pivotal role played by the notion of promise.

This project involves plunging into a different kind of literature: a commentary on the Psalms, set down by Luther while preparing and teaching his first lecture course in Bible at Wittenberg, 1513–1515. The texts under analysis no longer address themselves, in systematic fashion, to the general problems of hermeneutics. The object is rather to explain the meaning of particular biblical texts.

The question may fairly be asked, therefore: what basis for comparison does such a study provide? Is there any hope of drawing valid conclusions about Luther's relation to the tradition in this way, without also dealing with all the commentaries that Luther is known to have used? Although the ideal would certainly be to examine these medieval commentaries *in toto*, it would take years. In lieu of that, and in order to test my suspicions, where they arise, regarding innovations on Luther's part, I shall make spot comparisons between Luther and the tradition on crucial and specific exegetical points. In this way I shall provide supporting evidence for the conclusions I have drawn, while at the same time acknowledging the need for more evidence of this kind. My probes of traditional exegesis cover nine separate Psalms commentaries, eight of which Luther is known to have used. He mentions by name Augustine, the *Glossa Interlinearis* and *Ordinaria*, Lombard, Hugo Cardinal, Lyra, Burgos, Doering, and Faber. I have added Perez in my comparisons of Luther and the tradition.[1]

In the examination of Luther's prefaces already conducted, nothing was found that would indicate more than a radicalization of certain tendencies in late medieval exegesis. One finds there a stretching, but not a breaking, of old forms; a christological exegesis prevails, wherein Christ is the literal, "prophetic" sense of the text, meaning that the psalmist is the Spirit's mouthpiece for imparting information about Christ and the Church. The historical David all but vanishes behind this christological overlay, as does his Old Testament milieu.

The prefaces also reveal Luther trying to handle conflicting traditions in his peculiar and confusing use of "hystorice," whereby on the one hand it denotes the necessary and proper basis of the fourfold sense (as "literal" was in the medieval tradition) and, on the other, is branded as the carnal and improper sense, to which "prophetic" interpretation has to be opposed.

I propose to create here something of an abstraction, which I shall call the "medieval Luther." This construct will confirm my impression of the prefaces, and will further provide a *terminus a quo* for tracing with greater precision the development that takes place in the *Dictata*. My purpose is not to propose a new timetable for the appearance of Reformation theology, but rather to make clear the logical interrelationship of hermeneutical and theological ideas as they develop. I recog-

---

1. I follow Ebeling's list of Luther's medieval reference works, which include three more not used here: Jerome, Cassiodorus, and John of Turrecremata ("Luthers Auslegung des 14.(15.) Psalms in der ersten Psalmenvorlesung im Vergleich mit der exegetischen Tradition," *ZThK* 50 [1953], 280 n.1). The *Glossa* should be regarded as a unity, even though it is split up in the later glossed Bibles; the most probable author of the *Gloss* on the Psalter is Anselm of Laon, writing 1100-1130. (Smalley, *Study of the Bible,* pp. 56, 60).

nize the hazard of such a proceeding: the development goes on at many levels, and the whole thought-structure does not change all at once. Yet the notion of promise serves in a remarkable way to illuminate the inseparability of hermeneutical and theological ideas in the changing thought of the young Luther.

The "medieval Luther" is an abstraction in the sense that I take no account here of the elements of newness that are apparent from the very beginning of his preserved writings. However, my picture is a fair one in that it represents Luther's prevailing hermeneutical outlook throughout the early part of the lectures.

All the quotations used here come from Luther's comments on the first eighty-four Psalms.[2] According to Vogelsang's timetable, these run to about the end of 1514, or approximately sixteen months after the beginning of the course.[3] This procedure will show that a coherent grouping of hermeneutical ideas can be abstracted from the early part of Luther's lectures, that these ideas at first predominate but then become more and more inappropriate to, and inconsistent with, later material.

The starting point in this reconstruction is the broadest possible issue: the relation between the Old and New Testaments, or more precisely, the effect that basic hermeneutical assumptions have on the understanding, handling, and evaluation of the Old Testament itself. As has been shown, in the

2. I am not suggesting that something decisive happens at Psalm 84, nor was this Psalm chosen *a priori* as the final one. Rather, I chose to limit myself, in this chapter, to material that comes earlier than those texts which are decisive for the argument as a whole — mostly those after Psalm 100. This procedure serves to sharpen the contrast between earlier and later hermeneutical theory and practise. Psalm 84 happens to be the last source for any quotation appearing in this chapter.

3. Throughout this study, chronological observations are made according to the timetable suggested by Vogelsang, who proposes that by Christmas, 1514, Luther had reached Psalm 84 (*Der Junge Luther*, p. 40).

medieval tradition one of the bases of contrast was the fact that while the Old Testament promised only *temporalia,* the New promises *eternalia.* Another basis was that the Old Testament only *promised* grace and salvation, while the New *gives* it. In both cases, the effect is to downgrade the Old Testament: its promises and its people, by and large, are "carnal." Besides, that which it does promise is never given. In short, the Old Testament and its faith remain below the horizon of theological relevance.

The effect of the medieval view of the Old Testament-New Testament relation can be summarized by the observation that the coming of Christ serves decisively to cut the Old Testament out of the theological horizon. That is, the Incarnation marks the time of the first appearance of spiritual salvation, for only at that point in history appear the grace which fulfills the Old Testament law, the sacraments which provide that grace, the Church which dispenses the sacraments, and the New Testament scriptures which first reveal the normative-literal meaning of the Old Testament and of the pre-Christian history.

The hermeneutical expression of this religious situation is to refer to the Old Testament as "umbra," "figura," and "signum," which imply that its sole theological relevance is in its New Testament antitypes. Thus, its promises of *temporalia* are figures of the New Testament promises of *eternalia,* and only the latter have a currently valid meaning. Although it would have been unthinkable to deny that the Old Testament promised the salvation which appeared in Christ, there appears to have been little appreciation of the theological potential hidden in the notion of living *sub promissione.* Generally, such existence was unfavorably compared with living in the time of fulfillment, for the time of fulfillment made the time of promise irrelevant. Furthermore, under such assumptions, "faith" is exclusively Christian faith, "faith in Christ," that

New Testament faith which is "formed by love." In the medieval tradition, the promises were pressed to the service of this love above all else. Consistent with this view, the inspired Old Testament writer was usually conceived of as having belonged to a small, unique group, who was made to speak as a Christian doctor, to the Church, and who already must have had the New Testament *caritas* and spirit.

From Luther's handling of the first eighty-four Psalms one can reconstruct this entire picture. Again, it must be emphasized that this construction does not comprehend the whole of Luther's thought at the early stages of his Psalms course, nor is it intended to support the inference that the early part of the *Dictata* is not worthy of serious attention. Some scholars, for dogmatic reasons, hold that the writings of the period before 1519 "cannot be used alongside the works of the Reformation era," and argue that the Lutheran church "has followed the right instinct in owning as its true spiritual possessions only those writings of Luther which date from the year 1519 or later," since that which comes earlier is "sub-Reformation."[4] This opinion may be of interest to one who wishes to construct a system of Lutheran dogma, but it is irrelevant in an historical study of the emergence of Reformation theology. Furthermore, one might suggest that the "spiritual possessions" of the Lutheran church date back before 1519. With that *caveat,* it is possible to turn to the "medieval Luther."

Like every Christian theologian of his time, Luther believed that Christ is the *veritas* promised in the law.[5] And, like other medieval theologians, he was inclined to view the "time of

---

4. Uuras Saarnivaara, *Luther Discovers the Gospel* (St. Louis, 1951), pp. 125 f.

5. For example, WA 3.167.9-11 (Scholion [cited hereafter as Sch.] Ps. 30:7: "Odisti observantes vanitates"): "Quia deus veritatis est, juste odit vanitates . . . quales sunt omne quod est extra christum, qui, id est cuius fides et verbum est veritas olim promissa in lege." Cf. lines 2-4; WA 3.199.14-18, 37-40.

promise" as singularly lacking in theological or spiritual edification: he was glad to belong to the time when God "does mercy *in effectu,* not only *in promisso,* as with the Jews."[6] The pertinacious Jews are the "people of the promise," and they stubbornly refuse to give up the promise that God has now fulfilled. Promise belongs to the age of law and letter,[7] to the time of night now past.[8] The Old Testament was a time of promise, but Christians enjoy a time when God *hears,*[9] the time of fulfillment and the spirit.[10]

The Jews were given earthly and temporal promises, many of which were fulfilled. But the prophet, addressing Christ in the Spirit, knows that God's promised mercy is not to be hoped for in the promised land, or in any earthly thing, but in heaven.[11] In the Old Testament, God was a "promissor

6. WA 3.119.26 f. (Gloss [cited hereafter as Gl.] Ps. 17:51): *"et faciens misericordiam* in effectu, non in promisso tantum, ut Iudeis." In quotations from the glosses such as this, the italicized words are the biblical text.

7. WA 3.164.22–26: "Vanitates sunt omnia, que non iuvant spiritum ad vitam futuram, sed tantum iuvant carnem ad vitam presentem, ideo ista sunt litera occidens, hec autem spiritus vivificans. Unde et lex, cum sit tota umbra, non veritas ipsa, que est Christus in Euangelio: observantes eam vanitates observant, quia promissionem nolunt dimittere."

8. WA 3.241.10–13 (Sch. Ps. 41:9: "In die mandavit dominus misericordiam suam"): "in die (i.e. luce et revelatione novi testamenti) deus misericordiam suam in facto ostendit et omnibus mandat et denunciat, in nocte autem (i.e. umbra veteris legis) Canticum, i.e. prophetiam et psalmos ac promissiones de ea, nunciat."

9. WA 3.310.26–31: "Ubicunque in psalmis aut prophetis exauditio dei pronunciatur, tempus gratie prophetatur . . . non autem tempus legis veteris . . . Unde Isaie 65[:24]. 'Eritque antequam clament, ego exaudiam, adhuc illis loquentibus ego audiam.' Hoc enim promissionis verbum est. Quare non de legis tempore intelligendum est."

10. WA 3.311.5–8 (Sch. Ps. 55:20): *"Exaudiet deus,* id est tempus exauditionis veniet . . . Sed hoc fiet propter spiritum sanctum, qui datus est nobis."

11. WA 3.199.33–36: "Non ergo tua misericordia promissa est speranda in terra nobis danda, sed in coelo. Et veritas, i.e. impletio eiusdem misericordie, que per legem et prophetas significata est, non usque ad terram, i.e. terrestres et terrena sapientes pertingit."

bonorum temporalium," whereas in Christ he promises and pours out eternal goods (as well as evils).[12] For all the authentic promises of God are spiritual, even though the Jews want carnal things, and vainly simulate religion and obedience to God.[13]

To understand Old Testament prophecy, it is essential to understand that "all the words and deeds of the law are, as it were, only words and signs, whereas the words and deeds of the Gospel are works, and the very things signified."[14] In fact, especially in one ceremony, the Sacrament, God grants man everything, whereas formerly he gave his benefits only imperfectly, by sign, and intermixed with many carnal things.[15] Word, sign, promise, figure: all these are undifferentiated marks of the old age; but today, God has acted.[16] And even those words which God spoke to the people were veiled to all but the prophets; a "medium" was placed between God speak-

12. WA 3.436.35-437.3 (Sch. Ps. 68:25: "Effunde iram tuam"): "Mich.2[:11]. 'Et erit qui stillet populo huic,' id est promissor bonorum temporalium . . . Quia sicut populo Iudaico bona mundi promissa (que sunt stilla ad bona eterna), ita et mala mundi eis comminata sunt: ideo prophete stillare eis dicuntur. Christianis autem promissa sunt bona eterna et mala eterna. Ideo nunc non stillat, sed effundit utrunque in Christo et Apostolis suis."

13. WA 3.497.5-7: "omnia promissa dei . . . sunt spiritualia. Sed Iudei volunt ea carnalia: ideo . . . frustra literalem simulant religionem et obedientiam dei."

14. WA 3.258.8 f.: "Igitur omnia dicta et facta legis sunt velut verba et signa tantum: verba autem et facta Euangelii sunt opera et res ipsa significata." Cf. WA 4.6.25 f. (Sch. Ps. 84:4): "tunc erant omnia in litera et figura, scilicet iustitia, pax, meritum." The first of these quotations is reminiscent of Perez, for whom the Old Testament events, like its sacraments, were only signs, whereas those of the New are mysteries which in some sense contain what they signify.

15. WA 3.262.27-29: "Sicut modo in spiritu unica ceremonia, scilicet sacramento, omnia tribuit, que olim multis carnalibus et imperfecte, i.e. signo dedit."

16. WA 3.295.33-35 (Gl. Ps. 51:11: "Confitebor tibi in saeculum quia fecisti"): "Opus operatus est. Fecisti, verbum absolutum. Olim in lege dixisti. Tunc verbum, nunc opus, tunc promissio, nunc impletio, tunc signum, nunc res, tunc figura, nunc veritas."

ing and the people hearing. The prophets — a kind of spiritual elite — understood the spiritual meaning of the words, but because such meanings were veiled under temporal types, the people understood everything, even promises, only carnally, except perhaps when the prophets were expressly prophesying about future, spiritual goods.[17]

These assertions all presuppose that it was to Christ and to Christians that the Old Testament prophets addressed themselves.[18] Only those who share the same Spirit can understand their words properly; only those who are one with Christ receive the promises made to him. The question of how the contemporaries of the prophet were supposed to understand their words is scarcely raised; they seem to be left in the darkness

17. WA 3.347.29-37 (the context is a petition of the prophet for God to cease speaking "mediate," and to speak "immediate," as promised in Jer. 31:33 and John 6:45): "Sed quando mediate loquebatur, ut per Mosen et prophetas, tunc verbum eius mox erat velatum, et medium positum inter deum et populum, deum loquentem et populum audientem. Sicut et modo fit, licet aliter: Quia tunc erat medium *etiam quoad intelligentiam* [that is, "even as far as simple understanding was concerned"]: que prophetis erat clara, populo autem *velata sub typo temporalium* bonorum vel malorum. Quia omnia mala et bona populus *carnaliter intelligebat,* prophete autem spiritualiter . . . Aliquando autem ex persona propria expresse prophetabant de futuris bonis spiritualibus." (Italics mine.) This distinction is reminiscent of Perez' idea that sometimes the prophets spoke under temporal figures, and sometimes directly, of the same spiritual things.

18. WA 3.313.27 f.: "per omnes prophetas Deus promisit gloriam et exaltationem Christo et deiectionem inimicorum suorum." Cf. WA 3.312.20-23 (Gl. Ps. 55:9b: "posuisti lachrymas meas in conspectu tuo," that is, taken notice of them): "hoc enim Deus *soli Christo et suis* facit, sicut et promisit olim." (Italics mine.) In this early stage a remarkable number of the Old Testament promises are interpreted by Luther as having been made to Christ; via Christ, they come to mankind, according to the exegetical rule of the identity of Christ and his body, of head and members (the First Rule of Tyconius). For instances of the promise made directly to Christ, see WA 3.317.9-11, 412.15-18, 165.19-21 and 40, 237.10-13. Making Christ the object of the promises was a way of saying that all of God's blessings come to his people only in and through Christ. This is the message of the prophets, speaking "prophetice."

of carnal understanding, misled by words usually veiled under the figures of temporal things. Meanwhile, the prophet, privy to the christological import of his words, is inflamed by the fire of love that the promises excite.[19] For it is love, together with faith,[20] that distinguishes the old law from the new: the old law bound the hand, but "it did not bind the soul with love." [21] This last only the chains of *caritas* can do, which is given by Christ in his spirit.[22]

Not only the faith of Christ, and the *caritas* of Christ, but

19. *WA* 3.113.28-31 (Gl. Ps. 17:2: "Diligam te domine"): "In primo verbo huius psalmi [Luther refers to the "diligam"; vs. 1 is actually the title] exprimitur dilectio, quia amoris incentiva hic enarrantur . . . pro augendo isto igne amoris. Quia beneficia exhibita et promissa miro modo inflammant."

20. It cannot be denied that in the early portions of the *Dictata* Luther's emphasis on faith is already extraordinary, if not unique: see *WA* 55/2.31.4-32.10, where the Gospel is said to be the "law of Christ" only where it is grasped by faith, a faith uniquely stamped on the heart. The editors give a series of quotations which indicate that Luther's emphasis on faith is unparalleled (*WA* 55/2.31.9 ff.). It is noteworthy, however, that "faith" here is uniquely Christian faith; what may be designated "Old Testament faith" has not yet appeared in any positive sense. Furthermore, as following quotations show, *caritas* still holds a preeminent position in Luther's thought.

21. *WA* 55/2.115.11 f.: "nec [lex] ligabat animum amore, sed tantummodo manum exterius tenebat." For the witness of the tradition, collected by the Weimar editors, on this saying of Augustine (namely, that the old law bound the hand, not the will or heart), see *WA* 55/2.31.9 ff.

22. *WA* 55/2.7.1-6: "Licet enim lex per timorem penarum potuit manum prohibere et per spem bonorum [temporalium!] ad opera provocare, tamen voluntatem intus non potuit neque solvere neque ligare, Non inquam solvere ad libertatem neque ligare eius cupiditates. Hoc enim fit solum vinculis Charitatis, quam non lex, Sed Christus in spiritu suo dedit." "Spirit" and "caritas" are for Luther interchangeable terms in this context, for — with Lombard and against the Aristotelian-informed *habitus* doctrine of *caritas* — Luther had argued earlier that the *caritas* shed abroad in our hearts (Rom. 5:5) is the Holy Spirit himself concurring with the will (*WA* 9.43.2-8, Luther's marginalia on Lombard's *Sentences*, 1510-1511). Thus, in the *Dictata* Luther has the early Christians accusing the wicked Pharisees (Gl. Ps. 10:4: "Quoniam quae perfecisti destruxerunt"): "Quoniam 'destruxerunt' id in lege, quod est perfectum in ea, scil. *spiritum*,

also the word of Christ is unique, because it is accompanied by grace, whereas the Old Testament prophets' word was only a "naked word" which worked wrath.[23] The word of Christ not only teaches but "simul" is accompanied by the blessing and grace of God, a notion parallel to the Franciscan doctrine of the relation of the sacraments to grace: grace does not come so much through (*per*) the visible and outward signs as parallel to, or on the occasion of, their use, in virtue of God's *pactum* with the Church that he will "assist" them.[24] This benefit was not present in the Old Testament, and therefore one might even say that God did not speak in the law at all.[25]

---

immo quod Christus 'perficit' et implevit, i.e. *spiritum promissum olim*" (WA 55/I.86.15-17; italics mine). Cf. WA 55/I.18.19-22.

23. WA 3.258.29-37 (Sch. Ps. 44:3: "Diffusa est gratia in labiis tuis." The "tuis" are Christ and the apostles. The "calamus" referred to in Luther's comment relates to vs. 2: "Lingua mea calamus scribe velociter scribentis"; the "scribe" is identified as the Holy Spirit at WA 3.250.4): "Quia nec [Moses et al.] precipiunt nisi temporalia, et si preciperent invisibilia, nunquam persuaderent, quia non esset gratia, sed potius indignatio et ira in labiis eorum . . . Quia Mosi linqua non erat talis calamus, quando literam loquebatur: unde quando Iudeis in deserto aliqua suadebat absentia, futura aut difficilia . . . nulla erat gratia in labiis eius, quia non movebantur nisi *nudo verbo*. In nova autem lege Lingua mea, inquit que loquitur spiritum . . . semper est *diffusa per gratiam*." (Italics mine.)

24. Typical of this doctrine of the word, whereby in the New Testament it comes "with benediction annexed," is the following (WA 3.651.25-29): "Nam verba Christi spiritus et vita sunt, vivificantia per annexam gratiam et benedictionem . . . Quia quos docet, simul benedicit: simul plantat et incrementum dat deus." Cf. WA 3.262.30-33. Further investigation of the Franciscan sacramental doctrine of which the above is the hermeneutical parallel cannot be pursued here, but the following passage from Biel is illustrative of this tradition: "Statuit enim [Deus] quod adhibito tali signo [that is, the sacraments of the new law] . . . infallibiliter vult assistere suo signo producendo [simul!] gratiam si non ponatur obex in suscipiente sacramentum . . . Et de hoc fecit ecclesiam suam certam. Et ista ordinatio sive institutio divina vocatur *pactum Dei* initum cum ecclesia" (IV *Sent.* d.1 q.1 a.1 not.2 D; italics mine). As already shown with Saint Bonaventura, this *pactum Dei* was the decisive factor in distinguishing the sacraments of the new law from those of the old.

25. WA 3.347.13-15: "si ipse [Deus] loquitur, non carnaliter, sed

The total impact of this interpretation, and the point that must be made, is that the Old Testament, without New Testament resources, is theologically empty. The decisive moment is the actual coming of Christ: only then begins spirit, *caritas*, effective word, and faith. The interpreter looks back on the prior time as a mere time of promise, and the theological evaluation of that time is negative. The "hermeneutical divide" between letter and spirit, therefore, is between the Old and New Testaments. The New Testament provides all the theological content of the Psalms, revealing their total spiritual meaning. For as the medieval axiom has it, the law, spiritually understood, is the same as the Gospel; [26] that is, the Old Testament, spiritually understood, conveys just what the New Testament conveys. Only in the New Testament, however, is the message finally purged of earthly, carnal things — "sublimated from the letter," as Luther puts it.[27]

This may be theologically edifying, but it is exegetically devastating as far as the Old Testament is concerned, for proper interpretation depends not upon what it says, but upon how it is "understood." There is no incentive to understand

---

spiritualiter loquitur. Ideo non in Atrio legis, sed in Sancto Ecclesie loquitur." One must be careful in using these texts as indication of the theological emptiness of the whole Old Testament, since it is not always clear whether Luther means specifically just the Mosaic legislation or the Old Testament as a whole. My impression is that in this part of the *Dictata*, "lex vetus" and the Old Testament as a whole are practically synonymous (see *WA* 3.276.35–37). In Ch. XIII, an important change will begin to appear.

26. *WA* 55/1.92.19 f.: "Lex autem spiritualiter intellecta est idem cum euangelio." The Weimar editors have neglected to offer the medieval precedent for this notion, even though it is common enough and extremely important for Luther interpretation.

27. *WA* 55/1.92.7–94.2 (Gl. Ps. 11:7): "*Eloquia domini* Euangelica *eloquia casta* quia animam castificant: *argentum igne examinatum* metaphora est, quia probatio ignis est omnium fidelissima: *probatum terrae* hebreus: 'separatum a terra', i.e. sublimatum a litera." The marginal on "litera" (94.10): "i.e. non sapit terram aut terrena, Sed celestia tantum."

the Old Testament historically, since all matters of theological interest are found in the New. Consequently, what matters in Old Testament exegesis is not what the text clearly says or intends but how it is "handled" (*tractatur*) by the interpreter. Thus, Luther writes: "the law of Moses, although written with human letters, is also a living language to those who read and understand it spiritually. But it is only a 'pen,' or literature, to those who read it carnally." [28] And a few lines later: "Thus, the Gospel makes spiritual impressions spiritually; and living and eternal understanding, spiritually, in hearts that are living spiritually. On which account the law of Moses, whether spoken or written, when it is spiritually handled, is a living language and no longer a dead letter." [29] Thus, the requirements for Old Testament exegesis are that the interpreter have a good knowledge of the New Testament, as well as the living Spirit, who gives "eruditio" (spiritual understanding). The hermeneutical discussion is therefore removed from the problem of understanding the Old Testament, and has become a question of New Testament exegesis and Christian spirituality.

An accompanying fundamental characteristic of this type of Old Testament exegesis, one which, under present criteria of interpretation, makes real understanding of the text impossible, is that the interpreter does not place himself with the Old Testament writer in time. As long as the theological potential of Old Testament existence *sub promissione* and *sub lege* does not occur to him, he has no theological reason to

28. WA 3.456.29–31: "lex Mosi literis humanis scripta est etiam lingua viva iis, qui eam spiritualiter legunt et intelligunt. Sed est calamus seu literatura iis, qui eam carnaliter legunt."

29. WA 3.457.4–7: "Ita Euangelium facit spiritualiter impressiones spirituales, intelligentiam spiritualiter vivam et eternam in cordibus spiritualiter vivis. Quare lex Mosi, sive dicta sive scripta sit, *dummodo spiritualiter tractetur,* est viva lingua et non iam mortuus calamus." (Italics mine.) The principle enunciated here is almost identical to Perez' distinction between the "sensus in quo fit" and the "sensus quem facit."

project himself into the life, the faith, or the hope of Israel *ante adventum Christi*. As long as the post-Advent point of view is rigorously maintained, as by the "medieval" Luther, the Old Testament promise is void and empty of theological relevance, precisely because — like the *figura* and *signa* — it has come to an end. It must be spiritually understood. The time of fulfillment is here because Christ has come.

Of course, the Christian also lives under promise, but according to the prevailing medieval view the promises under which he lives are all different: they are all, and only, New Testament promises, promises of *eternalia*. The Old Testament promises of *temporalia* are nothing to him but *umbrae*, which have disappeared with the coming of *lux*. And consequently, neither are Old Testament faith and religion anything to him, since they are in every way inferior to his own.[30]

This frame of mind, with its attendant "contra Iudaeos" mentality, is more evident in the rigorously christological interpreters of the Old Testament, such as Perez and Faber. For them, the traditional Old Testament *lex* and *doctrina* — which gave at least some theological value to the Old Testament — became submerged under the axiom that the whole Old Testament is allegory, its whole meaning Christ.

30. See WA 3.200.35-37, speaking of the Old Testament people "qui nondum intelligebant gratiam Christi, sed tantum in pedagogo et umbra fidei et figura iustitie Christi vivebant." The significance of the synagogue is that it signifies the Church (WA 3.369.7 f.). Regarding the Mosaic dispensation, "sane non fuit intentio Dei in lege Mosi, ut umbra ista et figure aliter acciperentur nisi ut signa future veritatis aliquando finienda" (WA 3.515.39-516.1). Old Testament hope and fear are decidedly inferior: "longe differunt spes illorum et nostra, timor illorum et noster . . . illi speraverunt temporalia, nos spiritualia. Illi non timuerunt hostes corporales, quia submersi erant, nos spirituales, scilicet peccata et demones in baptismo submersos" (WA 3.595.4-10).

XI. LUTHER'S DEVELOPMENT: A PROJECTION

In the course of his lectures on the Psalms, Luther discovered that the Old Testament faith and religion were so much like his own that they could become exemplary for his own faith, and for the Church's self-understanding. As a preliminary to describing this process in detail, I will here indicate, via a sweeping survey, how Luther's reading of the Psalms underwent basic changes in its presuppositions and results. This sketch is intended to provide a glimpse of the *terminus ad quem* of my study and to provide a framework within which specific issues derive meaning. One may well ask what kind of framework can be imposed on a thousand pages of *ad hoc* exegesis, and how development and change in Luther's thought can be accurately measured.

The exegetical and devotional tradition is helpful here: it provides a framework in the seven penitential Psalms.[1] They can serve as a series of check-points throughout the Psalter at which Luther's progress can be tested as he proceeds. Because they belong to a single class of Psalms — those that are read and interpreted in the context of preparation for confession — Luther can be expected to approach them all in roughly the same fashion. Therefore, if a change emerges in the basic approach to these particular Psalms, broader hermeneutical changes may be expected to have occurred elsewhere, too. A span of almost two years separates the exegesis of the first and the last of these Psalms; even the brief analysis offered here

---

1. According to the Vulgate numbering, these are Psalms 6, 31, 37, 50, 101, 129, and 142.

will suggest elements quite different from the "medieval Luther" and will raise questions that beg answering.

Psalm 6. — In line with his radicalization of christological exegesis of the Psalms, already noticed in his "Preface of Jesus Christ," Luther departs from the tradition (Faber Stapulensis excepted) in making Psalm 6 an "oratio Christi" — a prayer of Christ himself.[2] The Weimar editors note that in most of the tradition the speaker is either the Church, or the individual Christian penitent, or both.[3] Luther, of course, agrees with the tradition that Christ does not share our *culpa* but takes upon himself our *pena,* suffering many things *sine peccato.*[4] It is noteworthy here that the Old Testament writer himself, and the meaning of the words to him, are conspicuously absent. The subject matter is Christ and the penitent, in tropological identity.

Psalm 31. — The general approach to Psalm 31 is more completely traditional: the subject is "the method of true penitence."[5] Christological exegesis plays no role, but neither does the Old Testament situation. In accordance with the title of the Psalm (*David Eruditio*), Luther makes the exegesis a discourse on Christian spiritual understanding: "To know that the son of God is incarnate for our salvation, and that outside him all are in sins: that is what this *eruditio* is, this *intellectus,* which no one knows except through the Holy Spirit."[6] David

---

2. WA 55/1.38.3-6: "Oratio Christi pro suis passionibus et peccatis membrorum suorum ut mediatoris inter deum patrem et homines." The editors provide Faber's comparable description, 55/1.39.13-15.
3. WA 55/1.39.15-20, with examples.
4. WA 55/1.38.13-15: "in isto Psalmo nulla fit confessio peccati, sed tantum questio penarum, ideo principaliter sunt verba Christi, qui sine peccato in multis tamen passionibus fuit." Thus, the fact that sins are not being confessed makes the christological starting-point convenient and not really as radical as a hallowed tradition in Luther scholarship suggests (for example, Ebeling, "The New Hermeneutics," p. 41).
5. WA 3.171.26: "de modo vere poenitendi."
6. WA 3.172.24-27: "Scire ergo filium dei esse incarnatum pro salute

is speaking here, removed from his own time, as a Christian theologian, and his meaning is explicated by glossing with the words of Christ and Saint Paul.

Psalm 37. — Luther returns to a partial christological orientation with Psalm 37, summarizing it as a "lament and complaint of our mediator in his passion." [7] Christ is remembering and confessing our sins *pro nobis* to God, and asking for our *liberatio*. Christians, in using this Psalm, must therefore pray it not "in themselves," but "in Christ." [8] Luther's emphasis is on the closest possible identity between Christ and the Church, head and members — especially in the very act of repentance. In this "tropological" identification, Christ does not share man's guilt; nevertheless, his *pena* signifies man's *culpa*.[9] The historical David is himself outside the scope of the exegesis, except insofar as he is named as author of the Psalm.

Psalm 50. — This Psalm is summarized by Luther as "the best possible *eruditio* and example for penitents and those who wish to confess." [10] For the first time, the Old Testament historical situation is accounted for, namely, David's repentance over the Bathsheba affair. Yet even while it is acknowledged that the *hystoria* is about David, "nevertheless, according to the prophetic sense (*propheticum sensum*) it ought to be

---

nostra et extra eum omnes esse in peccatis, hec est eruditio ista, intellectus iste: quod nemo nisi per spiritum sanctum cognovit."

7. WA 3.211.8 f.: "Planctus et querela mediatoris nostri in passione propter peccata nostra constituti."

8. WA 3.211.15-22: "Quia secundum apostolum Christus factus est pro nobis maledictum Gal.3[:13] et peccatum 2. Cor.[5:21] et peccata nostra ipse tulit Esaie 53[:12], ideo hic psalmus in persona eius dicitur, in quo commemorat et confitetur pro nobis Deo patri peccata nostra et querit liberationem sui (i.e. nostram per ipsum et in ipso). Ideo quicunque vult illum psalmum fructuose orare, debet eum non in se, sed in Christo orare et tanquam eum audire orantem, et sic ei suum adiungere affectum et dicere Amen."

9. WA 3.212.34 f.: "pena eius nostram culpam significat."

10. WA 3.284.2: "Optima penitencium et confiteri volentium eruditio et exemplum."

understood [as being spoken] in the person of human nature (that is, the church of Christ)." ¹¹ This means, in effect, that the history is an allegory or *figura* of the Psalm's "real" meaning. The Psalm is "not properly about David, but *prophetice* made in the person of the church," whereby David, having seized the occasion from his actual situation to make a "prophetic" utterance, speaks as "part of the church." ¹²

In the approach to these first four penitential Psalms, then, no departure can be detected from the presuppositions of Luther's prefaces and from the "medieval Luther." To get to the next penitential Psalm, however, we cross a 50-psalm gap — chronologically, more than a year. And changes are immediately evident.

Psalm 101. — Luther does not treat Psalm 101 throughout as a penitential Psalm, although he recognizes the propriety of the Church's decision to assign it as such.¹³ In his summary of the Psalm (a part of the printed edition he had prepared for his students in the summer of 1513), Luther called this "a prayer of the pauper when he was anxious" about the reality of God's presence and help.¹⁴ Who is the pauper? In his later gloss on the word, presumably made approximately at the time of his classroom treatment of the Psalm in the spring of 1515,¹⁵ Luther explains it as "the people before the advent of Christ." ¹⁶ Their prayer is an anxious petition for the coming

11. WA 3.284.27–29: "Potest quidem psalmus iste secundum hystoriam in persona David intelligi. Tamen secundum propheticum sensum debet accipi in persona nature humane (i.e. ecclesie Christi)."
12. WA 3.291.22–24: "Patet itaque psalmum istum proprie non de David, sed in persona Ecclesie prophetice factum esse: a David velut parte Ecclesie, sumpta occasione ex hystoria, que in titulo nominatur." The title is given as "Ad victoriam psalmus David," WA 3.284.4.
13. WA 4.152.30 f.: "recte pro penitentibus psalmus iste orandus deputatur."
14. WA 4.141.4: "Oratio pauperis cum anxius fuerit." This is the traditional summary for the Psalm.
15. According to Vogelsang's chronology (*Der junge Luther*, p. 40).
16. WA 4.141.4: "*Oratio pauperis* populi ante adventum Christi,

of Messiah.[17] "Tropologically" it is the same kind of prayer: a prayer of the Christian for Christ's spiritual advent in the situation of temptation.[18] An anagogical (eschatological) application is also made in the same vein: Christ will be called upon to rise up against the Antichrist.[19]

For the first time, then, the literal sense of the text con-

---

cum anxius fuerit." (The underlined words belong to the early, printed text; the rest is the later gloss.) Luther does this same thing at Psalm 122, where the printed summary reads: "Oratio fidelis populi ad Deum pro opprobrio divitum et superborum" (*WA* 4.407.19), and a later marginal gloss reads: "Est autem iterum petitio adventus Christi in carnem" (line 32). A probe of the tradition shows that following Augustine, most medieval exegetes had identified the "pauper" of Psalm 101 as Christ, speaking together with his members. The *Gloss,* Lombard, and Hugo do so (Burgos and Doering make no comment). Perez introduces his universal "Adam," the *homo mysticus,* who "expectavit et desideravit istum secundum adam celestem ut ipsum redimeret et liberaret." Thus, the Psalm is *"Oratio pauperis* adam . . . cum *anxiaretur* ante adventum christi existens in miseria. Qui cupiens redemi per christum . . . effudit precem suam ad christum." Faber labels the Psalm a "deprecatio ecclesiae, i.e. populi fidelis." It is Lyra who is closest to Luther, and Lyra uses Rashi's interpretation to support his own. Rashi, Lyra reports, said the Psalm was "de anxietate populi israel in hac captivitate positi orantis et desiderantis ab ea liberari per regem messiam venturum . . . et sic secundum eum loquitur de tempore christi." Therefore, Lyra concludes, the Psalm speaks "ad literam de anxietate populi israel cum desiderio deprecantis pro adventu christi." *Moraliter,* Lyra asserts, "potest exponi de quolibet vere penitente et ad deum clamante pro liberatione sua, per adventum gratie divine." Here is the first indication that Luther – almost in spite of himself – is moving toward the very medieval exegete whom he singled out for attack in his preface.

17. *WA* 4.141.18–21: "Et est oratio populi fidelis adventum Christi postulantis, qualis fuit tempore Herodis, quando et secundum carnem ab eo vexabatur, et simul per scribas, legis corruptores, multo peius vastabatur in vera intelligentia spirituali."

18. *WA* 4.141.25–27: "Tropologice autem est oratio pro adventu spirituali Christi, quando anima a demonibus oppressa viciis, etiam foris in carne a mundo vexatur."

19. *WA* 4.141.27–30: "Sic erit et circa finem mundi in adventu secundo . . . ut tunc exurgere postuletur dominus Ihesus et misereatur Zion, maxime tempore Antichristi."

forms to the historical order of things: attention is focused on the people "*ante* adventum Christi." The relation of the psalmist's own history and word to the Church's is not that of mere *umbra* to its *lux, signum* to *res,* wherein that which happened and was said is relevant only insofar as it can be put "prophetice" into the mouth of Christ or the Church, so that either Christ himself speaks, or else David speaks as "pars ecclesiae." Rather, the psalmist's own word, spoken out of his own circumstances, is the basis of the theological interpretation. He prays out of longing for the coming of Christ, who in three analogous situations is not yet present in the desired way.

Now Christ, rather than being the "prophetic-literal" sense, that is, the point of departure for a spiritual exegesis, becomes the goal or *telos* of the whole exegesis. And the *applicatio* springs not from the Christian's likeness to Christ, but from his likeness to the Old Testament speaker, with whom he shares the anticipation of the Coming One.

Psalm 129. — Like Psalm 50, Psalm 129 is treated by Luther as a penitential Psalm, and without the introduction of Christ as the speaker.[20] Like Psalm 101, this one is again a *petitio* for the coming of Christ in flesh, and therefore a prayer of the Old Testament faithful for redemption from sins. "But," adds Luther, "because everyone who is in sin is still under the law, therefore *moraliter* this is a prayer for any sins." [21] And so again a *petitio* is made prior to, and for, Christ's advent. Although the psalmist is viewed as a "prophet" who sees the redemption already accomplished in Christ, the interpretive standpoint is within the actual Old Testament situation. Also of interest is the identification here made between the man

20. WA 4.418.20: "Petitio veniae pro peccatis . . . in persona populi fidelis."
21. WA 4.418.35–419.18: "Est autem expressa petitio redemptionis populi a peccatis . . . Ideo primo intelligitur de redemptione per Christum facta toti generi humano. Sed quia omnis, qui est in peccato, est adhuc sub lege, ideo moraliter est oratio pro quibuscunque peccatis."

"sub lege" and the man "in peccato." As in his treatment of the previous penitential Psalm, Luther has seen a parallel, an analogy, of situations in the lives of the Old Testament faithful and the Christian. For the Old Testament believer to be under the law and asking for Christ is the same as for the Christian to be in sin and asking forgiveness.

Psalm 142. — The same new approach appears in Psalm 142, indicating a real shift from the perspective of Luther's earlier exegesis. In his original, printed summary, Luther had, as before, designated the Psalm as penitential in character.[22] But he makes a striking addition in his later gloss on the printed title ("A Psalm of David"): "This psalm in the spirit and in the prophetic sense is the voice of the people of the faithful synagogue . . . anxiously seeking the advent of Christ in the flesh."[23] This approach, Luther adds with apparent satisfaction, makes understanding the Psalm "easy."[24] Again, a new parallel appears between the Old and New Testament people: the signal for it is "the faithful synagogue," a rubric that appears with increasing frequency in the latter portion of Luther's lectures. The "faithful synagogue," the corporate people of God, await and pray for the coming of Christ; together with

22. WA 4.443.2: "Deprecatio penitentialis devota pro quolibet iusto et iustificari petente" (this being part of the printed text made in the summer of 1513).

23. WA 4.443.18–21: "Iste psalmus in spiritu et prophetico sensu est vox populi fidelis synagoge . . . petentis . . . anxie Christi adventum in carnem." My survey of tradition's handling of the title of the Psalm revealed that Luther alone uses the name "fidelis synagoge" as the speaker. Only Augustine, however, has Christ himself speaking: "Queramus . . . in hoc psalmo Dominum . . . Iesus Christum praenuntiantem se per hanc prophetiam." Perez' approach somewhat resembles Luther's: David, repenting, "petit liberari per Christum," and the Psalm is also "vox cuiuslibet peccatoris penitentis et desiderantis . . . liberari et iustificari." But Perez blurs the historical specificity of the Old Testament people by again introducing his "persona ipsius Adam" as the one in whom David speaks.

24. WA 4.443.21 f.: "et sic facilis est psalmus intellectu." Easier, certainly, than the *intellectus* described in n.6 above!

them and in like fashion, Christians also send prayers toward God "in the union and communion of saints." [25] This is how to apply the Psalm "moraliter." This moral application also includes the individual who "ardently desires grace" in the face of temptation.[26] Another striking feature of his exegesis is that the voice of the Old Testament people, their *petitio*, is no longer the carnal voice of the earthbound, unillumined Jew, but it is already spoken "in the spirit."

What, in summary, does this overview suggest? First, there is a noticeable shift in the basic material for exegesis — in the "literal sense" — from Christ and the Church as the subject matter and speaker to the actual Old Testament, pre-advent situation.

Second, as shown in the preface material, the literal, primary, and proper sense of all the Psalms is the "prophetic" sense. But if Psalm 50 is compared with Psalm 142, a fundamental change appears in the meaning of "prophetic." In the former Psalm, David's word is prophetic because he speaks "in the person of the Church," or as "part of the Church" — an interpretation consistent with Luther's prefaces. But in Psalm 142, the prophetic speaker is the "faithful synagogue" awaiting Christ's first advent. The voice of the Old Testament people, speaking as themselves, is now heard. This indicates a radical change from Luther's prefaces, where, in the tradition of Faber Stapulensis he had set up a total and qualitative opposition between "prophetic" and "historical" interpretation.

25. WA 4.443.26-29: "Et nota, quod moraliter hunc et omnes psalmos orare debes tanquam cum omnibus fidelibus devote orantibus eundem, ut scil. optes cum illis tuam quoque coram deo orationem venire et sic in unione et communione sanctorum."

26. WA 4.443.22-26: "quia ecclesia ipsum deputat pro poenitentibus, ideo moraliter intelligitur de adventu Christi in animam spirituali per gratiam . . . Igitur pone hominem, qui exemplum martyrum intuens et sanctos preteriti temporis, pressus confusione nimis ardenter desideret gratiam."

The question is: has this opposition collapsed? This will be answered later.

The identification of the speaker of the Psalms has changed: earlier, it was Christ himself or the "prophet," altogether removed from the Old Testament time. In either case, the exegesis is really New Testament exegesis. The Old Testament does not speak in its own right. In Psalm 142, by contrast, it is the "faithful synagogue" that speaks, solidly in its own time, *ante adventum,* yet *simul in spiritu.*

This change involves a striking difference in the *applicatio.* In the earlier exegesis, there was an identification (*tropologice*) of Christ and the believer as against the Old Testament figure, who either did not appear at all on the horizon of interpretation, or else (as in Psalm 50) prophesied and theologized as an on-the-scene New Testament theologian, and was therefore a radically "special person" elevated in prophetic isolation from among his contemporaries. In the later exegesis, by contrast, there is a communion of the *whole* people of God — the "communio sanctorum" — in their expectation and petition for Christ, and an accompanying tendency to broaden the Old Testament speaker to include, as it were, a "faithful remnant." While earlier the penitent was directed to identify himself with the vicariously penitent Christ, in word and *in affectu* (as in Psalm 37), later he is to identify himself with the petitioner of the "faithful synagogue" in *his* temptation and expectation (as in Psalm 142). Luther calls the former kind of application "tropological"; the latter, "moral."

Finally, a structural schema of multiple exegesis appears at Psalm 101, which is quite different from the traditional fourfold one. The traditional schema was built on the providential character of literal historical events as *signa,* whose *res* were, successively, Christ-Church (allegorical), grace-merit (tropological), and the *visio dei* (anagogical). Luther's schema is built on three comings of Christ: in flesh, in the soul, and eschatologically. The common goal (and therefore the single *res*) of the exegesis is Christ's coming.

What is the significance of these changes, considering the assumptions of the prefaces and of the "medieval Luther"? Has something fundamental happened in Luther's hermeneutical ideas? Or are the differences between the early and late penitential Psalms only accidental, and accountable in some other way? And what role does the concept of promise play in these changes? What follows will answer these questions.

XII. THE SENSES AND STRUCTURE OF SCRIPTURE

The task now is to trace in detail the changes that Luther's hermeneutical principles undergo in the *Dictata* and to show at each point the pivotal role of *promissio*. The argument must be built up piece by piece, since toward the end some serious questions are raised about leading trends in recent Luther research.

At the end of the Middle Ages the language used to describe the various senses of Scripture had virtually collapsed. One could no longer assume (especially after Gerson) that a reference to the "literal sense" meant the historical, grammatical meaning of the text. Prierias complained that under certain current definitions of the various senses, "literal" and "spiritual" had come to mean the same thing. Perez exhibited a chaos of terminology, and Faber attempted a sort of tour de force that defined "literal" in a way wholly removed from either grammatical or historical meaning, as far as the Old Testament was concerned.

The Sensus Propheticus

In Luther's preface, "prophetic" had been his label for the one proper sense of Scripture; it was radically christological, and opposed to "historical." But in his treatment of the penitential Psalms the meaning of "prophetic" changed, even though the term persisted.[1] What, then, does "prophetic sense"

---

1. Fritz Hahn indiscriminately mixes quotations from early and late *Dictata* in his brief explanation of *sensus propheticus* ("Die heilige Schrift als Problem der Auslegung bei Luther," *EvTh* 10 [1951], 415 f.)

mean by the end of the Psalms course, and how has its relation to historical and grammatical exegesis changed? Further, how is the notion of *promissio* involved?

Luther's exegesis of Psalm 118 provides a convenient focal point for answers. At the beginning of his glosses of this longest of the Psalms, Luther expresses his intention to apply a simple twofold interpretation: "prophetic" and "moral." [2] But strangely, there follow two quite different explanations of what both these labels mean. First, Luther explains himself as follows: *"prophetically,* the psalm is a *description* of the future faithful people in Christ pitted against the corrupting pharasaic people." This conflict has arisen between "true and faithful Christians," on the one hand, and "authors of their own righteousness, such as the Jews and heretics," on the other.[3] The moral interpretation that is paired with this prophetic one directs the message "against all the proud who, neglecting that to which they are obligated, do that which seems right to them." [4] This definition of "prophetic" fits Luther's prefaces.[5] The subject matter of the exegesis is not the Old Testament text and people, but the Christian church "in Christ."

But immediately following this gloss, in which the reader is supposed to be informed of the interpreter's basic approach to the Psalm, Luther adds another brief gloss of quite different import: "In the literal and prophetic sense, this psalm is a

2. WA 4.280.31 f.: "nos simplici sensu precedamus. — Dupliciter iste psalmus intelligitur, prophetice et moraliter." I found this distinction nowhere in the tradition of the interpretation of this Psalm.

3. WA 4.280.32–281.30: "Prophetice primo est *descriptio* populi fidelis in Christo futuri contra pharisaicas corruptelas . . . illi vere Christiani et fideles, isti autem sue iustitie auctores, ut Iudei et heretici." (Italics mine.)

4. WA 4.281.30–32: "Moraliter secundo contra omnes superbos, qui neglecto eo, ad quod tenentur, faciunt que sibi recta videntur."

5. Cf. WA 3.647.26–28, where the *sensus allegoricus* is described as the "prophetic sense of the [historical-] literal" and is referred to the Church.

petition for the advent of Christ, and a commendation of the church of Christ. In the moral and doctrinal sense, it is a petition for the spiritual advent of Christ through grace, and a commendation of his grace."[6]

In the first of these two glosses, "prophetic" means on-the-scene description of the Christian church; in the second, the petition of the Old Testament people. In the first gloss, the moral interpretation springs from and is modeled upon the conflict of primitive church and synagogue; in the second, upon the historical situation of the people of God prior to Christ's advent. Furthermore, "prophetic" is in the latter case paired with "literal," rather than being opposed to it.[7] My guess is that Luther, having written the first gloss and then proceeded to the actual exegesis, at length came back and added the second gloss. For it is the second, not the first, which fits the persistent line of interpretation running through all the glosses and scholia in Psalm 118.[8] This line interprets the whole Psalm

6. WA 4.281.35–37: "In sensu *prophetico et literali* psalmus iste est *petitio* adventus Christi et commendatio Ecclesie Christi, in morali autem et doctrinali est *petitio* adventus Christi spiritualis per gratiam et commendatio gratie eius." (Italics mine.) The spiritual advent of Christ is an important theme in the preaching of Bernard of Clairvaux, for whom Luther retained the utmost respect. See Bernard's seven sermons *In adventu Domini* (PL 183, 35–56). In *Serm.* 5, n. 1, he calls the spiritual advent the "medius adventus," in which Christ comes "in spiritu et virtute" (col. 50 D). This middle advent is the *via* "per quam a primo venitur ad ultimum" (col. 51 A). Rudolf Haubst surveys the systematic tradition, particularly Nicolas of Cusa, on the related theme of the threefold *nativitas* of Christ (eternal, historical, and spiritual; *Die Christologie des Nikolaus von Kues* [Freiburg, 1956], pp. 35–38). Haubst quotes a sermon of Cusa: "Man muss wissen, dass eine solche tägliche geistige Geburt, die man gewöhnlich als unsichtbare Sendung des Sohnes Gottes bezeichnet, nichts anderes ist als der Hervorgang (*processus*) des Wortes oder der gezeugten Weisheit von Gott dem Vater zum Geist (*mens*) einer vernünftigen Kreatur zu deren geistiger und gnadenhafter Erleuchtung" (p. 36).

7. *Doctrinal* is a traditional word for pairing with "moral," coming from Rom. 15:4: "quaecumque enim scripta sunt, ad nostram doctrinam scripta sunt."

8. Luther scholars who have studied the manuscripts agree that Luther

as *petitio* for God to fulfill his promises.⁹ And Luther can call this sense simply the "literal" sense of the Psalm, as in the second defining gloss he linked "literal" with "prophetic." A similar situation appears in the earlier exegesis of Ps. 97:4, a call for all the earth to rejoice in the Lord. Two quite different approaches to the text are suggested — both "literal." "The music here recited," Luther first writes, "can be understood *ad literam* as though he were saying: 'O you sons of Israel who are future, when you see that salvation, rejoice, sing psalms and render the honor which you give to God in your ceremonies to this one who has appeared in flesh, since he is true God.' " Here, the Old Testament prophet addresses the people of the New Testament time — in full cognizance of orthodox christology — and the interpretation, in conformity with the principles enunciated in Luther's prefaces, is called "literal." But then Luther adds a second alternative: "Or, it is the voice of the prophet exhorting the people *then present* to faith and hope in the future incarnation and advent of Christ, as if he were saying, 'Celebrate and rejoice, for behold, he will come to you; to you is *promised* the son of God, salvation.' " ¹⁰ Here, it is the Old Testament people who are

---

frequently made later additions and corrections to earlier interpretations. It is impossible to date these later insertions precisely. For a summary of the dating problems, see Vogelsang, *Der junge Luther*, pp. 39 f.

9. For example, WA 4.304.33–35: "Patet ergo, quod per totum psalmum nihil aliud nisi intellectum et gratiam, lucem et ignem, fidem et charitatem petivit et petit in Christo futuro promisso." WA 4.310.37–39: "totus psalmus est nihil alius nisi petitio, ut reveletur lex spiritualis, ut auferatur litera, proferatur spiritus, tollatur velamen et appareat facies, veniat Christus et transeat Moses." WA 4.312.34 f.: "Primo literali sensu generaliter propheta petit . . . spiritualem legem venire." The word *eloquium* appears twenty times in Psalm 118, and only seven more times in the whole Latin Psalter. In English translations the word is usually rendered "promise." In the Latin Psalter the word *promissio* occurs only once (Ps. 56:8). For a list of occurrences in the *Dictata* of the word *promissio* and of forms of *promitto*, see the Appendix. More than a quarter of the total occurrences are in the exegesis of this Psalm.

10. WA 4.121.3–9: "Ista musica hic recitata potest ad literam in-

addressed, and their joy is in the promise of the Coming One. The only difference between this and the Psalm 118 gloss is that here the label "prophetic" does not appear; only "literal" is used. But the content of the distinction is just the same. What is happening is that the prophetic — and therefore the proper theological — interpretation of the text has been given a qualitative turn toward a literal (in the ordinary sense of the word), historical interpretation. Luther has in fact reached a point where he can no longer oppose prophetic and historical interpretation as he did in his preface. And where this change occurs, *promissio* appears as the means by which the Old Testament exegesis becomes both theologically important and historically more credible. When the prophet turns to address his own contemporaries, his word becomes a word of promise.

Luther struggles to explain his new approach in the opening part of the scholion on Psalm 118. There he complains: "I have not yet seen this psalm explained in the prophetic sense by anyone, nor is there anyone who has observed the sequence and order of the narration in it without violence and distortion to the verses and words. They have not sought out, therefore, what I think must come first, because it is the prophetic — i.e. the literal — [sense] which is the *fundamentum* of the others, their master and light and author and font and origin."[11] This text cannot be used, as it was by

---

telligi, q.d. 'O vos filii Israel, qui futuri estis, quando istud salutare videbitur, iubilate, psallite et honorem, quem facitis deo in vestri ceremoniis, huic tribuite, qui in carne apparuit, quoniam est verus deus.' Vel [and this can be nothing but *ad literam* also] sit vox prophete exhortantis populum *tunc presentem* ad fidem et spem future incarnationis et adventus Christi, q.d. 'omnia festiva agite et laudate, quoniam ecce vobis veniet, vobis promittitur filius dei salutare.' " (Italics mine.)

11. WA 4.305.3–8: "Istum psalmum nondum vidi ab aliquo expositum in sensu prophetico, nec ullus est, quo seriem et ordinem expositionis in eo tenuerunt sine violentia et contorsione versuum et verborum. Quod inde puto venire, quia propheticum, id est literalem, primo non quesierunt:

SENSE AND STRUCTURE OF SCRIPTURE | 181

Ebeling, to illustrate Luther's use of the fourfold sense with a christological basis, that is, to speak of "Christ as the principle sense of Scripture, as the *fundamentum* of the others, their master and light," etc. Ebeling was viewing Christ as the first, or literal, sense, whereas in fact here, and in many of the later Psalms, Luther no longer treats the Psalm text in such a way that Christ and the Church are the "text." The *sensus propheticus* has changed its meaning.[12]

This change is clear in the actual exegesis of Psalm 118, where the psalmist now speaks in his own person (not in the person of another); he addresses his own contemporaries (not Christ or the primitive Church). Abandoning a full analysis of the spiritual affections of the prophet (the Spirit has reserved that understanding for himself), Luther proposes to examine the prophecy itself — the words of the text — to

---

qui est fundamentum ceterorum, magister et lux et author et fons atque origo." Psalm 118 is an alphabetical Psalm, and the *Aleph* standing at the head of it was interpreted by the tradition to mean *doctrina*, which was further specified as *doctrina moralis* concerned with *beatitudo*. This meant, for Lyra, that there was no need for a separate "moral" interpretation: "Ps. iste loquitur de beatitudine in spe . . . et sic patet quod sensus litteralis est simpliciter moralis." I found no reference to a *sensus propheticus* in the tradition. Perez again introduces "Adam," the *homo mysticus* and *peregrinus*: "Hunc ergo hominem mysticum et peregrinum introducit David loquente in hoc psalmo. Qui perigrinando querit Christum in v.t. . . . Sed postquam venit ad christum in n.t. perigrinando ad secundum adventum." Perez' *homo mysticus* is frequently found engaged in *petitio* for the first or second advents of Christ. I have not found in Perez reference to a "spiritual advent." Nor have I found that for him the "Old Testament man" is the historical Israel itself; rather, it is a *heilsgeschichtliche* Everyman "introduced" by David.

12. Ebeling, "Die Anfänge," p. 225. The newness of Luther's exegesis in the *Dictata*, as Ebeling formulated it in his dissertation, was not clearly seen. Ebeling stated that the uniqueness was "not that the book of Psalms is christological generally, and that the Old Testament was exegeted from the New Testament, but that with such energy and concentration an exclusively christological exegesis was established as a fundamental hermeneutical principle: that gives to Luther's hermeneutical theory already at the beginning of the Psalms exegesis a unique position over against the

discover its message.[13] He seems to observe, before long, that the words themselves are the key to the prophet's *affectus,* and that the prophet's *affectus* is, in a word, *fides.*

Under the impact of the promises of the future, the eyes of the psalmist have been opened to the temporary, provisional character of Moses' law,[14] and his mouth is opened in petition to God to act on his word of promise, to act in accordance with his stated intention.[15] He exhorts his own people to remain firm in their hope and faith in the coming of God's promised mercy.

What is important about Luther's new understanding of the *sensus propheticus* is that it makes the qualitative hermeneutical leap necessary for an eventual reuniting of the "theological" and "grammatical" senses of the Old Testament.[16] Luther

---

tradition" (*Evangelienauslegung,* p. 280). Extreme, yes, but not "unique" until the pre-advent *promissio* and *petitio,* rather than on-the-scene *descriptio,* become the pre-eminent way to speak about the Christ.

13. WA 4.305.12–18: "Sed nos . . . prophetiam scrutabimur: que erit facilius, quam morales affectiones per singula venari . . . quot, quando et qualiter atque quantum eant . . . plenarium intellectum moralem huius psalmi credo spiritum sanctum sibi soli reservasse."

14. WA 4.305.19–25: "propheta intuitus oculis spiritualibus legem Mosi, videns in ea latere et clausam esse legem fidei euangelium gratie et promissa invisibilia . . . petit hoc absconsum auferri et absconditum proferri in lucem, per totum psalmum relative loquens et comparative inter veterem et novam legem loquens ac distinguens." Cf. WA 4.325.17–25: " 'Statue servo tuo eloquium tuum in timore tuo' [vs. 38]. Semper prosequitur differentiam legis veteris et nove, seu litere et spiritus . . . [several examples are given such as] divites et avari sunt litram servantes promittentem terrena, sed pauperes, qui cor inclinant in testimonia et promissa futurorum."

15. WA 4.298.1–3 (Gl. Ps. 118:124): "*Fac,* non tantum dic, quia satis promisisti, *cum servo tuo* populo tuo *secundum misericordiam tuam* gratiam promissam, non secundum meritum."

16. In making this move, Luther is coming closer to the viewpoint of Lyra. Hailperin observes that even though Jews and Christians could not agree on the identification of Jesus as Messiah, Lyra (given his historical approach) and Rashi "could remain in the same historical mode as to

the interpreter has finally thought himself into the pre-advent situation, where he has found a rich theological reward.

Luther makes a distinction between the "figurative" and "spiritual" understanding of the Old Testament word that reflects the two meanings of "prophetic." Luther comments on vs. 129 ("Marvelous are your testimonies, Lord") that the testimonies of the old law are marvelous "in that one sounds forth *spiritualiter,* another *figuraliter.*" [17] The meaning of this distinction is that the spiritual interpretation and understanding of the text — when it involves *testimonium, eloquium, promissio* — does not necessarily require a figurative (non-literal) construction on the words of the text. This leads to the possibility of a marriage between historical-grammatical exegesis and theological (spiritual) interpretation.

The *spiritualiter-figuraliter* distinction appears to flow from Luther's apprehension that "testimonies," "promises," etc., bear intrinsic theological value as faith-inviting words, and therefore are edifying in themselves, without need of figurative construction. God's words are called testimonies, Luther writes, "because they testify to future goods. They are not the exhibition of present things, but testimonies of future things. And on that account, they make faith to be the substance of future things, not of things which appear. Thus, the grace of God was not yet apparent to the ancients, but it was being prophesied." [18]

---

what the prophet said in *his* day, since they both, the Jew and the Christian, saw messianic promises in the prophets" (*Rashi,* p. 53).

17. WA 4.298.34-37: "Non tantum antique legis testimonia sunt mirabilia, quod aliud spiritualiter, aliud figuraliter sonant, sed et nove legis, quod sub malis et passionibus tanta bona et guadia prestant ct multo maiora promittunt."

18. WA 4.310.28-32 (Sch. Ps. 118:14): "*In via testimoniorum tuorum delectatus sum* . . . 'Testimonia' porro dicuntur, quia testantur de futuris bonis: non sunt exhibitiones presentium, sed testimonia futurorum, ideoque faciunt fidem esse substantiam futurorum, non apparentium. Sic antiquis nondum apparuit gratia dei, sed prophetabatur."

A New Normative-Literal Sense?

Now, quite unexpectedly, Luther can refer to "testimonia" as a criterion for understanding *all* the words of the Old Testament. These testimonies begin to function in the same way that the normative-literal sense functions in the medieval tradition, as the standard by which all the words of the Old Testament are to be understood. This seems to be what Luther is getting at when he writes: "Or, the words of the Old Law, spiritually understood, are 'testimonies' which testify to nothing but the future Christ alone . . . Wherefore . . . the whole psalm is nothing but petition." [19]

Does this mean that the aim and goal of spiritual exegesis is to conform all the Old Testament words to explicit (literal) *testimonia* of the future? Does it suggest that for Luther the normative-literal sense of Scripture is promise and *petitio*, and therefore fundamentally different from the medieval tradition? Good evidence for this can be found late in the *Dictata*.

First, it is clear enough that throughout Psalm 118, *testimonia, eloquia,* and *promissa* or *promissiones* are all practically synonymous.[20] Second, the contents of this Psalm move Luther to make the sweeping assertion that all of Scripture, in its fundamental nature, is *testimonia,* and that recognition of the fact is absolutely essential for understanding the Bible. This is most clearly stated in the scholion on Ps. 118:24 ("Your

---

19. WA 4.310.33–37: "Vel 'testimonia' dicuntur veteris legis verba spiritualiter intellecta, que testantur nihil nisi solum Christum futurum . . . Quare . . . totus psalmus est nihil aliud nisi petitio."

20. For example, WA 4.325.17–25; 322.20–26 (Sch. Ps. 118:31: "Adhesi testimoniis tuis Domine"): "Scimus enim que fiunt et facta sunt, credimus que futura *promittuntur,* ut Abraham credidit deo promittenti &c. Et qui sic adheret *testimoniis* et *promissis* dei, non confunditur; quia implebitur promissum." (Italics mine.) WA 4.345.20 f. (Sch. Ps. 118:79): "*Convertantur* . . . *qui noverunt testimonia tua* (id est promissa tua futurorum)." WA 4.389.24 f. (Sch. Ps. 118:168: "Servavi . . . testimonia tua"): " 'Testimonia' autem sunt, que deus promittit et nos credimus." See also WA 4.303.25,38 f., 379.13–15, 388.30 f. Almost all

testimonies are my meditation"). Luther's comment, which may be without parallel, is: "But now we learn this: Holy Scripture is 'testimonies': first, to the Jews concerning the future Christ. For the law and the prophets were testifying to the righteousness of God in Christ . . . And it is called testimony for this reason, because it testifies and prophesies of future things." [21] The proud and the heretics wrongly "take everything not as testimonies, but as already finished and resolved truth," he adds.[22] A right and proper meditation on the testimonies is rather to recognize that they are signs and witnesses of future things. "For he who does not understand and implement Scripture with reference toward future things — that is, so that he always knows that what he should understand and do is ahead of himself, and so that he faithfully expects and desires at length to understand and to do — such a one certainly does not permit Scripture to be 'testimonies of the Lord.'"[23]

---

occurrences of *eloquium* in this Psalm are glossed as "promise": For example, WA 4.287.7 f., 288.10–12, 291.8 f., 296.13, 302.14 f., 304.7,11, 361.31–34. *Verbum* is also regularly so understood: see WA 4.291.3,27, 295.17, 296.8 f., 320.35 f., 347.4.

21. WA 4.318.33–40: "Nunc autem id discamus, quod Scriptura sancta est 'testimonia': *primum* [that is, according to the literal-prophetic sense] Iudeis de futuro Christo. Quia lex et prophete testificabantur iustitiam dei in Christo . . . Testimonium enim ideo dicitur, quia de futuris testatur et prophetat." Luther's exegesis of this passage is utterly unprecedented in the tradition as represented by the nine exegetes used here. Augustine glossed "testimonia" as *martyrdoms* (*martyria*) which, coupled with the love for enemies that they manifested, are examples for "meditation." The *Gloss*, Lombard and Hugo follow this interpretation; Lyra does not, being involved instead in a discussion of merit and grace, and without specific comment on *testimonia*. The same goes for Burgos and Doering. Perez has no comment on *testimonia* at this place, but at vs. 21 had glossed "in via testimoniorum": "i.e. in studio et observantia legis tue." Faber's interpretation is roughly the same.

22. WA 4.319.20 f.: "omnia non ut testimonia accipiunt, sed ut finitam et resolutam veritatem."

23. WA 4.319.34–37: "Qui enim Scripturam non relative intelligit aut operatur ad futura, scil. ut semper sciat sibi superesse, quod intelligat

Such an overall understanding of Scripture can also cover the "christological" sense, so that the Old Testament is not so much a cryptic description of Christ and the Church (prophetic sense as *descriptio*),[24] which conceals advance information about them, as a *testimonia* and *promissa* concerning the future to arouse the faith, the *expectatio*, and the *petitio* of the Old Testament hearers as a whole. In this framework, the Old Testament gets theological value not so much from the Christ it hiddenly describes as from the salvation it promises, and from the faith and expectation of the faithful whom this word invites.[25]

Another striking evidence that promise is taking over as the primary theological-literal sense now appears: *testimonia* and *eloquia* (= *promissiones*) have become so enhanced in Luther's mind that he can speak of them as the foundation not only of Christian hope but of faith and love as well. (Traditionally, the normative-literal sense was that which literally teaches faith, love and hope.) For example, Luther comments on Ps. 118:168 ("I have kept your *mandata* and your *testimonia*"): "Here it can be said that 'mandates' are those things which we promise to fulfill, and which God believes and accepts by these promises, though we very often fail him . . . But 'testimonies' are those things which God promises, and which we believe and receive *by believing, hoping and lov-*

---

et agat, atque fideliter expectet et desideret tandem intelligere et agere: hic certe non permittit ipsam esse testimonia domini."

24. A good earlier example of prophetic sense as *descriptio*: WA 3.384.33–36 (Gl. Ps. 67:4: "Et iusti epulentur"): the "feasting" is interpreted as early Christian participation in the Eucharist. Luther comments: "Et pro maiore parte iste psalmus *describitur* in actibus apostolorum." (Italics mine.)

25. Luther's new understanding of the Psalm word as "petitio" is clearly reflected in this from 1517: "Alle psalmen, alle schrifft *rufft nach* der gnaden, preisset die gnade, *sucht* Christum" (WA 1.212.9 f., from *Die Sieben Busspsalmen*, Ps. 142; italics mine. Cited by Hahn, "Die Heilige Schrift," p. 410). The "rufft nach" and the "sucht" reflect the understanding of the Psalm word as *petitio*.

ing." [26] Again, Luther can call God's *eloquia* the very "form and criterion (*forma et regula*) of Scripture." [27] Faith is being repeatedly defined not in relation to creedal propositions, but in relation to God's promises, and with reference to Heb. 11:1,[28] that is, not as *assensus* but as reliance on the promising God to do that which he has promised. The "truth of salvation" (*veritas salutis*) is understood as God's fulfillment of his promise to save.[29] And man is spiritual insofar as he adheres

26. WA 4.389.20-25: "potest hic dici, quod 'mandata' sunt, que nos promittimus implere, et promissionibus iis deus credit et acceptat, licet fallamus eum sepius . . . 'Testimonia' autem sunt, que *deus promittit* et nos credimus et acceptamus *credendo, sperando, amando*." (Italics mine.) I found two other similar texts: WA 4.399.23-26: "Quare ubicunque fides nobis occurrit, prima fronte . . . gaudet, quod promissus sit ei introitus in Ecclesiam. Nec gauderet, nisi vera esse *crederet, speraret, diligeret* ea [that is, the *dicta*, or *promissa ei*]." (Italics mine.) WA 4.380.35-37: "Omnis nostra laetitia est in spe futurorum et non in re presentium. Ideo enim gaudemus, quia promissionibus divinis credimus, et que promittit, speramus atque diligimus." See also WA 4.264.33, where faith is said to make (*facere*) "dilectionem et certam spem exauditionis" — although here faith is not explicitly linked with *testimonium*.
27. WA 4.390.36 f. (Sch. Ps. 118:170: "secundum eloquium tuum eripe me"): "non secundum uniuscuiusque opinionem, sed iuxta eloquium suum, id est secundum formam et regulam Scripture."
28. WA 4.322.18-21: "scientia [est] presentium et preteritorum, fides futurorum proprie . . . Scimus enim que fiunt et facta sunt, credimus que futura promittuntur, ut Abraham credidit deo promittenti." Cf. WA 4.271.24 31 (Sch. Ps. 115:10): "*Credidi [propter quod locutus sum]*. Intentio psalmi est docere tantum spiritualia bona in Christo expectare, et promissa in lege de spiritu et fide intelligenda esse, non de re temporali: contra insipientiam carnalium Iudeorum, qui fidem respuunt et rem expectant. Rem inquam temporalium: nam fides habet rem eternam. Dicit ergo: *Credidi*, id est fidem habui, et hec tota mea possessio, que est substantia, id est possessio rerum sperandarum, non autem substantia rerum presentium." WA 4.272.23-26: "fides est non apparentium, que non nisi verbo possunt doceri, ostendi, et indicari. Ideo vocatur 'argumentum (id est ostensio) rerum non apparentium,' quia ostendit nobis futura, que ex ipsa possidemus ut substantiam futurorum."
29. WA 3.412.17 f. (Gl. Ps. 68:14): "*exaudi me in veritate salutis tuae* promissa sive quam promisisti olim." A further marginal gloss on *veritas salutis* (lines 33-36): "Quam imples et reddis fideliter et vere, quia non fallit Deus promissa. Exaudi me in veritate salutis tue, i.e. per

to the *testimonia* of God's future vivification.[30]

Testimonia — promise — has thus become the normative meaning of the whole Bible. What has happened can be illustrated with a diagram (which may be compared to the one appearing in Chapter I):

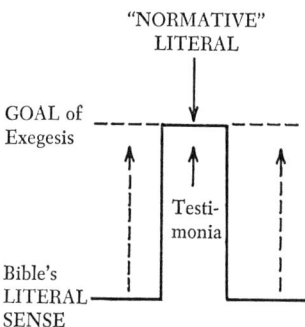

In view of the fact that the texts supporting my argument are taken from among thousands of individual interpretations of specific texts, corroborating evidence is needed, both negative and positive, showing other trends in Luther's exegesis that are consistent with the view here presented, namely, that for Luther, Scripture is seen fundamentally as *testimonia*; that this has become for him the primary normative-literal meaning of Scripture.[31] Such further evidence should also

---

impletionem salutis tue promisse mihi." Cf. *WA* 3.428.22-24 (Sch. on the same verse): "Differunt 'veritas salutis' (quia est fidelis impletio salutis . . .) et 'Salus veritatis vel vera' (est salus spiritualis et solida contra hoc, quia vana salus hominis)."

30. *WA* 4.320.32-36: "'Adhesi testimoniis tuis, domine' [118:31]. Quia secundum quod perfectus [= spiritualis] sum, adhesi testimoniis tuis ego totus, secundum quod autem imperfectus et adhuc carnalis, adhesit anima mea pavimento [118:25 'Adhesit pavimento anima mea']. Ergo tu magis magis [sic] *Vivifica me secundum verbum tuum.* Quia secundum promissum tuum peto id."

31. It is easier to prove that testimony-promise is normative than that it clearly belongs, in Luther's mind, to the grammatical meaning of Scripture. I have not found anywhere in the *Dictata*, including the later part,

show that the new trends in Luther's exegesis are in conflict with the understanding of Scripture revealed in his prefaces and in his "medieval" stage. The medieval answer to the question, "What is the Bible all about?" could be summed up in three words: *doctrina, lex,* and *promissio.* The Bible teaches us what is to believed (*credenda*), loved (*diligenda*), and hoped (*speranda*). The greatest of these is love, for, as Augustine had stated, the goal of the interpretation of Scripture is the "reign of charity" (*regnum caritatis*). As love is the goal of the law, so it is the goal of the use of Scripture.

With Luther, something different has now appeared: promise, or testimony, as Scripture's normative, theological-literal meaning, together with faith as the goal of interpretation.[32]

---

an open, complimentary word for literal-grammatical exegesis, although that is precisely what Luther is more and more engaged in. In the Scholion on Ps. 118:1, for example, where he tries to explain the literal-prophetic sense, he still opposes "grammatical" and "theological" interpretation: "verba una cum grammaticali sua significatione sunt velut caro Christi sine divinitate, litera sine spiritu, vana et vacua omnino. Sensus autem verus in illis [verbis] et theologica significatio est velut divinitas in carne Christi, spiritus in litera" (WA 4.306.32–35). It is as if he is still unaware of the distance he has come, even though he seems to be groping for expression of his new-found historical orientation to the Old Testament situation. For example, at WA 4.347.1 f., he speaks of a twofold "sensus theologicus," one "literalis" and the other "mysticus"; then he gives an interpretation that is both historically oriented (the prophet speaking to his own people) and theologically rich (urging hope in the *verbum promissionis*). He has discovered the theological relevance of the Old Testament history, without yet acknowledging its inevitable connection to, and consequent enhancement of, the Old Testament grammatical sense. For Luther's later acknowledgment of the grammar of Scripture, see Ebeling, "Hermeneutik," RGG III (1959), 251 f. A good test case could be set up here via a study of Luther's changing attitude to Lyra. In the polemical spirit of his thinly veiled attack on Lyra in the prologue, the first part of the *Dictata* contains numerous violent criticisms and charges of Judaizing, but these seem to be softened and much less frequent later on; in fact, Lyra is warmly complimented at WA 4.13.9 and 4.28.1.

32. Luther opposes the "sensus fidei" to the "sensus literae" in contexts where "letter" means not the grammar but the "sensus suus" of the

Scripture understood as testimony gives rise to the general principle that the understanding of Scripture is always infinite, and therefore relative, because our present is always transcended by the future. What is spirit today is letter tomorrow. It is possible to bring negative support to the thesis that *testimonium* is the normative sense of Scripture, by showing that *doctrina* (in the sense of *credenda*) is not. On the subject of *doctrina,* Ebeling has made it clear that although Luther's expectation of finding the word of God in and through the Scriptures is unparalleled in its intensity, the Bible is not for him a book of doctrine.[33] It is a book which places man himself *coram deo,* and exposes and subjects him to God's concrete judgment and mercy (*iudicium* and *misericordia*). Its effect is to drive the Christian always toward the future, out of that which he has attained in the present (letter), toward that which is still to be attained (spirit). Out of such thinking Luther could perhaps derive a theological rationale for doctrinal innovation, as he criticizes those who dissent to current developments on the basis of old tradition. He writes, "Truth has always, from the beginning, been revealed more and more."[34] He singles out for special criticism those who oppose the doctrine of the immaculate conception, the Bohemians for their views on the sacraments and the primacy, and the scholastic theologians. All share the same fault: failure to realize that "truth evolves."[35] "Therefore, he who does not wish to progress toward the future, he himself wishes to be stuck in the letter, like the Jews."[36] This point of view is in uneasy

---

unbeliever or the proud: for example, WA 4.289.18 f. Further, the "spiritual man" is said to be constituted by faith: "spiritualis homo factus per fidem" (WA 4.267.18). Cf. WA 4.320.32–37.

33. Ebeling, "Die Anfänge," pp. 181, 200.
34. WA 4.345.14: "semper ab initio magis ac magis veritas est revelata."
35. WA 4.345.29: "veritas transit a claritate in claritatem."
36. WA 4.345.34 f.: "Qui ergo non vult proficere ad futurum, ipse

balance with his more "conservative" statement counseling obedience to the tradition of the fathers, and asserting that "to expect new doctrine is a very serious way to tempt the Lord." [37]

Lex, together with *doctrina,* formed the core of the traditional normative literal sense. In accordance with the shifts noted in Luther's thinking about what the Bible's message is, one can detect indications that *lex,* as well as *doctrina,* can be harmonized with the notion that all Scripture is *testimonia* and *promissio.* Promises can be promises of evil as well as of good; that is, they can be threats.[38] In such contexts, "law" begins to take on the sense that the mature Luther gives it within the dialectic of law and gospel. Law also functions, in certain texts of the *Dictata,* to support the promise, in that its purpose is seen to increase all the more the petition for the advent of Christ. In this context, law is a testimony whose function is to "drive to Christ." [39]

The Promise-Advent Structure

The contention that promise has emerged for Luther as the focal point of Old Testament interpretation would be supported by the appearance of a comprehensive hermeneutical schema — an overall structure — which is different from the traditional fourfold one, and which better harmonizes with

---

vult literam perstare sicut Iudei." Cf. WA 4.365.11-13, where the Nicene doctrine of the Trinity was "spirit" in its own time, but is now "letter" unless living faith is added.

37. WA 3.578.38-579.1 (the context is a polemic against willful, innovating *heretici et superbi*): "Igitur nolle credere et omnia in dubium revocare ac sic novam doctrinam expectare: hec est gravissima tentatio domini. Cave ergo, o homo: sed humiliter disce sapere et ne novus author transgrediaris limites, quos posuerunt patres tui."

38. See WA 4.380.5-9, 15-18.

39. See WA 4.324.9-14. This is the clearest expression of such an idea that I found in the *Dictata.*

and serves the idea that Scripture is *testimonia*. The fourfold schema is inappropriate for this task, because in it the future-oriented, Old Testament word of promise scarcely functions theologically, being subsumed under the prevailing concept of *figura* which, once the *veritas* appears, is irrelevant. Thus, promise always suffers a negative theological evaluation. In the traditional hermeneutic, moreover, the function of words is to describe the theological relations that pertain between things already present and past; words do not in themselves, apart from these things, give any theological account of the future.

In Luther's interpretation of the penitential Psalms, however, another hermeneutical schema is at work which is more promising; a schema structured around the notion of Christ's "three advents" (Psalm 101). Still later in the *Dictata* such a schema is programmatically laid out, and for the first time it is explicitly anchored on the dual foundation of promise and advent.[40] The text is Luther's scholion on Ps. 113:1: "Not to us, Lord, not to us, but to your name give glory."[41]

40. In his sermons *In adventu Domini,* Saint Bernard grounds the spiritual advent in *election,* on the one hand, and in the requirement of *praeparatio in humilitate,* on the other. Thus, "medius [adventus] occultus est, in quo soli eum in seipsos vident electi" (*Serm.*5 n.1; PL 183, 50 D). Cf. n.3 (51 D): "Christum Dei Verbum recipiant singuli electorum." The only references to the promise in these sermons pertain to the eschatological advent (*Serm.* 4 n.1 [47 C], n.5 [48 A and C]). The poor and humble of Mt. 5:3–9 are to receive the promise. John 14:23 is the basic text that Bernard uses to instruct his hearers in preparation ("Si quis diligit me, sermonem meum servabit, et Pater meus diliget eum, et ad eum veniemus." *Serm.*3 n.4 [45 B]). The *praeparatio,* in summary, is as follows: "Diligit enim animam quae in conspectu ejus, et sine intermissione considerat, et sine simulatione dijudicat semetipsam. Idque judicium nonnisi propter nos a nobis exigit, quia si nosmetipsos judicaverimus, non utque judicabimur" (*Serm.*3 n.7 [47 A f.]). Saint Bernard derives the reference to *judicium* from Ps. 98:4: "Honor regis judicium diligit," to which he has responded; "Nihil quod in se est a nobis exigit amplius" (47 A).

41. *WA* 4.261.25 ff. The text: "Non nobis domine, non nobis, sed nomini tuo da gloriam." Luther's notorious scholion on this text is of

SENSE AND STRUCTURE OF SCRIPTURE | 193

Luther interprets this text in terms of three advents of Christ, each of which he grounds in a specific biblical promise. The following quotations make the overall pattern clear:

> Just as the advent of Christ in the flesh has been given out of the sheer mercy of the promising God . . . nevertheless it is still necessary that there be preparation and a disposition to receive him, as was done in the whole old testament through the line of Christ. Now, it was mercy that God promised his son, but it was his truth and fidelity that he presented him, as in the last chapter of Micah: "He will give truth to Jacob, and mercy to Abraham." [42]
>
> So also the spiritual advent comes through grace, and the future [advent] through glory . . . out of the sheer promise of the merciful God. For he promises as follows for the spiritual advent: "Ask and you shall receive, seek and you shall find, knock and it shall be opened to you." [43]
>
> And so for the future advent he promises, "that we may live justly and soberly and piously in this age, expecting a blessed hope." [44]

---

fundamental importance for understanding the relation of Luther to the Nominalist tradition regarding the question of *meritum de congruo*, to which Luther here refers favorably: see Oberman, "Facientibus quod in se est," p. 337 f. Here, I treat only the hermeneutical implications.

42. WA 4.261.25-31: "Sicut adventus Christi in carnem ex mera misericordia dei promittentis datus . . . nihilominus tamen preparationem et dispositionem oportuit fieri ad eum suscipiendum, sicut factum est in toto veteri testamento per lineam Christi. Nam quod promisit deus filium suum, fuit misericordia, quod autem exhibuit, fuit veritas et fidelitas eius, sicut Miche ultimo [7:20]: 'dabis veritatem Iacob et misericordiam Abraam.' "

43. WA 4.261.39-262.3: "Ita et spiritualis adventus est per gratiam et futurus per gloriam . . . ex mera promissione miserentis dei. Promisit enim pro spirituali adventu sic: 'petite et accipietis, querite et invenietis, pulsate et aperietur vobis' " (Mt. 7:7).

44. WA 4.262.7 f.: "Sic pro adventu futuro promisit, 'ut juste et

Finally, summing up, Luther writes:

> Hence, just as the law was a figure and preparation of the people for receiving Christ, so our doing what is in us (*factio quantum in nobis est*) disposes us to grace. And the whole time of grace is preparation for future glory and the second advent.[45]

---

sobrie et pie vivamus in hoc seculo, expectantes beatam spem'" (Tit. 2:12 f.).

45. *WA* 4.262.13–16: "Unde sicut lex figura fuit et preparatio populi ad Christum suscipiendum, ita nostra factio quantum in nobis est, disponit nos ad gratiam. Atque totum tempus gratie preparatio est ad futuram gloriam et adventum secundum." Luther's threefold promise-advent structure and his discussion of the *dispositio ad gratiam* are without precedent in the exegetical tradition examined on this and the next verse ("Non nobis . . . gloriam; super misericordia tua, et veritate tua"). Augustine and Cassiodorus put forth rival interpretations of *veritas*. For the former, it meant God's eschatological *severitas* against the *impius*, that is, those who refuse the merciful *vocatio*. For Cassiodorus, *veritas* refers to the certainty of the promise of beatitude, and the text is a *petitio* for grace. The *Gloss* makes a harmony of the two, and Lombard summarizes: God's *misericordia* involves the calling (Aug.) and sparing (Cass.) of sinners; his *veritas* is that by which he judges those who do not respond (Aug.) and by which he delivers the promised reward (Cass.). Lombard then elaborates on an idea only hinted at in the *Gloss*: *veritas* may refer also to the promises already fulfilled, "by which you have promised the advent of the Son." Here, the advent of Christ first enters the picture. Hugo adopts this point of view, but his moral interpretation does not repeat the promise-advent idea; rather, *veritas* means the correction of sins in penance by God's mercy, not man's merit. Anagogically also, it is God's mercy, not man's merit, by which he is saved. Lyra pursues a rigorous historical interpretation: God's *veritas* is the fulfillment of the promise to the patriarchs; it is also mercy that God kept his promise despite the constant defection of Israel. Like Hugo, Lyra then relates *veritas, moraliter,* to penance, but unlike Hugo he introduces a promise as well (Ezek. 18:23: God does not desire the death, but conversion, of the sinner). Burgos and Doering have no comment on these verses, but Burgos' *Additio* contains a classic medieval description of the "defectum" of existence under the Mosaic law, in which only earthly promises were given. Perez adopts Lyra's literal exposition as his starting point, but goes on to contrast the promises of the two testaments by making the fulfillments of the Old (such as the giving of the promised land) a *figura* of those of the New (such as Christ giving Peter the keys to the heavenly kingdom). The

To my knowledge, the eschatological advent is always called the "second" advent by Luther, even where the "three-advent" scheme appears. This is probably because of the inseparable bond he sees between the advent in flesh and in grace, which together can be treated as part of the "first" advent.[46]

The following characteristics of this structural scheme are noteworthy. First, the text is interpreted "christologically," but in a way different from the early treatment in the prefaces, whereby Christ himself speaks, or the prophet describes Christ and the Church in New Testament fashion. Here, Christ is the one who is promised and awaited, so that in all times, God's word to his people is the promise: God comes to man in Christ. This view, of course, harmonizes well both with the new formal definition of "prophetic" sense found five Psalms later (Psalm 118), and with the idea that promise, or testimony, functions as the normative-literal sense of the Bible.

Further, Christ in this schema does not fall into line as the sign of something else — for example, of our penitence — as in the traditional fourfold exegesis; rather, he is the goal of the entire exegesis. This lends new weight to the notion that Christ pre-eminently and ultimately "is," while we and all else "signify."[47] Christ is "the goal of all things and the thing

---

systematic unity and apparent originality of Luther's exegesis is striking against this background; for him, Christ himself is in all times the promised *res*, and *expectatio* and *preparatio* are in all times the proper response.

46. Thus, WA 4.298.6-8 refers to God's "tempus faciendi" (Ps. 118:126): "[tempus] implendi que promisisti, mittendo Christum *et gratiam* pro adventu primo, et eundem pro adventu secundo." (Italics mine.) However, the spiritual is called the "second" advent at WA 4.19.35.

47. WA 3.368.22-24: "Christus est finis omnium et centrum, in quem omnia respiciunt et monstrant, ac si dicerent: Ecce iste est, qui est, nos autem non sumus, sed significamus tantum." The same thought comes through at WA 4.248.39-41: "Et hec est ratio, quare ps. 18 et 118 verba Dei dicuntur 'iudicia' et 'iudicia iustificationis,' quia iudicant et iustificant diversos. Et hoc totum, quia Christum predicant, qui est iudicium et iustitia."

signified through [rather than signifying] all other things."[48] In the fourfold hermeneutic, this is not the case.

Attention has also been turned to finding an Old Testament warrant for "christological" interpretation.[49] Under the fourfold schema, one operated on the assumption that the New Testament events alone reveal the providential sign-character of the Old Testament events. It was not necessary for the interpreter to think himself into a pre-advent situation, since the prophet himself did not even really belong to that situation, or speak to it. By contrast, the promise-advent scheme needs textual support for some kind of christological interpretation within the Old Testament itself, since the interpreter has now placed himself (and the Old Testament speaker) solidly within the pre-advent situation, under the promise of the future Christ, who has not yet come with his Spirit and grace.[50]

But this implies that the actual appearance of Christ in history (with his grace, Spirit, sacraments, etc.) is no longer determinative for theological value to be accorded to the Old Testament text, and to the historical situation of the Old Testament people. In that sense, Christ is *not* the "center of Scripture." The New Testament does not have to be the exclusive text and source of spiritual or theological content. The Old

---

48. WA 3.375.32 f.: "ipse finis omnium et res significata per omnes res."

49. It will be recalled that in his prefaces Luther found warrant in the New Testament, in the actual death of Christ. The logic was: if the Old Testament can be understood in itself, then Christ died in vain.

50. Thus, for example, Luther later argues that because unfulfilled promises remain outstanding in the Old Testament, one is allowed – indeed, "compelled" – to find their fulfillment in the New Testament (WA 4.408.24–26): "Omnis Scriptura prophetarum primo de Apostolis intelligitur, quia sic *cogit* promissio dei, qui promisit populum Israel exaltare super omnes gentes." (Italics mine.) The interpretive logic has changed to read: if Christ had not come, the promise would have been given in vain, and the faith of the Old Testament people broken.

Testament can be the text, and Old Testament faith can inform the Christian community. But this in turn implies that the absolute "hermeneutical divide," formerly located between the Old and New Testaments, has been broken down. The distinction between carnal and spiritual, mere grammatical and theological, if it is still to be maintained at all, must somehow be rooted in the Old Testament itself. As shall be shown later, Luther's discovery of the positive (rather than negative) theological value of promise is of decisive significance in this shift.

Furthermore, whereas in the usual tropological exegesis (in which Christ is the literal meaning) attention is invited to the identification of the believer with Christ. One then expounds on the *imitatio Christi*, that is, on obedience and humility, or (to use a favorite expression of Regin Prenter and others [51]) on *conformitas Christi*, wherein God conforms man to Christ. But now, in Luther's new scheme, the identification comes between Christians and the Old Testament faithful rather than between Christians and Christ. All the faithful are seen living expectantly under the testimonies and promises of Christ's coming. And all alike are threatened and tempted to despair.

51. Regin Prenter, *Spiritus Creator*, trans. J. M. Jensen (Philadelphia, 1953), pp. 9–11 *et passim*. Scholars who see Luther's use of tropological interpretation as the gateway to the Reformation doctrine of justification are anxious to conjure up some radical difference between *conformitas* and the "medieval" idea of *imitatio*. The classic document here is Vogelsang's *Die Anfänge von Luthers Christologie*, for example pp. 101 f. See also Gerhard Rost, "Der Gedanke der Gleichförmigkeit mit dem leidenden Christus in der Frömmigkeit des jungen Luther," *Lutherischer Rundblick* 11 (1963), 2–12. It seems to me that Luther's *conformitas* is simply *imitatio* purged of Pelagian tendencies, so that rather than man's actively imitating Christ, God "imitates" his action in Christ by doing the same to man. No change in hermeneutical principles is involved. Bernhard Lohse's findings regarding the influence of Augustine, already in the *Dictata*, is relevant: "Bei Augustin konnte Luther . . . manches über die Bedeutung Jesu Christi als des Exempels des göttlichen Gnadenwirkens lernen" ("Die Bedeutung Augustins für den jungen Luther," *KuD* 11 [1965], 133).

This kind of "applicatio," which is labeled "moral" by Luther, invites much greater emphasis on faith and hope, two virtues absent in the Christ of medieval orthodoxy.[52]

Finally, the function and import of the "Word" has come in for a qualitative change from its use in the fourfold exegesis. There, the word was only a descriptive *signum* that designates an Old Testament *res,* which in turn — when the New Testament time comes — is discovered *ex post facto* to be itself a *signum* of a New Testament *res.* This use of "word" allows no spiritual or theologically valid understanding of its import until the New Testament events have already occurred. It inevitably implies that the Old Testament hearer was in the dark (in mere letter) about its meaning, and raises the problem of deception on the part of the Old Testament prophet (or, for that matter, on the part of God), who always spoke in figures to his own people, so that one thing was said, but another was to be understood.

Now, the word is losing its character of describing the future under figures, in favor of promising and petitioning for it openly. The prophet is becoming less a seer, and more a preacher who urges faith in the God who has committed himself to a future redemptive deed. His is a word whose spiritual, theological meaning is already available, because to the one who hears it, it points beyond present *res,* creates expectation, and arouses the *petitiones* of those who hear it with faith. The Old Testament time can still be called *figura,* as before, but it

---

52. The "moraliter" label seems to become more frequent than "tropologice" late in the *Dictata,* although the latter does not disappear. The three-advent schema is one of the ways Luther summarizes the whole of Psalm 118 (*WA* 4.305.31–35): "quicquid in hoc psalmo et aliis quoque dictum est de adventu christi primo in carnem, debet etiam intelligi *moraliter* de adventu eius quottidiano per gratiam . . . Tercio de futuro adventu per gloriam, quia tunc videbimus verbum eius, eloquium, testimonium in sua claritate." (Italics mine.) The christological-tropological mode was hampered in developing the notions of faith and hope became Christ was not believed to have had either.

now means a real, historical time of preparation, a disposition for, and expectation of, the future, and not merely a shadowy existence as *signum* of a solely New Testament *res.*

For Luther, the faith of the Old Testament people has — quite unexpectedly — ceased to be just carnal, just a *figura.* It has become a model for Christian faith! The Old Testament struggle for faith in face of all the *contraria* of Israel's historical existence is taking on fundamental significance for Luther's own faith as well as for his interpertation of the faith and proper self-understanding of the Church itself.

XIII. THE NEW HERMENEUTICAL DIVIDE

The "hermeneutical divide" between letter and spirit undergoes a fundamental shift in the course of Luther's Psalms lectures. When this happens, the "divide" no longer lies between the testaments, but begins to appear as a distinction grounded in the Old Testament itself — between its law and its promise, between "two testaments" found there, between the "law of Moses" and "the law of the Lord." [1]

1. The last of these distinctions must be used with care, since it also appears early in the *Dictata*. Decisive here is whether an Old Testament, pre-advent perspective is operative. My approach to this problem is quite different from that of Ebeling, who tends to confuse the issue. He sets up the problem by first asserting that the New Testament's exegesis of the Old Testament provides the model for Old Testament interpretation; then he states that there are *two* basic ways in which the relationship of the testaments can be viewed. The first is prophecy and fulfillment — in broadest terms, *figura* or *umbra* and *veritas*. According to Ebeling, this scheme embraces not only the indirect correspondences — that is, the allegorical structure — of the Old and New Testament relationship, but also the direct prophecies (which, I presume, must also include promises) ("Die Anfänge," pp. 210 f.). I have shown in my treatment of the medieval material — especially of Perez — that the *figura-veritas* scheme, whereby the whole Old Testament is allegory, is quite different from a promise-fulfillment scheme. Perez himself was aware of the difference. But Ebeling wishes to lump these together in order to clear the field for his second kind of relationship: *litera* and *spiritus*, "which originally (ursprünglich) designates the opposition between Law and Gospel" (p. 210). Ebeling does not explain the historical referent of his "ursprünglich," but it is that which he sees Luther developing, in order to bring out properly the "antithetic" (rather than the positive) relationship between the two testaments, and between the two peoples represented. "The people of the Old Testament and the people of the New are related to each other as flesh and spirit" (p. 211). This, I maintain, is precisely the prevailing medieval view that Luther overcomes. It is correct that Luther opposes two "testaments" to one another, but this

Early in the *Dictata,* when Luther mentions the "eternal testament" or the "eternal law" of God, he gives no indication that he conceives of these as having been a living reality in the old Israel, except to prophets and such spiritual elite as were able to penetrate to the real meaning of Israel's religion.[2] Any reference to something "eternal" triggers in Luther's mind thoughts of Christ, the Church, and New Testament faith. A good example of this response to the text is Luther's handling of Psalm 88, which deals largely with the "perpetuity and stability of the reign of David," according to Luther's summary. For Luther, that phrase means "the spiritual reign of David, *i.e., of Christ.*"[3] Thus, the words wherein God makes great promises to David are pressed by the interpretation into promises made to Christ. For example: *"I have sworn to David* to Christ from the seed of David, *'I shall establish your seed forever . . .* which he does not do with the literal David . . . *And I will build up* spiritually *from generation to generation* from one to another *your throne'* your militant church."[4] The interpretation continues in the same way, so that God is all along swearing and promising to Christ and the Church that the promises and covenant will remain stable and not be "terminated," as was the covenant with "the synagogue and Moses."[5]

---

antithesis, in the end, ceases to correspond to the relationship between the two testaments, or between the two peoples, and finds its basis in the Old Testament itself — both in the text and in the faith of the people. Just that relocation of the hermeneutical divide marks the genuine difference between Luther and the tradition, for which the Old Testament/New Testament relation (with Christ, grace, sacraments, etc.) remained the fundamental divide-point.

2. This holds true despite the fact that he early calls the "covenant of faith" (*pactum fidei*) eternal (WA 3.491.10 f.).
3. WA 4.37.2: "De stabilitate et perpetuitate regni David spiritualis, *id est Christi.*" (Italics mine.)
4. WA 4.37.15-19.
5. For example, WA 4.40.13-15 (Gl. Ps. 88:29): *"Ineternum servabo,*

However, at one point, the testament made with Moses is contrasted with *"my* [God's] testament," identified as the promises made in the prophets, which will be fulfilled.⁶ It is not here specified to whom these promises were made — whether to the Old Testament people, to a few "special persons," or, as most of the material of the Psalm, to Christ. But the text touches off a lengthy marginal comment on the difference between the old and new laws. Because the old covenant was based partially on the works of the people, it was broken; indeed, Jeremiah says that the people themselves broke it. But not so the *pactum Christi*. It stands on the sheer promise and grace of God. It cannot be broken, even if the Church sins.⁷

It is clear, then, that although the main dividing line seems to be between the old and new laws, meaning between the entire old dispensation up to Christ, and the new that began with Christ,⁸ yet the very foundation and basis for the inviola-

---

non sicut synagogam et Mosen terminabo, *illi misericordiam* gratiam *meam*: *et testamentum meum* promissiones et pactum, quod feci cum eo, *fidele ipsi* permanens et stabile."

6. The gloss to vs. 35 (WA 4.41.1-3): "*Neque prophanabo,* sicut prophanavi testamentum Mosi, *testamentum meum,* non legis pactum: *et que procedunt* promissa *de labiis meis* in prophetis, *non faciam irrita,* sed implebo fideliter."

7. WA 4.41.15-23: "patet, quod lex nova non ex operibus et meritis nostris incepit . . . sed ex mera promissione et misericordia et veritate Dei incepit, stat et perstabit. Vetus autem lex non. Quia data fuit sub conditione tali, scilicet si implerent ipsam, staret, si autem non implerent, rueret. Quia erat fundatum in operibus eorum et non in misericordia et promissione pura Dei, sed cum inclusione operum illorum. Unde Iere.31 [:32] 'pactum quod irritum fecerunt' . . . Sed non sic [pactum] Christi, quod nullus homo potest irritare quantumvis omnes peccent, quia stat in gratia Dei."

8. For example, WA 3.276.35-37: "Et ita tota lex vetus est tantum vox vel sonus, quia solum sensibilia tradens ac sine verbo mystici sensus." A frequent traditional contrast between the old and new laws consists in the fact that the grace-endowed "law of the Lord" cleanses the soul and the will, while the bare law of Moses controls only the hand: WA 55/1.92.18 f.; 3.128.17-19; 4.9.33-35, 323.6 f., 28 f.

bility of the new law is found in the Old Testament itself — in its promises. Thus, the Old Testament contains both the fundamental principles here introduced to contrast the old and new laws, that is, both a covenant dependent partly on works, and an inviolable promise resting on the sheer mercy of God.

But if this great promise is already given in the Old Testament, to the people, alongside the law of Moses, then the way is open for interesting new developments. In the exegesis of Psalm 88, Luther does not go further into the possibilities latent in the fact that the Old Testament is not only the book of the old, past, broken, and forgotten covenant, but also the place in which irrevocable promises were made. He does not ask whether, among the Old Testament people themselves, this duality was understood. If it were understood and known, then two kinds of response would be possible, depending upon which of the two arrangements the person adhered to as constituting his relation to God. The Moasaic law demanded obedience and was susceptible to ruin through disobedience. But the promise demands faith only, and is susceptible to ruin only if God fails to do what he has promised. Later on, this last idea becomes the crux of the proper Old Testament "covenant," a promise that can be made empty (*irritum* is the customary word) only if God fails.[9]

"Promise" is beginning to emerge as a unique theological concept in Luther's exegesis, and his growing preoccupation

9. In the present text, the *pactum Christi*, guaranteed by the promise, cannot be made void by any man: "nullus homo potest irritare" (WA 4.41.23). Later, the promise itself becomes the focus of attention: Israel's faith is challenged by unbelievers, and would have been broken (*irrita*) had Christ not finally come: WA 4.262.26–29; cf. 4.296.14–17, where the psalmist prays that God would not confound him, "which could happen, if you did not fulfill your promises, which I believe . . . for then faith would be *irrita*, and confusable in the face of unbelievers." So also WA 4.322.25 f. (Sch. Ps. 118:31): "*Noli me confundere*, id est fidem meam illusam permittere fieri et irrita promissa tua."

with it can be traced. But the investigation confronts a confusing situation. When Luther is discussing the Old Testament promises, it is not always certain whether he means the "temporal" promises acknowledged to be "in" the law of Moses (and therefore part of the breakable covenant), or whether he means to abstract specific Old Testament promises, separating them from the law and promises of Moses in order to oppose them to each other. This problem is clarified by examining relevant passages.

The Temporal Old Testament Promises

Late in the body of material representing the "medieval Luther," he raises the question of the purpose of the promises of *temporalia* that appear in the Old Covenant. The text being examined is Ps. 77:7 ("He has raised up a *testimonium* in Jacob . . . in order that they might put their hope in God"). This verse, Luther maintains, accuses the Jews, who have promises of temporal things in the law and who have come to trust in God *because* of those things — and therefore trust "in them more." But God gave the Jews these promises to teach them to hope in Him, whether in good or bad times, for Christ was to come, teaching poverty and humility and "naked hope in future goods. Therefore he sent the law first, in which he promised and gave temporal goods, so that thus nourishing them with milk, they might learn from temporal things to have hope in the Lord." [10] It appears here that the idea has not yet occurred to Luther that the Old Testament has a dif-

10. WA 3.561.6–13: "Hoc maxime arguit Iudeos, qui habent in lege promissiones temporalium. Ideo in deum confidunt propter illa: ergo in illa magis. Sed tamen deus ideo eis ista concessit, ut per ea discerent in ipsum sperare. Sperat autem in Domino, qui tam in copia inopia temporalium deum non derelinquit: futuram enim erat, ut Christus veniens doceret paupertatem et humilitatem et nudam spem futurorum bonorum. Ideo premisit legem, in qua temporalia promisit et dedit, ut sic lacte eos nutriens, a temporalibus discerent spem in domino habere."

ferent kind of promise, not implicated with Moses, his law, and mere *temporalia*. At least, no mention of such promises is made. But Luther does not want to rest in the above interpretation; shortly afterward he suddenly has the prophets preaching to their own people, trying to recall them to the truth, "especially lest the people of Israel expect the promises of God carnally in this life." [11] This is the earliest place in the *Dictata* in which Luther clearly states that Israel was told by its own prophets that the promises were not to be awaited "carnally," indicating that (even though Luther never denies that the Old Testament promises *temporalia*) he has awakened to a "proper" Old Testament promise, which is gaining in theological importance. In Psalm 90 he argues that the law only "seemed" to promise glory, riches, or power.[12] And at Psalm 93 Luther writes that it was the "carnal" understanding of the law current among most of Israel that resulted in their rejection of Christ, for they supposed that worldly prosperity was the sign of God's favor. "If Christ had come in the pomp of this world, they would have received him as sent from God." But misled by their false understanding of the law, they killed him.[13] The suggestion is getting stronger that Israel should

11. WA 4.50.19–21 (Gl. Tit. [= Title] Psalm 89): "Deplorat miseriam humane nature, ut omnes revocet ad veritatem, maxime autem ne populus Israel promissiones Dei in hac vita exceptaret carnaliter."
12. WA 4.70.24–26 (Sch. Ps. 90:6: "sagitta in die volans"): "[quo] docet literam occidentem et de iis que sunt in die humano, de gloria, divitiis, et potestate mundi: que in lege promissa *videbantur*." (Italics mine.)
13. WA 4.94.25–29: "Deum autem non credebant, quia non nisi magnifica et prospera in deo sapiebant ex legis auctoritate, *licet false intellecte*. Si enim Christus in pompa mundi venisset, tanquam a deo suscepissent. Sed quia humilis venit, ideo non a deo esse credebant." (Italics mine.) Cf. WA 4.92.2–7: "Iste psalmus [93] contra eos loquitur, qui Christum nec deum nec ultorem putabant, Iudei scilicet . . . Quia cum legis *promissa non nisi carnaliter* intelligerent, atque ea sententia posita mox sequitur, quod eos, qui prospere agunt secundum carnem, deo gratissimos iudicent, et qui infoeliciter agunt secundum carnem, deo odibiles, nullo respectu spiritum habito." (Italics mine.)

have known better. The problem is, how could they have, as long as the word they had been hearing was veiled, and therefore misleading?

The Inviolable Old Testament Promise

Up to this time in the *Dictata,* there has been little hint that the Old Testament prophets promised anything *more* than "temporalia" to Israel. But now there begins to appear the idea of a second Old Testament promise, or covenant, and the name of Abraham is tied to it.[14] This is a promise that does not "titillate the flesh" but "recreates the spirit." [15]

One can say that here the "spiritual" promises of the Old Testament — chief of which is the promise of Christ — are functioning now as the "normative-literal" sense of the Old Testament. However, it is not certain yet that Luther has firmly in mind a distinction between what he thinks are clear, literal promises of a future beyond the Old Testament time, on the one hand, and on the other, promises of *temporalia* which sound temporal but are to be interpreted as figurative of those promises that are already both literal and "spiritual." He still holds that the Old Testament promises always *sound* "temporal," although they are intended to be *understood* spiritually.[16] A certain irreducible ambiguity remains. Neverthe-

14. WA 4.117.31–118.2 (Gl. Ps. 97:3): *"Recordatus est,* quam olim promiserat patribus, *misericordiae suae* gratie gratis promisse, que est Christus promissus, Gen. 12[:3], 'In semine tuo benedicentur omnes tribus terre,' *et veritatis suae,* sic enim Abrahe, Isaac et Iacob promiserat: *domui Israel* exhibendo ei illam ad salutem eius."

15. WA 4.159.11 f.: "Nam litere promissa titillant carnem, sed promissa spiritus spiritum recreant." Notice that the last phrase attributes a spiritual creativity to the promising word.

16. WA 4.160.16–19 (Sch. Ps. 101:19, but commenting on a reference in vs. 15 to God's taking pity on the earth): "Ideo secundum spiritum necesse est eam [vs. 15] accipere, ut nos accipimus. Eodem modo de omnibus promissionibus legis et prophetarum, ubi semper assumuntur nomina de rebus temporalibus. Et in hoc Iudei occiduntur litera, et tamen sub illis spiritualia intelligi vult."

less, Luther is finding a duality in the Old Testament text: the promise of an "eternal testament" is becoming more prominent, and is being opposed to the "temporal" covenant of the law.

An important passage of this type occurs in Ps. 104:8–10, where Abraham and Isaac are mentioned in the text itself as recipients of an eternal covenant. This, Luther explains, was the promise of the future grace of Christ. The "blessing" is the "benedictio fidei" promised to Abraham in all nations. God, the text says, established this covenant "for a precept," which means that the Old Testament people were held (*tenentur*) to believe in Christ. And on the basis of this word of faith, promised and at length fulfilled, "they would have eternal life. For faith is the 'eternal testament,' i.e., of eternal things, because it gives eternal goods, not temporal ones as the testament of the law gave." [17]

This passage is not without ambiguity either. But clearly there is emerging an idea of great consequence: the faith of the Old Testament fathers, resting on only the word of promise, is at the theological heart of the Old Testament. And equally important, this kind of faith is not only still valid, but will become normative.

In the marginal glosses to the passage given, faith is defined

17. WA 4.193.10–22 (Gl. Ps. 104:8–10): "*Memor fuit* exhibendo sicut promisit *in saeculum testamenti sui,* in quo promisit gratiam Christi futuram: *verbi* fidei future, *quod mandavit* suscipiendum pro mandato posuit, ut qui crediderit, salvus erit [Mk. 16:16]. Benedictio fidei enim promissa est ei [to Abraham] in omnes gentes: *in mille generationes,* in omnes generationes huius seculi. *Quod* verbum fidei *disposuit* Gen. 22 [:18]. 'Benedicentur in semine tuo omnes gentes' *ad Abraam:* et iuramenti sui *ad Isaac* Gen. 26[:4]. 'Benedicentur in semine tuo omnes gentes terre.' *Et statuit illud* illud verbum fidei promissum *Iacob* filiis Iacob *in praeceptum,* quia credere in Christum tenentur: *et Israel* populo ex Israel *in testamentum aeternum,* i.e. quod ex verbo fidei promisso et tandem implcto ct exhibito, si ipsum servarent pro precepto, haberent vitam eternam. Fides enim est eternum testamentum, i.e. eternorum, quia dat eterna bona, Hebr. 11, non temporalia sicut testamentum legis."

(in reference to Heb. 11:1) as "the word of *future* things, i.e. their argument and sign and covenant." [18] There is no opposition posed here to "new-testament" or Christian faith as the word of *present* or fulfilled things. Further, Luther notices that even in the book of Exodus, in which the giving of Moses' law is recorded, God was already teaching the people that they should "await the promise of their fathers." [19] In short, the people were really being instructed as to what faith was all about.

But Luther cannot explicate these thoughts further without eventually getting trapped in a difficulty of language. For now, faith in the naked promise is being suggested as valid, right faith; yet earlier Luther had unfavorably contrasted the "naked word" of the Old Testament to the New Testament word, which comes endowed with vivifying grace. This kind of opposition worked all right when it was drawn between the naked command of Moses (law) in contrast to the grace-filled word of Christ (gospel). But now the Incarnation doesn't stand as the hermeneutical divide, and therefore it can no longer be New Testament grace that alone constitutes words as spiritual or efficacious. For there is already a deep theological divide among Old Testament words themselves, between its earthly, temporal provisions and the eternal covenant of faith made with Abrham and those who shared his faith and who longed for the future that God had promised. Luther tries to explain that faith further in Psalm 111: "Although they did not yet have the revealed [New Testament] faith,

18. WA 4.193.31 f.: "Et fides verbum est rerum futurarum, i.e. argumentum et signum et testamentum."

19. WA 4.193.33 f. (a marginal note to "Et statuit illud . . . in preceptum"): "In libro Exodi hoc fecit, cum populum doceret expectare promissum patribus eorum." Summarizing the whole passage, Luther adds that it was because God remembered this promise to the fathers that he continued to show favor to the people under the law until he fulfilled his promise in the advent of Christ (lines 34–37).

which directs one immediately to God through Christ, nevertheless, what they had was *not a naked letter,* but a letter which was hiding those things which are spirit." [20] But exactly what sort of Old Testament "letter" can it be that is not altogether "naked" but "hides" spiritual things? The answer is the promise, as the next sentence shows: "For with simple literal faith (*simplici fide literali*) they were waiting for the promises of God." [21]

Now, the question arises, were these faithful Israelites — without grace or Spirit (the hallmarks of the Christian people) — somehow more than mere figures and signs of Christians? Were they more than merely *sub lege* and carnal? By all means! Their existence under promise, caught, as it were, between the "already" and the "not yet," is replete with theological significance for Christians. For the word that describes the existence of both peoples is "simul." The tension of old and new, present and future, grips them as it does Christians. "Therefore it is *simul* true that they were 'upright' and yet not yet (*tamen nondum*) illuminated; *simul* upright and still in shadows; *simul* upright and not yet righteous with the perfect righteousness of faith. So also are we now [upright] in relation to those things which we have; and yet, in regard to those things which we do not yet have, we are in shadows." [22]

20. WA 4.251.1-4 (Sch. Ps. 111:2: "Generatio rectorum benedicetur"): "'Recti' isti dicuntur fideles primo in synagoge . . . qui licet nondum haberent fidem revelatam, que immediate in deum dirigit per Christum, tamen habuerunt *non nudam literam, sed literam abscondentem ea, que sunt spiritus."* (Italics mine.)

21. WA 4.251.4 f.: *"quia simplici fide literali* expectabant promissa dei." (Italics mine.) The "hypocrites," by contrast, were trying to establish the letter from which the spirit had been "extruded," so that they expected temporal blessings — or nothing at all, which was worse (lines 5-9): "Sed hypocrite, qui literam extruso spiritu statuebant, pravi facti sunt. Et non nisi temporalia, sicut litera sonat, expectabant: immo aliqui nihil amplius exspectabant [sic], sed carnem tantum sapiebant."

22. WA 4.251.10-15: "Quare *simul* verum est, quod erant recti et tamen nondum illustrati, *simul* recti et adhuc in tenebris, *simul* recti et

Luther has discovered a common theological ground upon which the Old and New Testament faithful both stand — a ground, moreover, that can take into account the actual historical situation of the Old Testament people, *ante adventum Christi,* and discover in it great theological value for the present. Luther himself summarizes this parallelism of existence a few lines further on: "For just as it has not yet appeared to us what we shall be, so also it had not yet appeared to them what the future deeds were to be. Hence it is clear that they are called 'upright' because their hearts were directed to the future, awaiting what was invisible, not content with present, visible things." [23] Like Christians, they had to stake everything on the veracity of the promising God. With them, as with Christians, *"sola fides rectificat."* [24]

Even "Lex," in certain contexts, is interpreted to serve this idea, with the result that — just as there are two "testaments" in the Old Testament — there are two interpretations of "law" that can be found next to each other: law as the promise of mercy to those who wait for God, and law as the old law which, together with sin, functions as man's oppressor.[25]

---

nondum iusti iustitia fidei perfecta. *Sicut et nos modo* sumus [recti] in iis, que habemus, et tamen ad ea, que nondum habemus, in tenebris. Nam sicut nos ad gloriam futuram dirigimus cor nostrum et ita sumus recti: ita illi ad gratiam et ita erant recti." (Italics mine.)

23. WA 4.251.17–20: "Sicut enim nobis nondum apparuit quod erimus [1 John 3:2]: ita et illis nondum apparuit, quod futuri facti sunt. Unde liquet, quod ideo 'recti' dicuntur, quia corde sunt directi ad futura et invisibilia expectantes, non contenti presentibus et temporalibus."

24. WA 4.247.21 f., the gloss on this same verse (Ps. 111:2).

25. WA 4.419.8 f. (Gl. Ps. 129:4: "Quia apud te propitiatio est, et propter legem tuam sustinui te, domine"): *"propter legem tuam,* in qua promisisti misericordiam expectantibus te." Here, *lex* means God's promise of mercy (not the *lex Mosi*). But just six lines later, in the gloss on vs. 7, *lex* and *peccatum* are paired off against mercy and grace (lines 15 f.): *"Quia apud dominum* te domine solum *misericordia* gratia, sed apud nos lex et peccatum." The law that is "apud nos," then, has the connotation of "killing" law, an idea that is fairly frequent throughout the *Dictata.*

With reference to the "hermeneutical divide" separating letter and spirit, improper and proper understanding, the discovery of the theological and religious efficacy of promise, and its appropriateness for Christian faith, has opened up for Luther a theological and spiritual dimension of the Old Testament that was completely absent at the beginning of the *Dictata*.[26] The Old Testament prophets are now pictured as preaching proper understanding of the promises to their own contemporaries. Those who grasp the promising word are grasping not a mere naked letter, as are those who observe the bare command and count on temporal rewards promised. The Old Testament faithful are directed to the ancient promises made to their fathers. In these, they may know God's intention for the future, his "eternal testament." And the people who trusted that promise were not mere shadows of Christians — unlike them — but rather "simul" carnal and spiritual — like them. Now the way is open for a surprising turn of exegetical events: the Old Testament *community* ("the faithful synagogue") and Old Testament *faith* (hope, trust, expectation) will be enhanced to the point of becoming a model and example for the self-understanding of the Christian community, and the Christian believer.

26. This is the root of Luther's later definition of a sacrament as a sign to which is added a promise (rather than grace). Recognition of the validity of Old Testament faith prepares for Luther's later recognition of the validity of the Old Testament sacraments, and thus for his thorough criticism of the traditional contrast between the sacraments of the two dispensations, whereby those of the old covenant were mere signs. See *De captivitate Babylonica ecclesiae*, 1520, where Luther draws a sharp distinction between the "legal figures" of Moses, on the one hand, and the faith-demanding "signs" of the fathers, on the other. "At nostra et patrum signa seu sacramenta habent annexum verbum promissionis, quod fidem exigit et nullo opere alio impleri potest: ideo sunt signa seu sacramenta iustificationis, quia sunt iustificantis fidei et non operis, unde et tota eorum efficatia est ipsa fides, non operatio . . . fides in promissionem, cui iuncta fuit circuncisio, iustificabat et implebat id quod circuncisio significabat" (*WA* 6.532.24–32).

XIV. THE DISCOVERY OF THE FAITHFUL SYNAGOGUE

So far I have dealt largely with abstractions. Now for something concrete: Luther's discovery and ever-increasing occupation with the Old Testament people and their faith, under an exegetical rubric that would have been impossible for the "medieval Luther" — a rubric that Luther calls "the faithful synagogue" and which denotes Israel at once under promise and law, before the advent of Christ. I have found no occurrence of this designation in an investigation of the tradition's handling of five texts in which Luther uses the term.[1]

In the medieval tradition and in the medieval Luther, the Old Testament prophet was a "special person," who belonged to, and spoke to, an age not his own. The general development that I wish to show here is from this "elitist" view to the idea of a "remnant" — an exemplary part of God's people whom Luther calls the faithful synagogue.

The Elitist View

The essence of the elitist outlook is that since the prophet is really speaking not to his own people (except in "figures") but to the Church, his contemporaries are in the dark as to the true import of his words. This view was illustrated in the passage where Luther spoke of the "medium" placed between the prophet and the people even as regards the mere understanding of the words, so that the people understood every-

1. The five Psalms texts checked were 88:40, 118:81, 118:123, 121:1, and 122:1, according to the nine medieval commentators (listed in Ch. X) who for this study represent the tradition.

thing carnally.² It is obvious that under these conditions, faith-creating promises to the people of Israel themselves are scarcely imaginable.

I am not going to suggest that Luther suddenly abandoned all ideas about special gifts whereby the prophet saw the future in a way that the Israelite on the street did not.³ My argument is rather a positive one, a further elaboration of the shift whereby the prophet begins to be less a seer, and more a preacher to his own people.

Under the old view, God's *novum pactum* is secret, the mystery of the new law, which God reveals only to the worthy.⁴ Or, Luther can write that the prophet understands his own history "mystice" and so sits down and writes "de Christo"; David becomes Christ speaking.⁵ "Before," Luther writes, "the 'word of the Lord' was not being 'done' to the people, but only to the prophets. Now it is being done to all, through preachers." ⁶

2. WA 3.347.29-37.
3. As late as WA 4.288.24 f. (Ps. 118:62) Luther repeats the traditional explanation of why the prophet often speaks in the past tense, not the future: it is so clear to him that he speaks as though it had already happened. This form of speech is peculiar to the prophetic mode, as traditionally understood. Cf. WA 4.21.2, 50.30, 120.16 f. The last has a new element, however: Luther marvels at the great faith of the prophet, who so firmly believed and hoped for the promised future that he "speaks the future as an accomplished fact — much more devoutly than we." The faith and hope of the prophet have become exemplary for ordinary Christians. When the prophet begins instructing his own contemporaries about this, the "elitist" viewpoint has been broken down.
4. WA 3.144.22-25 (Gl. Ps. 24:14): *"Firmamentum* secretum, vel consilium Domini i.e. mysterium nove legis . . . *est dominus timentibus eum . . . et testamentum ipsius* i.e. novum pactum suum, ostendet eis *ut manifestatus illis* et solum talibus."
5. WA 3.188.12-16. Cf. the approach to Psalm 50 as described above in Ch. XI. David is described as a mystic. WA 3.185.26 f.
6. WA 4.165.38 f.: "Olim enim non ficbat verbum Domini ad populum, sed ad prophetas tantum, nunc autem ad omnes per predicatores." Here Luther has been asserting that the word of God was only *promised*

Prophets Become Preachers

Of special interest is the text, given earlier, in which Luther juxtaposed two interpretations of the prophet's speech — one in which he addresses the future Church, the other in which he exhorts his own people to rejoice because Christ is promised to them.[7] In the moment that the prophet-psalmist turned to address his own people, his word became a word of promise: "Enjoy all gaiety and rejoice, for behold, he will come to you; to you is promised the son of God, your salvation." The prophet, deploring the human condition in general, was also concerned "especially lest the people of Israel await the promises of God in this life, carnally." [8]

In Psalm 118, where one is virtually bombarded with the "eloquia Dei" — the promising words of God — Luther gives a general view of his understanding of what the prophet now intends, as he speaks to his own people and time: "And thus the prophet intends in his own meaning [9] that the people of Israel be prepared by the Lord like a wineskin, stretched out in hope through the word of promise, so that they may receive the evangelical wine in the future Christ. But behold what happens when Christ is delayed: meantime the Pharisees come, and shrink this people from that hope of future things to an enjoyment of present things, in order that they might not hope for the wine, the spiritual things, but . . . become shrunken." [10]

---

to the Old Testament people, "but now *fit et exhibetur in facto* through the ministers of Christ" (lines 36 f.).

7. *WA* 4.121.3-9.
8. *WA* 4.50.19-22.
9. "in suo sensu vult": here, the intention of the human author clearly appears as a control on the interpretation. This is the classic definition of *sensus literalis* among the followers of Saint Thomas.
10. *WA* 4.347.3-8: "Propheta itaque in suo sensu vult, quod populus Israel a domino velut uter paratus et per verbum promissionis in spe dila-

The Remnant, the Faithful Synagogue

For Luther, the hermeneutical situation is now ripe for the "faithful synagogue" to be born. This same kind of thinking leads Luther to introduce the notion of a "remnant." In a prophetic lament about the physical destruction of his people, Luther hears the following message: " 'You have turned the testament away from your servant' [Ps. 88:40], that is, you have turned away from his covenant (*pactum*) with you, namely, from the *major part of the people,* because of their unbelief, as well as from us, by not helping us in persecutions. For thus, in the same words, the prophet describes and laments the destruction of the whole people: one part of them (namely, *the remnant*) are destroyed, rejected, etc., according to the flesh, and outwardly only. But the other part (namely the reprobate) according to the spirit, and inwardly — and in fact, finally, in both ways." [11]

Next, in the exegesis of Ps. 118:81 Luther makes a connection between the remnant and the "fidelis synagoga," a

---

tatus, ut vinum Euangelicum in Christo futuro susciperet: sed ecce dum differetur Christus, interim veniunt pharisei et populum istum ab ista spe futurorum contrahunt ad fruitionem presentium, ut non vinum nec spiritualia spiritualia sperarent, sed . . . contraherentur."

11. WA 4.49.3-9 (Sch. Ps. 88:40): *"Avertisti testamentum servi tui,* id est pactum eius tecum avertisti, scilicet *a populi maiore parte* per incredulitatem illorum, et a novis per non auxilium in persecutionibus. Sic enim eisdem verbis describit et lamentatur totius populi destructionem. Cuius una pars (scilicet reliquie) sunt secundum carnem et foris tantum destructi, repulsi &c. Altera autem (scilicet reproba) secundum spiritum et intus, immo hec tandem utroque modo." (Italics mine, excluding *Avertisti . . . tui.*) *Reliquiae* is the Vulgate word for the well-known "remnant" passages in the prophets (for example, Isa. 10:19, 21f.; 37:32, et al.). The word does not occur in the Psalms in that sense (nor does "remnant" occur in the English Psalter). It may be recalled that Luther interpreted this Psalm as addressed to Christ and his people; thus, here also the "remnant" includes the few Jews who have converted and the Christian martyrs in New Testament times. It first designates a genuinely Old Testament remnant in the next passage dealt with in my text.

term that now appears with increasing frequency.[12] The text reads, "My soul faints for your salvation, and in your word I have hoped exceedingly."[13] Luther comments first that "again, the faithful synagogue calls for Christ, and waits for the gospel of grace." Then, two sentences later, he notes that the prophet is crying out on behalf of the "remnant of Israel, as he does through the whole psalm."[14] It is in this faithful

12. The earliest occurrence I found is at WA 4.78.34 (Gl. Ps. 91:2, just three Psalms after the introduction of the "remnant" idea). The occurrence under discussion (Sch. Ps. 118:81) is at WA 4.346.15. See also WA 4.301.19 (Gl. Ps. 118:147, but without "fidelis"), 349.37 (Sch. Ps. 118:87), 364.28 (Sch. Ps. 118:123), 373.26 (Sch. Ps. 118:145), 396.30 (Gl. Ps. 120:1, without "fidelis"), 399.24 (Sch. Ps. 121:1), 400.1 f. (Sch. Ps. 121:2; without "fidelis"), 407.29 (Gl. Ps. 122:12), 443.19 (Gl. Ps. 142 title).

13. "Deficit in salutare tuum anima mea: et in verbum tuum supersperavi."

14. WA 4.346.15 f.: "Iterum fidelis Synagoga Christum vocat et euangelium gratie expectat." Lines 23 f.: "pro reliquiis Israel . . . clamat iste propheta, sicut per totum psalmum." In probing the medieval tradition on the exegesis of these two passages where Luther resorts to the idea of a faithful Old Testament "remnant" (at Pss. 88:40, 118:81), I found a few remarks that harmonize with the idea, but no occurrence of the term *reliquiae* itself. In the traditional handling of Ps. 88:40, Augustine's explanation of the apparent failure of God's promises is that "David positus erat, cui promitterentur haec omnia in semine eius, quod est Christus, implenda." The *Gloss,* followed by Lombard, adopts from Cassiodorus this solution, as an alternative to Augustine: "promissa Iudais lata sunt ad gentes." Lyra keeps to the history, referring to the putting off of the temple-building until Solomon: *moraliter* the text can be referred to the delay in attaining promised blessings. From Burgos and Doering there is no comment. Hugo has adopted Cassiodorus' solution: "promissa iudeis ad gentes transtulisti; destruxisti vetus testamentum." The old covenant, with its promises, is destroyed. Perez writes that it was revealed to David that all would be fulfilled in Christ, "nam regnum david fuit figura regni christi, et salomon inquantum filius et heres david fuit figura christi." The Jews are excluded altogether: "Et avertisti testamentum eius ut a iudaeis non recipiatur in verum regem et messiam." Faber gives a strictly New Testament interpretation: "legem Christi tui infirmam fecisti: sancti eius in terra conculcati sunt." In the traditional exegesis, then, there is nothing to suggest the idea of an Old Testament remnant, although for the rest, Luther's interpretation

remnant, and in the apostles, that the promises to Israel are to be fulfilled.¹⁵ The word *expectare* occurs with increasing frequency in these texts — indeed, Luther says it is a *proprium* — an inalienable attribute — of the faithful people.¹⁶ And along with this expectation comes *petitio,* also with increasing frequency.¹⁷

Luther now begins to argue that both the Church and the existence of the believer are to take the faithful synagogue as a model and norm for their faith. The promise under which the synagogue lives involves pain and anxiety because it is delayed. Luther meditates on the pathos of existence which waits entirely on God's promise. In doing so, Luther assumes the burden of giving theological expression to the perpetual crisis of faith, in every age, when God does not seem to be doing anything in the world. The situation was particularly acute in post-exilic Israel — and, one might add, in the post-

---

seems close to Augustine and Faber. One comes closer to the remnant idea in Ps. 118:81: Augustine speaks of the "genus electum, regale sacerdotum, gens sancta . . . desiderans Christum," and designates Simeon as an example. This people is refrred to as the "ecclesia" (not "remnant" or "synagogue"). The *Gloss* and Lombard follow this, both mentioning Simeon. Lyra and Faber pursue moral interpretation, Lyra observing that the contemplative "defecit" from external acts. Perez' "peregrinus" (*homo mysticus,* Adam) "petit proficere in lege euangelica quam a christo accepit et per quam fuit justificatur"; he has already attained the New Testament situation. The link between the tradition and Luther in this exegesis thus seems to be the figure of Simeon: in his comment three verses later Luther refers to him as a New Testament example of the loyal persistence of the faithful synagogue (Sch. Ps. 118:84; WA 4.348.8-11, 21).

15. WA 4.408.24-29: "Omnis Scriptura prophetarum primo de Apostolis intelligitur, quia sic cogit promissio Dei, qui promisit populum Israel exaltare super omnes gentes, quod in Apostolis *et reliquiis* Israel implevit." (Italics mine.)

16. WA 4.388.10.

17. WA 4.147.10, 149.14, 196.35, 203.39 f., 277.27, 302.36 f. ("peto, quero, pulso . . . Semper petit"), 304.5, 320.35 f., 328.15, 20, 25, 27, 30, 35; 344.15 ("petitur semper"), 369.17, 390.25 ("semper petendus"), 407.32-36, 418.35, 445.26.

Schism church to which Luther belonged, and over which he lamented frequently in the *Dictata*: "Therefore, because the promise is being delayed, it works affliction for him who hopes, and groaning for him who expects it. And — if I may again digress a bit — this prophecy, the expectation here described in the whole psalm in the same way, and in others, ought to be referred above all to the approaching time of the advent of Christ, and the prophet should be understood as speaking in the person of faithful such as these. And the reason for this is that already then, the time of the promise was approaching, and the period of weeks was nearly ended, and the prophecy of the departure of a leader coming from the tribe of Jacob was fulfilled. The people were being oppressed by impious tyrants — more than that, they were being seduced by impure teachers and scribes . . . Therefore, seeing that these things had come about, they — or the spirit seeing for them — begin to wonder why the Christ is not yet come. And so they complain about the delay of his advent, and the more anxiously they wait, the nearer his advent is. For from the Gospel it is very evident that they had waited with great sadness of soul, for example Simeon and Joseph and Anna, of whom it is said that they were awaiting the kingdom of God and the redemption of Israel.

"Moreover, just as Simeon and Anna and Zacharias prayed, there is no doubt that in the same way others also were appealing for Christ with the greatest anxiety. And it is really their voice that sounds forth in all the prophets, where they aspire to the church, to the gospel, as this psalm [118] especially does." [18]

18. WA 4.347.36–348.12 (Sch. Ps. 118:84): "Igitur quia differtur promissum, facit sperantem afflictum et gemebunde expectantem. Et ut iterum paulo digrediamur: ista prophetia et expectatio hic descripta per totum psalmum similiter et in aliis debet maxime referri ad tempus propinquum adventus Christi, et quod propheta in talium fidelium persona loqui accipiatur. Et ratio est, quia tunc iam tempus promissionis instabat et

Not only sheer delay and waiting, but defectors within the ranks make faith an arduous thing: "Perhaps even I [the prophet says] would have failed along with them, did I not have 'exceeding hope' (*supersperavi*), that is, hope beyond hope. For you have delayed in sending him for a long time; and therefore I have fainted, and am driven to extend hope into hope. For this is 'to hope exceedingly,' i.e., to depend on the word of promise from hope to hope, against all that is contrary to it." [19]

Under the promise, they know not only sheer endurance and hope against hope, but they also receive joy and certitude.[20] Luther's strongest expression of this in the whole *Dictata* comes at Ps. 118:111 ("I have obtained your testimonies as a heritage forever, for they are the joy of my heart").[21] Those who get an inheritance of lands, he observes, have visible presence

---

finita erant proxime spacia hebdomadarum [Dan. 9:24] et impleta prophetia de defectu ducis de femore Iacob [Gen. 49:10], et populus ab impiis tyrannis oppressus, insuper ab impuris magistris, scribis seductus: que omnia prophetata prius fuerant. Ideo videntes hec fieri, vel spiritus pro eis, incipiunt mirari, quod non veniret Christus. Et ideo querulantur dilationem adventus eius, tanto egrius expectantes, quanto vicinior erat adventus eius. Nam ex Euangelio clare patet eos expectasse cum magna anime tristitia, ut Simeon et Ioseph, Anna, de quibus dictum est, quod expectabant regnum dei et redemptionem Israel [Luke 2:25, 38]. Sicut autem Simeon et Anna oraverunt et Zacharias, sine dubio eodem modo et alii quam plurimi anxie vocaverunt Christum. Et horum proprie est vox in omnibus prophetis, ubi suspiratur ad Ecclesiam, ad Euangelium, sicut maxime facit hic psalmus." Following Karl Meissinger's correction, I read "totum psalmum" in line 38 f. (*Luthers Exegese in der Frühzeit* [Leipzig, 1911], p. 9). The Weimar text has "tot psalmos."

19. WA 4.346.25-29 (Sch. Ps. 118:81: "Deficit in salutare tuum anima mea: et in verbum tuum supersperavi"): "Et defecissem forte etiam cum illis, nisi quod in promissum tuum supersperavi, id est spem supra spem habui. Quia diu differs illum mittere: ideo defeci et spem in spem coactus sum prorogare. Hoc enim est 'supersperare,' id est verbum promissionis de spe in spem continuare contra omne contrarium."

20. WA 4.287.2-9, 343.6-11; 399.18-27.

21. "Hereditate acquisivi testimonia tua inaeternum, quia exultatio cordis mei sunt."

and possession of present things, not testimonies of the future. To have joy in mere testimonies "does not arise from the infirm faith and hope of men." [22] But for those who believe God, this is a *"felix hereditas* . . . for the promises of God make their heart happy who believe and hope in them. Meanwhile, therefore, we rejoice in the faith and hope of future things which God promises to us. Moreover, we rejoice because we are certain that he does not lie, but will do what he promises, and will take all evil away from us . . . For who will not rejoice if he is certain that his body will be clothed with glory and immortality, brightness and virtue, etc.? But he is certain, if he believes. It [his joy] is so great, I take it, because there is no doubt that what he expects will be done." [23]

The Church's Conformity to the Faithful Synagogue

The passage just cited, wherein the third and first person — "he" and "we" — are used interchangeably, indicates that in the context of these thoughts, the move from explanation of the text directly to application in the present is very easy for Luther. He now suggests that the faith of the synagogue, resting on the promise and waiting for it, is a proper and normative model for Christian faith and hope. For example, where the psalmist says, "Our feet are standing in your gates, Jerusalem" (Ps. 121:2), Luther comments: "For they stand who

22. WA 4.359.35-39: "Immo qui in terris hereditatem acquirunt, exultatio cordis eorum non sunt testimonia futurorum, sed exhibitio et possessio presentium. Non enim signis rerum, sed rebus ipsis noverunt gaudere. Testimonia autem sunt signa et verba, non res ipse: et hec pro hereditate sibi estimare et gaudere in illis non est infirme fidei et spei hominum."

23. WA 4.360.5-13 (on the same verse, 118:111): "Felix autem hec hereditas, quia eterna: dicit enim 'hereditate acquisivi ineternum.' Promissa enim dei cor letificant eorum, qui credunt et sperant in ipsa. Igitur interim exultamus in fide et spe futurorum, que nobis promisit deus: ideo autem exultamus, quia certi sumus, quod non mentitur, sed faciet quod promisit, et auferet a nobis omne malum . . . Quis enim non exultet, si

wait expectantly, that it might be opened to them, and they might enter. But those who do not believe [the promise] go away instead . . . From which it is evident that the person of the synagogue is speaking. Not only the synagogue, however (as I have often said), but everyone who is progressing ought to feel and speak like this, *as if he were in the synagogue*. For as long as we do not receive the promises, we have not entered Jerusalem, but we stand and await our entrance." [24]

Such parallels are frequent. And they not only teach conformity of Christian faith to Old Testament faith, but also, in the process, serve greatly to enhance the evaluation put on the Old Testament faith itself. In fact, "this people also [the faithful synagogue], who cry out here, were not without salvation and light and grace. But the promised future they did not yet have, to which they were being held as something still to be had, to be sought, to be desired. For they were being held closed up in the faith to be revealed. So all of us are in the midst of grace which is had and yet to be had." [25]

---

certus est, quod induetur corpus eius gloria et immortalitate, claritate et virtute &c.? Certus autem est, si credit: tantum est, ut expecto, quia sine dubio fiet, quod expectat." This outburst seems unprecedented, on the basis of a probe of traditional exegesis on this verse. Augustine, as he did before, interprets the *testimonia* as martyrs who are thereby made "testes dei," who rejoice in their suffering. He is followed by the *Gloss*, Lombard, and Hugo. Lyra and Perez connect the rejoicing to the understanding of the law of God that is revealed in the Gospel and typified by the parable of the hidden treasure, Mt. 13:44 (Perez: "exulto et letor in possidendo intelligentiam legis," followed by the Matthew reference). Faber attributes the *exultatio* to the presence of grace and the Spirit which is the answer to prayer. Nowhere but in Luther did I find the idea of sheer joy arising from trust in the promise.

24. *WA* 4.399.30 400.5: "Stant enim, qui expectant, ut eis aperiatur et intrent. Qui autem non credunt [promissionem — see 399.25], abeunt potius . . . Quo patet, quod persona Synagoge loquitur. Non solum, autem, sed, ut sepe dictum est, omnis proficiens ita sentire et loqui debet, *ac si in synagoga esset*. Quia quamdiu promissiones non accepimus, non intravimus in Ierusalem, sed stamus et expectamus introitum." (Italics mine.)

25. *WA* 4.375.4-8 (Sch. Ps. 118:146: "Clamavi ad te, salva me"):

Luther had earlier come to understand the whole Old Testament as — in essence — *testimonia*. Now he shows how Christian existence, and the Church itself, is to be conformed to that understanding. Just as scripture is *testimonia*, its understanding both relative and infinite, so also the life of the faithful is open-ended, "without limit, end or measure."[26] This openness, in fact, defines the Christian "spirit of liberty" for which there is no law, "for it does more than it is commanded to do, so that if one were permitted to live forever, he would strive eternally to understand and to do, nor would he ever turn back. Such is the man whose meditation is the *testimonia Domini*."[27] A faithful reader of Scripture does not try to make it conform to his wishes, but rather, lets the testimony of Scripture shape his own understanding.[28]

So comprehensive in application is this future orientation,

"Nam et iste populus, qui hic clamat, non erat sine salute et luce et gratia. Sed futuram nondum habuit, promissam, ad quam tenebatur habendam, querendam, desiderandam. Tenebatur enim clausus in fide revelanda [cf. Gal. 3:23]. *Ita omnes sumus* in medio gratie habite et habende." (Italics mine.) Cf. the "simul" of their existence and the Christians', WA 4.251.10-15.

26. WA 4.320.3-6 (Sch. Ps. 118:24: "Nam et testimonia tua meditatio mea est: et consilium meum iustificationes tue." Luther engages in a word study here; the following is part of the exposition of "meditatio," beginning at 319.27): "Non quod necesse sit nos omnia intelligere et agere in hac vita, sed quod paratus debeat esse animus, nunquam velle desistere ab amplius agendo et intelligendo usque ineternum, nullum scire limitem, nullum finem, nullum modum."

27. WA 4.320.6-9: "Hos est enim esse in spiritu libertatis, cui non est posita lex et statutum, quia amplius facit quam sibi precipitur, ut si ineternum vivere liceret, ineternum intelligere et agere studeret nec unquam retrocedere. Hic est, cuius meditatio est testimonia Domini."

28. In the scholion on the same passage, Luther polemicizes against the "proprietarii" of their own opinions, who pervert and twist everything "so that the *testimonia domini* is not their *meditatio,* but, on the contrary, they want their own *cogitatio* to be the *testimonia domini.* Indeed, as though Scripture ought to say to them: 'Your meditation is my testimony'" (WA 4.317.32-36). Cf. WA 4.353.37-354.2, which reads in part, "But let us twist our *sensum* into the *testimonia dei*, in which future goods are testified to."

prompted by the promise, that even the law — the commands — are interpreted so as to serve it: "Hence often in the old law and prophets, God commands that he be worshiped and his law kept with our whole heart, even though the law was not able to give those things, because it was letter.[29] But he commanded it anyway, so that they might long for Christ, and beg for its fulfillment." [30] Here is one of the earliest expressions of Luther's fundamental idea that the function of the law — both before and after the advent of Christ — is to "drive to Christ" and to the future. Thus, Luther does not go on to mention Christ's fulfillment of the law, nor does he argue in terms of "the love of God *super omnia*" which is now possible with the coming of grace. The application of the text to the present situation is rather as follows: "So also now, he commands that he be loved perfectly, even though this cannot be done in this life, in order that he might drive us to long for the future life, in which we will fulfill all these things." [31] This interpretation fits the parallelism of the "promise-advent" structure of exegesis: just as the Old Testament command drove the people to long for Christ's first advent, so also the New Testament command drives man to long for the eschatological advent, in which everything will be fulfilled. Thus, even the law as command serves, in a negative way, as testimony to the future.[32]

29. For Luther law is now "letter," not because it is a *figura* of the New Testament law, or the same with an addition of grace, or *caritas,* to fulfill it. Rather, the law is established in its own right as law; it has a permanent, abiding, although negative purpose in relation to Christ.

30. WA 4.324.9–12: "Unde sepe in vetere lege et prophetis precipit deus ex toto corde se coli et legem suam custodiri, quod tamen lex illa non potuit dare, quia erat litera. Sed ideo tamen precipit, ut Christum optarent et peterent pro impletione eius."

31. WA 4.324.12–14: "Sicut et nunc precipit perfecte amari, quod tamen fieri non potest in hac vita, ut cogat nos optare futuram vitam, in qua implebimus hec omnia."

32. The idea is near at hand that the real purpose (not just an accidental side-effect) of the law is to convict of sin. In the medieval tradition (Bonaventura, for instance) it did this "accidentally," its real purpose being

Finally, when Luther confronts a text (Ps. 121:4) in which the Old Testament tribes themselves are called "a testimony of Israel," the interpretation is no surprise: Israel, if it understands rightly what it is, sees that it is not "the real thing, Israel (*quid Israel*)," but only a testimony of it. Even here, Luther's application to the Church is not by way of contrast, so that the synagogue is the *figura* and the Church is the *res*, the "quid Israel." On the contrary: "The Church is also a testimony, not the real thing (*reale quid*), for it does not exhibit itself, but only gives testimony to the sort of things which have been promised in it and about it. For its goods are future; it cannot exhibit them in the present." [33]

This text is perhaps most striking for showing the contrast to the traditional exegesis of the Old Testament: the Church, exactly like the synagogue, is a testimony of what God intends for the world. It continues the mission of the "faithful synagogue." It is not yet what it will be. Although it is true that the Church is the result of the fulfillment of a promise, it in turn must understand itself as a promise, a testimony addressed to the world, of the coming city of God.[34] To understand itself

---

to lead (with the aid of grace) to salvation. Earlier in the *Dictata*, where there is less differentiation between "law" and "Gospel" than in this later portion, a certain confusion is evident. Luther writes, on the one hand, that those who "do not use it rightly" are convicted of sin by it, but that it is "testimony" to those who use it rightly, "because Christ is shown to them in it, to whom they ought to flee in order to be justified" (*WA* 3.551.23-28). But why flee to Christ, unless they are convicted of sin? And are they not using it "rightly" if it convicts them?

33. See the whole passage, *WA* 4.402.19–403.22. The portion quoted (403.4-6): "etiam est Ecclesia testimonium et non reale quid, quia non exhibet se talem, qualia promissa sunt in ea et de ea, sed solum testimonium dat. Quia futura sunt eius bona, que non potest in presentia exhibere."

34. *WA* 4.403.7-11: "ergo ipsa remanet testimonium incredulis et credulis, sed incredulis in testimonium et scandalum, credulis autem in testimonium et surrectionem. Per eam enim deus testatur toti mundo futura bona. Ideo est testimonium dei ipsa Israel ad mundum, sed nondum exhibitio: exhibebit autem eam in futurum, et cessabit ipsam habere in testimonium."

as anything else is to be like the "carnal," the unbelieving Israel.

It is not as though no difference at all now remained between the "faithful synagogue" and the Church. The Church has the promise not only of future goods and a future advent, but also of Christ himself to be present to it.[35] Nor is it as though no difference remained between the individual Old Testament believer and the Christian. For the Christian lives in the promise of Christ's "spiritual advent" and in the certain hope of the resurrection of the dead. This last relation evokes the question: how does Luther's emerging doctrine of promise affect the definition of the structure of Christian faith? How does the idea of faith as grounded in promise harmonize with the much-heralded idea of faith as grounded in the tropological relation of Christ and the believer?

35. This promise is the ecclesiological parallel of the promise made to the individual of Christ's "spiritual advent." Thus, for example, when the psalmist calls on God to "be mindful of your word to your servant, in which you have given me hope" (Ps. 118:49), Luther writes, "This is explained either of the hope of the fathers for the promised advent of Christ, or of the hope of the church in the words [promises] of Christ about his own presence, help and [finally] future glory" (WA 4.332.10-12.) A series of New Testament promises are then adduced; "therefore the church holds the promise of Christ regarding the help of his grace in its necessities."

XV. TROPOLOGY, PROMISE, AND FAITH

Considerable evidence has been adduced to show the increasing gap between Luther and the hermeneutical tradition in which he matured. Two of the most critical changes in Luther's thinking have been shown to involve, first, his definition of the *sensus propheticus* and, second, the manner of *applicatio* of text to Christian. The *sensus propheticus* of the Psalms has changed from Christ to the Old Testament text itself as *testimonium* and promise, and the application has moved from "tropological" identification and conformity with Christ to a "moral" identification with the Old Testament faithful — not in "morality" but in the quality of their faith.

It is fairly obvious that I believe these changes are of paramount importance for the genesis of Reformation theology. But this places me in contradiction with some of the best contemporary scholarship on the young Luther: according to Gerhard Ebeling, "the intimate connection between the sensus litteralis (Christus) and the tropological sense (fides Christi) became the original form (*Urform*) of the reformation doctrine of justification."[1] In this, he agrees with a whole tradition of scholarship which has tried to unlock the secret of the genesis of Reformation theology via Luther's cryptic axiom, "Christ, tropologically understood, is faith."[2] It is a well-known fact that, for Luther, tropology is not "quid agas"[3] —

1. Ebeling, "Hermeneutik," col. 251.
2. The best study on this subject is still that of Erich Vogelsang, *Die Anfänge von Luthers Christologie*, esp. pp. 50 f., 55, 73-75.
3. I refer to the traditional ditty explaining the four senses: "Littera gesta docet, / Quid credas allegoria, / Moralis quid agas, / quo tendas

a moralistic "what you do" in response to Christ. Rather, it is what God does in conforming you to Christ, particularly to the cross. As Ebeling notes, Luther's ruling idea in tropological interpretation is "that God makes all his saints to be conformed to the image of his son." [4]

I am convinced that it is more appropriate to understand this tropological method of *applicatio* as the "Endform" — quite extraordinary to be sure, but still the "Endform" — of the medieval doctrine of justification, rather than as the "Urform" of the new theology. To prove my point, I shall first examine what the words Christ and faith mean in the christological-tropological system of interpretation, and then set against that system the meaning of promise and faith as they emerge in the late *Dictata*.[5]

The Medieval Pedigree of Tropology

Several arguments can be adduced to undermine the inflated significance attributed to Luther's tropology in the emergence of his reformed theology. First of all, it is well known that tropological exegesis presupposes the medieval fourfold sense, which Luther was to abandon in 1517.[6] Second, tro-

---

anagogia" (among other places, in Lyra, *Prologus in moralitates bibliae,* fol. 4ʳᵇ).

4. Ebeling, "Die Anfänge," p. 226. He cites WA 3.46.32 f.: "deus facit omnes sanctos suos conformes fieri imagini filii sui." Within this system of interpretation, christological analogies to Christian life abound, for example, WA 3.468.17–19: "Sicut enim Christus de spiritu sancto conceptus est: ita quilibet fidelis nullo opere humano, sed sola gratia dei et operatione spiritus sancti iustificatur et renascitur."

5. Although my argument involves criticism of Ebeling, I am only following through on his own convincing demonstration that hermeneutics and theology in the young Luther are changing together. My aim is to show that the hermeneutic of tropology is ill-suited to the theology of promise appearing late in the *Dictata*, and hence requires and undergoes fundamental revision.

6. Ebeling, "Hermeneutik," col. 252.

pology is ultimately predicated on the first hermeneutical rule of Tyconius, "according to which," as Augustine explains, "it is understood that sometimes the head and the body, that is, Christ and the Church, are indicated to us as one person."[7] Or, as Luther repeats over and over, "as with the head, so with the body" (sicut in capite, ita in corpore).[8]

Third, Luther's peculiar use of tropology is predicated absolutely on the assumption that Christ is the *sensus literalis* (*propheticus*) of the Psalms,[9] an assumption he at first shares with Faber Stapulensis. But this assumption is being abandoned in the later part of the *Dictata*. Fourth, as the editors of the new Weimar edition of the *Dictata* point out, Luther's designation of the tropological signification of the work of Christ as "faith" is not unique in the tradition. The editors find it also in Augustine, the *Gloss,* and Lombard.[10] And fifth, as Ebeling himself has noted, "faith" is not Luther's only designation of what Christ signifies. The incarnation, Luther can write, "signifies . . . nothing else but obedience in works."[11] Or — to cite the most frequent definition of Christ's signification that can be found in the early part of the lectures — Christ's suffering and death signify man's

---

7. Augustine, *On Christian Doctrine* III, 31, 44; trans. p. 106.
8. For example, WA 4.179.13.
9. In Ebeling's succinct sentence, "Christ is now the text" ("Die Anfänge," p. 225).
10. WA 55/1.93.36–38, where the editors are commenting on Luther's first such application (92.12–14). Augustine, *De fide et operibus,* c.16 n.27 (PL 40, 215): " 'fundamentum . . . quod est Christus Iesus,' si autem Christus, procul dubio fides Christi." Lombard, III *Sent.* d.23 c.3 n.3: "unde Augustinus . . . Fundamentum est Christus Jesus, id est Christi fides, scilicet, quae per dilectionem operatur, per quam Christus habitat in cordibus, quae neminem perire sinit . . . Fides enim sine dilectione inanis est . . . nam et 'daemones credunt . . .' " I found this gloss also in Henry Totting (p. 62.22, taken over from the *Gloss,* PL 114, 525).
11. WA 3.155.20 f., cited by Ebeling, "Luthers Auslegung des 14.(15.) Psalms," p. 298 f., n. 2.

humiliatio under the *iudicium* of God, the place of man's justification.[12]

Two questions therefore arise. If the Reformation doctrine of justification is "by faith alone," it is not at all clear how this tropological method could have given rise to its *Urform*. Would not such a claim, to be credible, have to show how tropology at least worked in favor of concentrating on *fides*, to the ultimate exclusion of other elements? And second, would it not also be desirable to see some unique notion of "the Word" emerging from within this structure? [13] I think so.

But neither of these things happens via tropology. In fact, it is precisely the notion of faith that *cannot* be developed tropologically as long as, and insofar as, Christ remains exclusively the literal sense. For then one must willy-nilly speak of Christ's own faith, and although Luther stretches that idea as far as he can within the limits of an orthodox christology, Christ's faith cannot serve as a proper model for man's faith. The reasons will be given in a moment.

Furthermore, the tropological application nowhere calls for an exclusive reliance upon "God's word." Rather, it depends

12. See esp. *WA* 3.171.20-23: "[Christus] in summa exultatione patiendi clamavit: 'ut quid dereliquisti me?' et hoc est proiectum esse a Deo. *Tropologice* autem *significat*, quod omnis qui se proiicit et humiliat coram deo, ille magis auditur." (Italics mine.) See also *WA* 3.345.29 f. (confession of injustice a precondition of justification), 431.40 f. (the Christian dies and goes to hell "in affectu"), and 647.23-25 (the cross signifies sufferings of the saints). Frequently in this context the *iustus* is defined as the *accusator sui* (*WA* 55/2.24.8 f., 33.1; 3.185.6 f., 288.31, 291.14 f., 27 f.; 322.15 f., 370.18). "Impossible est enim, quod qui confitetur peccatum suum, non sit iustus" (*WA* 55/2.34.2 f.). Hence, *iustitia* can be defined as "concrucifixio Christo" (*WA* 3.202.24) or "humilitas" (*WA* 3.575.25). The interminable arguments of Luther scholars over this kind of text does not alter the fact that herein lies Luther's basic metaphor for understanding justication throughout the *Dictata*.

13. To this textent I am in accord with the insistence of Ernst Bizer in *Fides ex Auditu*, 3rd ed. (Neukirchen, 1966), on the centrality of "the (external) Word" in the development of Luther's reformation theology.

upon an understanding (*intellectus*) of the correspondence of things — Christ, the Church, and his people — as set forth under the rubrics of the fourfold scheme of interpretation.[14] "The word," as long as it functions in harmony with the fourfold structure, necessarily presupposes a notion of grace which becomes inappropriate to Luther's new understanding of the biblical mode of speech.

The Limits of Christ's Faith

Luther offers a great deal that is both suggestive and specific regarding Christ's faith. In the early part of the *Dictata* he frequently interprets the Old Testament promises as having been made to Christ. In Ps. 85:7, it is Christ who "cries out" for God to hear him in his tribulation and hope, and in a gloss Luther ascribes to Christ "fiducia," giving two possible grounds: that Christ had experienced being heard by God in the past, or that God had foreordained, or promised via the prophets, to hear him.[15] A little later, Christ is again made to appeal to the promise of God to raise him from the dead.[16]

14. As acknowledged earlier, I owe to Ebeling the clue that Luther's new understanding of language is intimately involved in his new hermeneutic. I was stimulated to a hermeneutical orientation for this study of *promissio* in part by Ebeling's lecture at Harvard Divinity School in December 1963, the substance of which appears in his article "The New Hermeneutics" of 1964. I even suspect that, had he come to this insight earlier, the results of his pioneering articles on Luther's *Dictata* might have been different; he might have attached less importance to tropological exegesis, and more to *promissio*.

15. WA 4.21.1–3: "*In die tribulationis meae* passionis mee future *clamavi* clamabo, preteritum pro futuro, *ad te, quia exaudisti me* in hoc, quod sequitur." The marginal gloss (lines 27–29), commenting on the reversal of the natural order of the two propositions – "I have cried out because you have heard me": "Vel ideo permutat, quia expertus prius erat se exauditum, unde animatus etiam nunc se clamasse dicit, eadem fiducia se exaudiri sperans. Vel 'Exaudisti,' i.e., quia preordinasti exaudire seu promisisti, ergo clamavi."

16. WA 4.22.32: "redde promissa [Christ says], scilicet suscitando a morte et glorificando." Cf. WA 3.313.27 f.

Further on, the suffering Christ pleads with God that an exhibition of his wondrous works only to the dead would be "in vain." [17]

All this, of course, lends itself beautifully to tropological application — which is just the point of Luther's exegesis at these junctures, since he believes that all Christ's sufferings are "ordained" toward such existential application, as God conforms the Christian to his Lord. But Luther is fast coming to a boundary, to a limit beyond which he cannot go. And it is precisely *beyond* that limit that a quite different dimension of faith awaits discovery.

The tradition taught that Christ had the fullest measure of grace and *caritas,* but not faith or hope. Luther is exerting considerable pressure on that doctrine. But how far can he push it? He reaches the limit in his exegesis of Ps. 115:10 ("I have believed, on account of which I have spoken"). Luther comments: "The whole psalm can be understood as being [*literaliter*] about Christ, except for the first word [*credidi*]. For it is denied that Christ had faith, since he was a *comprehensor* at the same time [that he was a *viator*]. Nevertheless, if we wish to say that just as he had hope, so also faith [, then we may], for there is no doubt that he hoped for the glorification of his own body, which he did not yet see in the present. Therefore, he also believed." [18] Precisely here, Luther has

---

17. *WA* 4.34.8-14, 23-31. The christological assumption, to put it crudely, is that Christ has to be saved, in order for men to be saved. Everything depends on the Savior being saved (*WA* 4.34.28-31): "Quia cum Christo omnes resurgunt, quia resurrectio Christi causa est omnium resurgentium. *Quare si ipse non resurrexisset, nulli resurrexissent.* Et ita mortuis fecisset Deus mirabilia. Et frustra misericordiam et veritatem dedisset. Ergo ut hoc non fiat, petit resuscitari, ut et in ipso resuscitentur omnes." (Italics mine.)

18. *WA* 4.266.23-267.3 (Sch. Ps. 115:10. This is in fact the first verse of the Psalm and therefore the place where introductory observations are made): "*Credidi, propter quod locutus sum* &c. De Christo per omnia posset intelligi psalmus, nisi primum verbum. Quia Christus negatur fidem habuisse, eo quod fuit simul et comprehensor. Si tamen velimus dicere,

reached the limit of making Christ his "text" on the subject of faith, for he can push Christ's faith no further. The idea of faith, resting on the *mera promissio* (especially with no divine nature to fall back on [19]), so powerfully emerging in this part of the lectures, cannot be developed with Christ as its subject,[20] and therefore not tropologically either. For

---

quod sicut spem habuit, ita et fidem [the sentence is incomplete; hence my insertion]: sine dubio enim speravit sui corporis glorificationem, quam tamen nondum vidit in presentia: ergo et credidit." Faber is the only one in the tradition to give this Psalm a christological interpretation. He first asserts that the same approach applies here as to the previous Psalm, namely, "Ps. de christo domino. Propheta in spiritu in persona Domini loquitur." In his *Expositio continua* on the first verse (= vs. 10; "Credidi, propter quod locutus sum; ego autem humiliatus sum nimis"), Faber comments, "spem certam indubitatamque habui placiturum me domino in regione vivorum, quam ob causam orationem fidenter fudi, nam vehementer afflictus sum." Luther's observations may well have sprung from consideration of this reference to Christ's hope. In his *Adverte*, Faber acknowledges that most of the tradition interprets the Psalm *de ecclesia primitiva*. This interpretation, he allows, provides "pia meditatio"; yet he prefers his own approach: "sed de veritate [Christ] quae de imitatione intelligentia pientior . . . Nam et imitatio veritatis ipsius gratia est." Augustine heard in this Psalm the *vox martyrum*; the *Gloss*, Lombard, Burgos, Hugo, and Perez concurred. Lyra, again following Rashi, explains the literal sense *de David*, an interpretation criticized by Burgos as judaizing. Doering strikes a compromise: Lyra's interpretation is right *ad litteram*; Burgos is right about that which is *figurata* by the letter, namely, *mysteria ecclesie*, especially its *predicatio* and *martyrium*. Both Lyra and Hugo, citing Bernard of Clairvaux, interpret this *moraliter* as a penitential Psalm.

19. The force of this remarkable passage about Christ's faith is in fact blunted by the last clause, omitted above: "ergo et credidit, non obstante, quod eam [that is, his *glorificatio*] clarius vidit in verbo, quam nunc videt in proprio genere" (WA 4.267.3-5). Trying to make sense out of this passage, I would set aside the obvious comparative construction ("clarius . . . quam") and translate: "therefore he also believed, even though in the Word [that is, in his divinity] he saw quite clearly that which he now [in glory] sees in its own kind [that is, as an accomplished fact, namely, his glorification]."

20. It therefore seems no accident that just here, in the scholion on Ps. 115:10, where the development of the notion of Christ's faith has hit its limit, Luther launches one of the most eloquent expositions of the essence

Christ is neither *purus homo* nor *in culpa*. And therefore, the abyss of despair and nothingness, the threat of ultimate abandonment and *desperatio*, which for man in sin is a real threat, cannot in Christ come to genuine expression. In fact, *conformitas* has no place here; on the contrary, the real distance between Christ and man is disconcertingly exposed. Christ *literaliter* goes through hell (and Luther's expression of this is unparalleled in the tradition), but he knows he will not stay there. Trust in the naked word of promise is not the sole ground of his hope. As *deus-homo* he is not, at this most crucial point, one of us men.

The consequence is obvious: exposition of the structure and essence of faith must be developed along completely different lines. Christ as the subject of faith (as the one who believes) must cease to be the text. Faith — unlike obedience or humility — is exposed as precisely the point at which Luther's idea of *conformitas* via tropology is exhausted and inadequate. There can be no complete identification of Christ and men as believers. Nor of course need there be such identification, once the discovery is made of the faithful synagogue and its faith as a model for Christians. Therein, Christ can become the object of faith rather than its exemplary subject.

The Warrant for Tropological Faith

The next question concerns the nature and ground of one's faith in Christ (*fides Christi*), according to Luther's tropological interpretation. If Christ's own faith cannot serve as faith's model, what then is it really like? How does it arise, and on what does it actually depend?

First of all, Luther's revision of tropology from a moralistic

---

of faith, which relies totally on the promises of God: "All our goods are only in words and promises" (*WA* 4.272.16). His *sensus litteralis* here shifts from Christ to the Old Testament speaker himself. This, in my opinion, is the wave of the future in Luther's theological development.

"quid agas," what *you* do, to "opus Dei," what *God* does, puts considerable strain upon the traditional hermeneutical structure, for it shifts the critical problem from an anthropological to a theological focus. That is, the question now is not *my* capacity to act (which involves the questions of free will and possession of grace), but rather: what warrant or assurance can I find for presuming — believing — that *God* so acts, and is acting redemptively, with me? How do I know, for example, that the mere *fact* that Christ was raised from the dead effects my "spiritual" resurrection, as tropological interpretation proclaims? Does the hermeneutical insight suffice, that his resurrection "signifies" mine, that his resurrection, tropologically, or "mystice," is "faith in the resurrection"? [21] On what ground can I trust that God really acts in the same way that this tropological exegesis works?

Without an answer to these questions, *fides* is on extremely hazardous ground. The trouble with tropology, as a matter of fact, is that it already presupposes in its very structure that these questions are favorably disposed of. This is evident in Ebeling's own exposition of the fourfold sense, where he raises the question of how the individual reader may come into possession of the Psalm word so as to speak and pray it as his own word. Ebeling replies: "According to Luther, this question could only be answered as follows: the Psalms are understood primarily as having been spoken in the person of Christ [*sensus literalis propheticus*]; therefore, the individual is included in them insofar as his own person has its place before God in the person of Jesus Christ." [22] Existential appropriation of the text

21. WA 4.34.37–40: "Mystice autem [propheta] vult, quod cum fideles non possint resurgere in spiritu nisi per eius resurrectionem (i.e. per fidem resurrectionis eius): ideo dicit . . . mea resurrectio faciet illud."
22. Ebeling, "Luthers Psalterdruck," p. 97. The insertion in brackets is of course my own, a reminder that Ebeling — mistakenly, I believe — takes Luther's early, preface understanding of the prophetic sense as definitive for the whole *Dictata*.

as my own, then, already presupposes that I have a "place before God in the person of Jesus Christ."

But that seems to pose precisely the same question already raised, the question of the warrant for believing that God acts with Christians as he acted with Jesus Christ. How am I brought to this favored place *coram Deo*? Ebeling seems to pass over this question, but it is necessary to discover how the fourfold hermeneutic as used by Luther really answers it.

The Logic of the Fourfold Exegesis

The medieval hermeneutical structure rests on a historical basis, which provides the warrant for its use. The basic clue to the system is in the warrant for the first of the spiritual senses, the allegorical, since this warrant provides the model for all the rest.

Allegory arises from the juxtaposition of the Old and New Testaments in the canon. The mere fact of what happened, as recorded and interpreted in the New Testament, raises questions about the significance of the Old Testament for the Church (assuming one wishes to include it in the canon). The conclusion was arrived at that the *gesta veteris testamenti* were intended to prefigure, to "signify," the New Testament events. The New Testament reveals, in Perez' words, that the Old Testament was not intended "gratia sui," but is an allegory (that is, a letter to be allegorized) of the New Testament. The Old Testament, as a whole, albeit hiddenly, signifies the New Testament. "The Law, spiritually (i.e. allegorically) understood, is the same as the Gospel," to quote a medieval axiom. Likewise, the sacraments of the old law are signs and figures of the sacraments of the new law.

It is important to observe that this interpretation (regardless of whether its reading of the intention and purpose of the Old Testament was justified) had in its favor the indisputable fact that the New Testament events did happen, and that its authors (with canonical authority) provided some warrant for reading the Old Testament allegorically. Therefore, the intention of God seemed clearly to have been revealed at this point.

The same logical grounds underly the allegorical and tropological exegesis of the New Testament. It is a simple fact that the Church came into being: therefore, the *gesta Christi* are intended to signify — allegorically — the Church and its sacraments. It is also a fact of history that the Church became peopled with individual martyrs and saints who were conformed to their Lord, even to death; therefore the *gesta Christi* are intended to signify, tropologically, the individual believer as well.[23]

Thus, when questioned about the propriety of such exegesis, the Christian can argue: if the Old Testament can be understood without the New, then the New Testament was given in vain.[24] And if the New Testament can be understood apart from the Church, sacraments, and Christian people, then it was given in vain.

Now, suppose it is true that Luther's use of tropology is exceptional in that it raises the question, for faith, not merely of man's capacity to act, but of God's intention to conform him to Christ in a redemptive way — to justify him. What warrant would Luther give in response to this question?

He answers with a logic that is exactly parallel to the general logic of the fourfold system: if Christians are not justified by the coming and work of Christ, then his advent is in vain.

---

23. This scheme was clearly laid out by Saint Thomas and repeated by Paul of Burgos. Especially in Burgos, and programmatically in Gerson, it was also clear how the New Testament letter could step into the place of the Old Testament letter as the basis of fourfold exegesis — even when one was ostensibly interpreting the Old Testament. All it required was a Faber Stapulensis to assert that the Psalms were *literaliter* about Christ. The logic of the whole system made that step very natural.

24. Luther makes this point, WA 55/1.6.26–28.

Luther's most succinct expression of this line of reasoning appears in his interpretation of Psalm 84: "But I believe that the tropology of the psalm, from what has often been said, is readily apparent. For whatever is said about the first advent in the flesh, is understood at the same time (*simul*) of the spiritual advent.[25] In fact, the advent in flesh is ordained and done on account of the spiritual advent." ("On the basis of what reasoning, what *intellectus,* do you say this?" one asks. Luther answers:) "If this were not the case, *it would have profited nothing.* Hence, these words also, 'misericordia' and 'veritas' cannot be said about Christ except for the sake of the second advent, on account of which it was chiefly *intended. For what would it have profited God to become man,* unless we could be saved by believing in him?" [26]

This text is transparent to the fourfold scheme: the advent of Christ (*litera*) is intended to signify his spiritual advent, which is man's justification by faith (*tropologia*) and eventually, anagogically, his salvation. Christ, tropologically understood, is faith; faith, anagogically understood, is salvation.

But the problem lies precisely in the legitimacy of these identifications: How do I know that God "is" in fact (as well as in theory) justifying me and "intends" to save me? Luther gives the only answer tropology can give: "if this were not the case, the Incarnation would have profited nothing." So a man's

---

25. Notice that Luther is not yet working with the "promise-advent" scheme programmatically sketched in Ps. 113:1. The theological reasoning in Psalm 84 is entirely different.

26. WA 4.19.31–37 (Sch. Ps. 84:14: "Iustitia ante eum ambulavit: et ponet in via gressus suos"): "Tropologiam autem psalmi credo ex sepe dictis facile apparere. Nam quecunque de adventu primo in carnem dicuntur: simul de adventu spirituali intelliguntur. Immo adventus in carnem ordinatur et fit propter istum spiritualem: *alioquin nihil profuisset.* Unde et ista verba 'Misericordia et veritas' [referring to vs. 11: 'Misericordia et veritas obviaverunt sibi'] non possunt de Christo dici nisi propter adventum secundum: quare iste principaliter intenditur. *Quid enim prodesset* deum hominem fieri, nisi idipsum credendo salvaremur?" (Italics mine.)

faith in Christ — *fides Christi* — is supported by a sort of "necessary reason," which is logically a *post hoc* fallacy. One may wonder whether Luther, in the midst of the sort of penitential self-annihilation that he frequently prescribes in the early part of the *Dictata,* might not have asked himself, "But how much would it spoil the 'profit' of God's becoming man if I myself were not being justified and saved? My *intellectus,* my tropological schema, convinces me that God intends to save men by this means. But does he intend to save *me*?" [27]

At this point, Luther could call upon another bit of hermeneutical wisdom: the insight that the biblical language is "causative." [28] This notion comes through in the next two sentences of the Psalm 84 passage last quoted to explain tropology. Luther argues: "Christ is not called our righteousness, peace, mercy and salvation in his own person, except causatively (*effective*). But faith in Christ (*fides Christi*) is that by which we are justified, pacified, through which he reigns in us." [29] In short, *fides Christi* must be justifying and saving

27. But this opens up the question of election, which appears, interestingly enough, right in the exegesis of the same Psalm, two verses earlier (Ps. 84:12: "Veritas de terra orta est, et iustitia de coelo prospexit"), in a text that makes interesting comparison with the "promise-advent" scheme of Psalm 113. Here in Psalm 84 the first advent of Christ is already seen as the result of God's Old Testament promise: "that he comes to us, the promise has affected (*promissio fecit*)." But the parallelism to the spiritual advent, first found in Psalm 113, whereby it too is effected by the promise, is here missing. Instead, Luther goes on (and his text, admittedly, suggests the interpretation) to state that *iustitia,* the purpose for Christ's coming, "remains in heaven, and looks down from heaven, electing and granting itself only to the elect (*eligens et electis tantum se tribuens*)" (*WA* 4.17.41 f.). This is comparable to the reference to election in Saint Bernard's explication of the "middle advent," noted in Ch. XII above.

28. See Siegfried Raeder, *Das Hebräische bei Luther untersucht bis zum Ende der ersten Psalmenvorlesung* (Tübingen, 1961).

29. *WA* 4.19.37–39: "Quocirca Christus non dicitur iustitia, pax, misericordia, salus nostra in persona sua nisi effective. Sed fides Christi, qua iustificamur, pacificamur, per quam in nobis regnat." Cf. *WA* 3.183.3–5: " 'Verbum Domini rectum' [Ps. 32:4]: in seipso primum, deinde quia

men, because Christ's advent would otherwise have been pointless, and because biblical words are not merely descriptive but causative.

In response to this analysis of Luther's understanding of tropological faith in Christ, one might object that I have ignored the conception of the word of God that Luther is already developing. Is it not "the Word" that gives the warrant, the certainty, being sought here? Without doubt, Luther has a very interesting doctrine of the word at this stage. But does the word "do it" for Luther; does the word break through the impasse he has reached? Luther's word theology deserves closer investigation at this stage.

The Sacramental Word

An interesting feature of the above passage from Psalm 84 is the absence of *allegoria,* which in the full fourfold schema is occupied by Church and sacraments. Luther makes no appeal in his argument to the mediating position between the acts of Christ and the believer's justification (that is, between *litera* and *tropologia*), which the sacraments, and the justifying grace they impart, may bring to support his contention that Christ's advent effects man's justification. One might have expected Luther to do so. Traditionally, and for the youngest Luther on record, it is not the word itself that places one safely in Jesus Christ. Rather, it is the sacraments that do so. For example, in a very early writing, Luther explains what it means that Christ is a *sacramentum* (an efficacious sign): his cross is a sacrament because it signifies the death of the soul in penance.[30]

---

rectificat"; WA 55/1.92.7 f. (Gl. Ps. 11:7): *"Eloquia domini* Euangelica *eloquia casta* quia animam castificant"; WA 55/2.115.16 f. The editors cite Augustine and Perez to the same effect, WA 55/1.93.22-94.34.

30. In the exegesis of one of the penitential Psalms (Psalm 31) Luther was seen to interpret Christ's *pena* as signifying man's *culpa.* Luther had

Here occurs the existential, ecclesiological locus of tropological exegesis: in the sacrament of penance. In that sacrament the soul dies to sin just as Christ died on the cross. His death "significat" the soul's death to sin.[31] There is, then, in response to the question of how one comes to stand before God in Christ, a structural — a factual — dependence of tropology upon the sacraments.[32] This harmony and interdependence of hermeneutical and sacramental structures is what traditionally bridges the real gap between Christ and Christians. In just the same fashion, allegory, signifying Church and sacraments, normally stands in the hermeneutical gap between the letter (the record of *gesta Christi*) and tropology (application to individuals).

already given clear expression to the rationale for this view in the marginals on Lombard's *Sentences* (1510–1511), WA 9.18.19-23: "Crucifixio Christi est sacramentum quia significat sic crucem poenitentiae in qua moritur anima peccato [, et] exemplum quia hortatur pro veritate corpus morti offerre vel cruci." It will be recalled that for Perez, the whole range of the *gesta Christi*, in contrast to the Old Testament history which is only *signum*, is *sacramentum*, containing the grace signified in its letter.

31. Luther's "theologia crucis" is built on this foundation. Bizer uses this passage as part of his argument that Luther's theology is still essentially "medieval": "der Tod Jeus am Kreuz zeigt uns die Demut [rather than *fides*] als den weg des Heils" ("Die Entdeckung des Sakraments durch Luther," *EvTh* 17 [1957], 66). My point is rather to show the admirable structural congruence of the fourfold hermeneutic (in particular, of tropology) and medieval sacramentology. Just as the concept of promise subverts and supplants tropology, so promise also changes the meaning of a sacrament from "sign" to "promise," or "testament." Scholars such as Gerhard Müller ("Neuere Literatur zur Theologie des jungen Luther," *KuD* 11 [1965], 335), who point to Luther's early designation of Christ as *sacramentum* to indicate a new sacramental theology, ignore the purely medieval meaning that word had for Luther at the time.

32. One can miss this interdependence, as I think Ebeling does, by assuming *a priori* a post-Reformation point of view, whereby technical hermeneutics must deal with the existential dimension of justification itself, because the encounter with the Word effects justification – a view not normally represented by the medieval sources, and certainly not held by Luther in 1510.

Luther gives a clear illustration in his discussion of Ps. 110:4: "He has made his mighty acts to be remembered." These mighty acts (*mirabilia*), Luther explains, "have been done fundamentally and causally (*radicaliter et causaliter*) in the passion of Christ, to whose example (*exemplum*) all must be formed (*formari*). Therefore, the sacrament of the eucharist is [the sacrament] of the passion, i.e., the 'memory' of his 'mighty acts.' "[33] This can be hermeneutically organized to mean that Christ's passion (*litera*) "causally" signifies the sacraments (*allegoria*), and that through them Christians are "formed," conformed (*tropologia*), to Christ.

But Luther seems reticent to plant the sacraments so firmly "between" Christ and us. He appears rather to be trying to understand words themselves, not as "mere signs" (*signa tantum*), but as efficacious signs, which is exactly what sacraments are. In this way, he attempts to develop a hermeneutic modeled on the traditional one, but without the relationship of dependence upon the sacraments to actualize and make present the "grace" signified or intended by the letter.[34] The dependence is lacking because the word itself is being understood as sacramental. As evidence for this, Luther's appeal to the "causative" nature of biblical language may be recalled. The following passage is also pertinent, because Luther inserts "the Gospel" into the interpretive structure at the point where Penance and the Mass would ordinarily fit: "Sacrifice is the goal of the law and the gospel. For what else does the gospel

33. WA 4.243.14–16. For further explication of the medieval understanding of the relation of Christ and Christians as one of "exemplary causality," see M.-D. Mailhiot, "Le pensée de S. Thomas sur le sens spirituel," *Revue Thomiste* 59 (1959), 647.

34. I would not insist that Luther is being unique here, although research might show that he is. Nor do I wish to isolate this hermeneutic at one clearly delimited chronological stage. Rather, it is a logical stage, characterized by the coherence of certain hermeneutical ideas found in the texts from this time, together with their compatibility with the medieval understanding of the working of the sacraments.

do but *kill and mortify us* according to the flesh [cf. Penance], and so *offer us to God,* vivified according to the spirit [cf. the Mass]?" [35] Since Luther maintains that "the Gospel" does these things — since he does not mention Penance and the Sacrifice of the Mass — I think he is working with a "sacramental" doctrine of the Gospel word, or of preaching. But note that this understanding of the word still fits into the traditional hermeneutical structure.

That it does so is confirmed by an examination of the theological logic that Luther brings forth to support the claim of the word's sacramental efficacy: it is the "classic" logic of the fourfold schema, previously uncovered. "Grace," as spiritual "benediction," must accompany the word when it is preached, for "unless cooperating grace at the same time (*simul*) [36] comes to the hearer, they [the spoken words] would profit nothing." Why not? Because the "Gospel," in this early view, consists of "invisible and incomprehensible things" which cannot be understood, and of commands which cannot be fulfilled, without the special aid of grace.[37] Without grace, then, the words are as dark and unhelpful to Chirstians as the prophetic

---

35. WA 3.282.6-8: "sacrificium est finis legis et Euangelii. Quia quid aliud facit Euangelium, quam quod nosipsos *mactat et mortificat* secundum carnem et sic *offert deo* vivificatos secundum spiritum?" (Italics mine.) I believe this "sacramental hermeneutic" also helps explain Luther's marked reticence about the sacraments themselves throughout the *Dictata.*

36. Cf. the parallel "simul" in the quotation giving the rationale of tropology, WA 4.19.31-37, discussed earlier.

37. WA 3.259.9 f. (Sch. Ps. 44:3: "Diffusa est gratia in labiis tuis"; Luther commenting here on the preaching of Christ and the apostles): "Quia talia predicant [that is, *invisibilia et incomprehensibilia,* 258.26] que, nisi gratia *simul* cooperans auditori accesserit, *nihil proficiant.*" (Italics mine.) Cf. WA 3.258.26-29: "Quia cum Christus et Apostoli predicaverint invisibilia et incomprehensibilia, que oculus non vidit &c., et iusserint pro istis omnia visibilia contemnere, tam bona quam mala: nisi in verbo eorum fuisset gratia attrahens, nunquam prevaluissent." See also WA 3.641.28-38: unlike Moses, God (in Christ) is a "legislator" who "jubet *simul* et dat benedictionem, ut implere possint" (italics mine); and WA 3.651.25-29.

word was to carnal, unspiritual Israel! Just here may be seen how the sacramental model is still in full force: a spiritual *res* must be conferred along with the external *signum* (the words). This *res* is invisible grace, or spirit. What the *res sacramenti* is to sacramentology, the *res verbi* is in this hermeneutic.[38]

But how is one to specify exactly what sort of *res verbi* (grace) is meant? Applied to the Gospel words as Luther understands them at this stage, grace must serve two functions — as *intellectus,* or (to use the Vulgate word) *eruditio,* for penetrating the "invisibilia et incomprehensibilia" preached by Christ and the apostles, and as *caritas* for fulfilling the commands of the new law. These two themes are understandably frequent in the early part of the *Dictata;* [39] grace must be received with the word — grace as *intellectus* to penetrate the

38. The doctrine of the word operative in the well-known "fides ex auditu" passage at Sch. Ps. 84:8 f. (WA 4.8.32-35: "Nunc enim [Christus] ostenditur nobis per fidem . . . Ideo hic per auditum . . . fides enim ex auditu est. Et ita Christum esse dominum ex auditu tantum habemus in fide"), although it might as well have been written by the later Luther, is still embedded in a hermeneutical structure that is in formal conformity with the traditional sacramental theory. This is clear from the context when, a few lines later, Luther defines the difference between the law and the Gospel: "lex est verbum Mosi *ad* nos, Euangelium autem verbum dei *in* nos. Quia illud foris manet . . . istud autem intus accedit . . . Ita verbum fidei penetrat ut gladius anceps in interiora et spiritum erudit et sanctificat. Verbum autem legis tantum carnem crudit et sanctificat" (WA 4.9.28-35, italics mine). It is not really the plain hearing and grasping of what the word says, then, or the difference in content of law and Gospel, but the inner *eruditio* of man's spirit, effected by the New Testament grace now available, which distinguishes the Gospel from the law. Formally, this relation is exactly the same as that traditionally said to pertain between the sacraments of the old and new laws.

39. For the "medieval Luther," see n. 37 above. *Eruditio* is defined as spiritual information and understanding, which is *revelatus* (WA 3.235.16-20); cf. 293.25 f.: *eruditio = spiritualis informatio,* opposed to *hystoria.* For the necessity of *eruditio,* see WA 3.262.30-33. It is given only by the Spirit (WA 3.172.26 f.). See also WA 3.176.10 ff., 246.22 f., 249.11-16 & 31, 251.2, 254.3-5, 257.32-34, 488.5 f., 507.34-36. On the need for grace to fulfill the law, see WA 55/2.7.1-6; 3.223.12, 641.28-32; 4.2.28 f.

spiritual meaning of the words,[40] grace as *caritas* to love and to realize what it commands.

But how does one acquire the grace? This question has to be answered in some way with reference to the word itself. One cannot appeal to the sacraments, for then one would have not a "sacramental" word but a "naked" word, which depends utterly upon some outside source for the grace to bring it to concrete realization. Grace must come with, or through, the words themselves. But how, if the words are incomprehensible, and the commands impossible? It simply must be — *ex opere operato,* if you will, just as grace comes through the sacramental signs. Otherwise, all the Scripture and preaching would be in vain.

Thus, one stumbles on just the same problem as that which was met in connection with justification itself: granted that the words were intended and ordained to be grace-endowed, sacramental, or accompanied by benediction in themselves, how does one know that the words he hears are accompanied by grace — by *intellectus* and *caritas* — for him personally? It must be concluded that this sacramental doctrine of the word is of no help at all, for it cannot provide a satisfactory answer to the question raised by Luther's peculiar use of tropology — the question of whether God is in fact acting upon a person in the way that the *gesta Christi* signify he is acting. Adding Luther's present notion of the word to the system, then, merely aggravates the problem, rather than alleviating it.[41] The only answers, in summary, which tropology can pro-

40. Doering's position in opposition to Burgos was the same as that represented here by Luther: certainty of spiritual understanding comes only through the inspiration of the Holy Spirit.

41. The temptation to quote the later Luther is irresistible: "O stulti, o Sawtheologen! Sic ergo gratia non fuerat necessaria nisi per novam exactionem ultra legem" (*WA* 56.274.14 f. [1515–1516]; repeated in *WA* 8.54 f. [1521]). In Luther's early hermeneutic, precisely as in the Nominalist theology of law and grace that Luther so vehemently attacked later, "grace" functions as "a new exaction beyond the law" because one *must* have grace as *intellectus* and *caritas*. Grace is the stumbling-block in this

vide in this hermeneutical emergency are "necessary reasons" and hermeneutical axioms, to wit: Tyconius' first rule, whereby (in Luther's adaptation) God is conforming his saints to the image of his Son, so that words about Christ can be applied also to men; the supporting rationalization that, were this not the case, Christ's advent and the preaching and sacraments would be in vain; and the supporting linguistic insight about the causative nature of the biblical language.

Enter Promissio

There is a certain irony about the inefficacy of the tropological scheme of interpretation for solving certain crucial problems, because the avenue toward their solution lay so near at hand — in the promise. Yet promise remained for a time unnoticed, because Luther was using it to lead himself astray. So long as the christological-tropological system of interpretation remained intact, the promises of the Old Testament could be read "prophetically" as having been made to Christ. The reason is that, in virtue of the Tyconian axiom that God conforms all his saints to the image of his Son, it was already assumed and argued that God must be doing the same thing in his people as He was doing in Christ.[42] The promises were thus becoming man's via a hermeneutical axiom.

It is ironical that the text from which Luther was getting these Christ-directed promises was the Old Testament, since

---

whole hermeneutical structure; thus, Ebeling is beside the point when, in his *Evangelienauslegung*, p. 299, he characterizes the medieval system as sacramental and hermeneutical "*Werk*gerechtigkeit" (quoted with approval by Werner Jetter, *Die Taufe beim jungen Luther* [Tübingen, 1954], p. 132).

42. WA 4.22.15 f. (Gl. Ps. 85:17): "*Fac mecum* signum resuscitando et glorificando in fidelibus meis," that is, make of me (Christ) an effective, causative *signum* (= a *sacramentum*) of the resurrection of my members, the faithful. This is said in a context in which Luther has Christ appealing to God's promise to raise him from the dead, WA 4.22.10, 32.

they were not being made to Christ at all, but to the people of Israel. Luther could not yet see that, however, because his intensely Christian hermeneutic told him that "Christ is the text." The fact that Christ did not at all need the promises does not seem to have occurred to Luther.[43] He couldn't get theological help from the Old Testament, because for him the hermeneutical divide between bare letter (bad) and spirit (good) was drawn between the testaments; therefore, nothing of decisive theological or spiritual consequence could be expected from the Old Testament.

It is fruitless to try to pinpoint one moment of insight, or one single idea which at this time made everything fall into place. Such a "moment," which for a long time was the Holy Grail of much Luther study, is more the figment of historians' imaginations than a datable historical occurrence. Luther is churning with new ideas all through the *Dictata*; they roll in upon one another like waves, so that it is difficult to tell which belong to the incoming tide of the Reformation, and which to the ebb tide of the Middle Ages.

But somehow Luther grasped the fact that all those promises he was finding in the Old Testament were being addressed to the people who were then hearing them. How could he so long have failed to see something so obvious? His first axiom of the Prefaces stood in the way, namely, that Christ was the real "text." His original definition of *sensus propheticus* kept him from getting the Old Testament sense.

43. After all, Christ merits his resurrection (WA 4.264.38; 3.166.39 f., 171.20–24); man does not. And the promises given him are not made in spite of his demerit; with man they are (WA 4.258.6 f.: "fac quod promisisti propter gloriam nominis tui [the psalmist prays], nec meritis nostris dando, nec demeritis negando"). Futhermore, Christ is *deus-homo*, while man is *purus homo*. All these factors threaten the security of the assumption that promises made to Christ, and their fulfillment in his resurrection, are so easily to be transferred to man via a hermeneutical principle.

Then also, Luther was at some point arrested by the fact that the inviolability and therefore the superiority of the new covenant itself was rooted right there in the Old Testament, in its promise. But this notion required shifting the traditional hermeneutical divide so that the Old Testament promise, the *testimonia,* could sound forth, and the Old Testament emerge out of the limbo of *umbra* and *figura* into its own reality.

Just as Luther's development of the notion of Christ's own faith was reaching the boundary-line beyond which it could not go, when he was trying to grasp the meaning of Ps. 115:10, "I have believed, therefore I have spoken," he perhaps heard the authentic sound of fully human expectation, hope, and prayer in the word of the psalmist himself, leading Luther to write: "All our goods are only in words and promises. For heavenly things cannot be shown as present; they can only be proclaimed by the word. Therefore, he does not say, 'I see, therefore I show it by a work,' but 'I believe, and therefore I speak.' But those who boast of their own goods, and glory in something present — they do not have faith of those things, but sight. But we believe, and thus cannot show it by a work. That is why we only speak and bear witness. For faith is the reason why we cannot do other than to show our goods by the word, since faith rests in what does not appear, and such things cannot be taught, shown and pointed to — except by the word." [44] And that empathy with the psalmist might have

---

44. WA 4.272.16–24: "omnia nostra bona sunt tantum in verbis et promissis. Coelestia enim ostendi non possunt sicut presentia, sed tantum annunciari verbo. Ideo non ait: 'Video, propter quod opere ostendo,' sed credidi, propter quod loquor.' Illi autem qui sua bona jactant et in re presenti magnificant, non habent fidem illarum, sed visionem. Nos autem credimus, et ideo opere ostendere non possumus. Quare tantum loquimur et testificamur. Fides enim est causa, quare non possumus aliter quam verbo ostendere bona nostra, eo quod fides est non apparentium, que non nisi verbo possunt doceri, ostendi et indicari." As indicated earlier, this line of interpretation of the passage is simply without precedent in the tradition.

helped cut him loose from Christ as the model for faith, and drawn him toward the "faithful synagogue" and the expectant, petitioning Israelite, the *purus homo* who is altogether like other men, who "faints" and "hopes exceedingly against hope." It is with him that tropological (or rather "moral")[45] exegesis finds a new locus of identification, conformity and *imitatio*, a new "sicut . . . ita." It is for his sake that the prophets become preachers, and the whole Scripture becomes *testimonia* for the whole *communio sanctorum*. To be sure, the Christian and the Church continue being conformed to the cross and suffering of Christ, just as described in the tropological exposition.[46] But faith itself is now extricated from the toils of tropology and regrounded in the word of promise. And with that word as its focal point, faith's canon of Scripture is instantly expanded: it has found a new text for its edification in the Old Testament.

I have completed my argument that tropology worked

45. "Moral" seems to be replacing "tropological" as the exegesis shifts off its christological base and uses the Old Testament as its text. See *WA* 4.349.13–20, where the letter is the faithful synagogue, "moral" is the Christian under temptation, "allegorical" the conflict of the Church (which very frequently used to be the literal), and "anagogical" the woes of the end-time. For other occurrences of "moraliter": *WA* 4.329.31, 349.15, 357.26, 375.31, 407.35, and the texts noted from the penitential Psalms: *WA* 4.418.38, 443.23, 26 f. In this context, comparison with Lyra would be most interesting. At the beginning Luther singled out Lyra for acid criticism (*WA* 55/1.8.3–7) and avoided the "moraliter" rubric, probably just because it was Lyra's general mode of spiritual application. Now, later in the *Dictata*, the attack on Lyra lets up, and Luther is using "moraliter" more frequently. Thus, Ebeling's assertion that Luther intentionally avoids "moraliter" and is in fundamental opposition to Lyra ("Luthers Psalterdruck," p. 97 f.) holds only for the early part of the lectures.

46. These themes by no means disappear from Luther's mature theology. On the contrary, they are developed further, but in the realm of vocation, where the descriptive character of this whole *theologia crucis* can be developed in its full richness, without having to carry the burden of being faith-engendering, or that upon which faith relies. See Gustaf Wingren, *Luther on Vocation*, trans. C. C. Rasmussen (Philadelphia, 1957).

against the development of Reformation theology, because it worked against faith alone as the basis of Christian life, as long as Christ was the "text," and because the word of God played no effective role in Luther's original hermeneutic when it came to answering the critical question of how one could count on being included among those whom God was described as conforming to Christ and justifying, so that in Christ one could stand securely *coram Deo*. In short, tropology could not answer the questions that Reformation theology deserves its name for answering. Luther had to break out of the traditional hermeneutic to see that whatever one needs to stand before God — for example, righteousness — comes because it is promised by God himself, and by Christ himself, not because Christ is a "sacrament" that mystically contains it and conveys it to man. The promise-advent schema that appeared at Ps. 113:1 illustrates the new hermeneutic at work: God in the Old Testament promises the first advent, in which Christ himself, in the New Testament, promises his spiritual advent.

The word now appears as a promise made by God rather than a hermeneutical axiom made by Tyconius; and what it requires is not grace-as-intellectus, but a trusting hearing of the promise, that is, faith. Perhaps the following diagram will help clarify and summarize the qualitative difference of the two ways of exegesis, and the two ways of appropriating the text as one's own:

A. Sacramental Hermeneutic

TEXT: The NT (Res^I). . . .*Tropologice*. . . .*Justitia Christi* (Res^{II})
significat
↑
FAITH

B. Promise Hermeneutic

TEXT: The OT Promise ----- *facit* -----→ NT *Res* & *Promissio*
↑   ↑
(OT) FAITH. . . .*Moraliter*. . . . . .(NT) FAITH
significat

The critical changes between *A* and *B* are, first, that the text ceases to be the *gesta Christi* in the New Testament and becomes the Old Testament word of promise; second, that faith is grounded not in the *intellectus* of some causally significative relationship supposed to obtain between Christ and Christian, but in the *ipsissima verba* of the text itself; and third, that spiritual exegesis, when it is describing what faith is, no longer functions so much tropologically between Christ and Christians, but rather "morally" between the faith of the Old Testament people, based on the promise of Christ's advent, and the Christians' faith, also grounded in a similar promise.

Furthermore, in *B* Christ is no longer the one who signifies but the one who uniquely is, and who promises. One no longer bothers with the idea that Christ is the one who receives the promises, and that this event, tropologically, is man's justification and resurrection; rather, one takes Christ as the Lord who promises to Christians what they will be, and who can be trusted to keep his promises. Faith now depends not on some interpreter's gnosis about signification but on Christ's person and word.[47]

In this qualitative revision lies the ground for finally abandoning the hermeneutic and doctrine of the word which was modeled on the sacraments. The new hermeneutical ideas that emerge are both tailor-made for the peculiar nature of words and thoroughly appropriate to the Old Testament text that Luther was for two years trying to understand and teach.[48]

---

47. My interpretation harmonizes with and explains a statement attributed to Luther in 1532: "per epistolam ad Romanos [that is, in 1515 and 1516] veni ad cognitionem aliquam Christi. Ibi videbam allegorias non esse, quid Christus *significaret*, sed quid Christus *esset*" (*WA Tischreden* 1.136.15–17 (no. 335), cited by Karl Bauer, *Die Wittenberger Universitätstheologie und die Anfänge der deutschen Reformation* [Tübingen, 1928], p. 23). (Italics mine.)

48. The first half of this statement is Ebeling's own idea, but I do not

Faith, with the word of promise as its *fundamentum* and the "faithful synagogue" as its Old Testament model, can now come to eloquent expression. Some of these expressions have already been shown, not least revealing of which was the clearest expression of certitude of salvation in the whole *Dictata*, resting solely on God's promise and the conviction that He does not lie.[49] Certitude that sufferings are redemptive, Luther has discovered, comes not from the fact that Christ himself was raised from the dead (although that is *conditio sine qua non*), but that man is promised it. A Christian now hopes, not that the "causal signification" of Christ's resurrection extends also to him, because it does so hermeneutically, but rather that Christ's promising word is good. As long as the promise was absent from this picture, the mere fact of Christ's resurrection could serve as well to drive one to despair, since the conditions of Christ's suffering (especially as *deus-homo* and sinless) only opened up the gulf between him and others.

---

know whether he would now also accept the second part — "appropriate to the Old Testament" — since he has invested much in the christological-tropological hermeneutic, which is anything but appropriate to the Old Testament or to a "word-hermeneutic." This is why I wondered earlier whether the results of his articles of the 1950's would have been different had he at that time already developed his insight into Luther's unique notion of the nature of speech, which he published in 1964 in "The New Hermeneutic." The following steps can now be seen in the development of Luther's hermeneutical thought: the attempt to work out a hermeneutic and a doctrine of the word on the old sacramental model; then, abandonment of that model in face of its bankruptcy and in favor of a constellation of ideas more suited to the nature of words; and later (perhaps not until 1518, as Bizer argues in "Die Entdeckung") a discovery — or rather a rediscovery — of the sacraments, but now modeled on the new, word-oriented hermeneutic, so that the chief thing in the sacrament becomes the promise (see, for example, the *Small Catechism* on the Lord's Supper: "He who believes the words, 'Given and shed for you for the remission of sins,' has what they say and declare, namely, the forgiveness of sins"). The categories of external sign-invisible grace have no function any more.

49. WA 4.360.5-13.

Promise overcomes that distance — and yet preserves it. Tropology was unable to do either.

The Unique Quality of Words

Words, Luther is finding out, are not like sacramental signs. As late as Psalm 89, Luther was representing the nature of theological language in a way that was fully consonant with the medieval idea of words as mere signs. The hallmark of this idea is that the word is disjoined from its theological meaning, as "letter" from "spirit." Thus, "the spirit latent in it [the word], and signified through it is, as it were, the meaning of that word. But they [the carnal] hold only the word; others, however, have the meaning: those the letter, these the spirit." [50] The prophetic word, to be sure, can be called the instrument (*organum*) of the Spirit in this view — but *not* because what God means is given in the plain meaning. Rather, the word is an instrument because the Spirit secretly instructs hearts while the prophet speaks, in "simul" fashion.[51] Such an understanding of theological language of course lends itself to analogy with sacramental theology. But it is such an analogy or parallelism that Luther is destroying. A subtle indication of Luther's new thinking appears in a statement he makes at Psalm 109: "Words are the vehicle and the feet through which truth comes into us and over us . . . yet, it [the word] has no other feet but its voice and syllables, which are materially the word in which the formal word — that is, its meaning

---

50. *WA* 4.58.16–18: "Spiritus autem in illa [sermo] latens et per eam significatus est velut sensus illius sermonis. Sed illi tantum sermonem, alii autem sensum tenent: illi literam, isti spiritum."

51. For example, *WA* 3.262.30–33: the Spirit is freed to instruct hearts as to the true meaning of the Psalm text now that Christ has come and the letter has been laid aside, "for the spiritual meaning is the *proximum instrumentum* of the Holy Spirit . . . but the letter is *remota et tarda.*"

— goes to the heart of the hearer." [52] The sound and the syllables are now important because they are the carriers of the words' meaning.

Understood in the old sacramental sense, words are like the outward sacramental actions, namely, intrinsically ambiguous as to their significance (for example, is Baptism a sign of drowning or of cleansing; is the cross a sign of defeat or victory? of salvation or damnation?). Words (to use Augustine's classic definition) have to be added to make these signs into sacraments. Thus, if a doctrine of the Scripture word is conceived on a sacramental model, one must hold to a doctrine of the obscurity of Scripture — also represented by Augustine.[53]

By contrast, what is happening with Luther explains why he later must insist that Scripture is the clearest book in the world, as he does in 1521: "Es ist auf Erden kein klärer Buch geschrieben, denn die heilige Schrift." [54] Signs may be ambiguous, but Luther in the *Dictata* has discovered that words by themselves are disturbingly unambiguous and clear. God threatens. God commands. God promises. Once Luther discovers it, he can scarcely contain himself. In Psalm 118 he exclaims: "Oh if we were only able to weigh, with the *affectus* that we ought, what it means to be saying, 'God is speaking,' 'God is promising,' 'God is threatening'! Who, I ask, would not be shaken to the very depths? This is a great word, a great sound, and one to be feared: 'Behold, the Word of God!' " [55]

---

52. *WA* 4.229.38–230.3 (Sch. Ps. 109:1): "Verba enim sunt vehiculum et pedes, per que in nos et super nos veritas venit . . . tamen [, verbum] alios pedes non habeat nisi vocem illam et syllabas, que sunt materialiter verbum, in quibus formale verbum, id est sensus vadit ad cor audientis."

53. See Augustine's authoritative explanation and justification of such a doctrine in *On Christian Doctrine* II, sections V and VI.

54. Given in Bauer, *Universitätstheologie*, p. 30.

55. *WA* 4.380.15–18: "Quanquam o si debito affectu possimus per-

But this discovery carries with it tremendous consequences. Words, Luther is learning, do not, like signs, need some hidden "grace" to be "causal." Words are intrinsically causal: they cause expectation, fear, doubt, hope, or trust in the one who hears what they say. Not because a concealed grace comes with them, but simply from what they say as "naked words." [56] Marveling at the perseverance of the saints under persecution, Luther notices that mere words accomplished it, and he cites Isa. 50:4: "The Lord has given me a learned tongue (*linguam eruditam*), that I may know how to sustain with a word him who is weary." Noting that the prophet has only "a naked word," Luther stands in awe at this "wondrous permutation, whereby words prevail over things — even the most contrary and powerful things!" [57]

Grace, then, on the sacramental model, is becoming inap-

---
pendere, quid sit dicere, 'deus loquitur,' 'deus promittit,' 'deus minatur'! Quis queso non funditus contremisceret? Magnum verbum est, magnus et metuendus sonus dicere: 'Ecce verbum Dei'!"

56. WA 4.380.5-9 (Sch. Ps. 118:161: "Princes persecuted me without cause, but my heart stood in awe of your words [*a verbis tuis formidavit cor meum*]"): "Magna gratia hec est, tu verba dei plus quam verbera hominum timeantur, plus moveant future pene comminate quam presentes inflicte . . . Quis hoc facit, nisi perfectissima fides futurorum?" Notice here that "grace" denotes the faith of the heart which takes with ultimate seriousness God's threat. Grace then is not functioning as special *intellectus*; the meaning is clear from the word itself. Cf. lines 29-31.

57. WA 4.381.36-42: "in medio persequentium principium et minantium plus letitie habet [Ecclesia] intus, quam doloris foris: plus firmant verba Dei spiritum, quam infirment verbera hominum carnem: hec affligitur poenis tortorum, ille consolatur virtute eloquiorum [= promissorum; see the text given below, this note]. Mira permutatio, ut verba prevaleant rebus et rebus contrariis atque fortissimis! Sicut promisit Isaie: 'Dominus dedit mihi linguam eruditam, ut sciam sustentare eum qui lassus est, verbo.' *Verbo* inquit, scilicet nudo sine re exhibita, sed non sine re exhibenda." The text being commented on is Ps. 118:162 ("Letabor ego super eloquia tua: sicut qui invenit spolia multa"), upon which the scholion begins: "Omnis nostra letitia est in spe futuorum et non in re presentium. Ideo enim gaudemus, quia promissionibus divinis credimus, et que promittit, speramus atque diligimus" (WA 4.380.34-37).

propriate, because words are no longer like signs, requiring grace as *intellectus* to discern their meaning. Luther's notion of the word is inexorably undermining the notion of that special endowment of *intellectus* which was before required for spiritual exegesis: "faith requires *affectus*, not *intellectus* . . . faith does not illuminate the *intellectus* (indeed it makes it blind), but the *affectus*, for it leads the latter to where it may be saved, and this through hearing the word."[58] This text is from Psalm 118, where "the word" has become the promises. And spiritual things are no longer so much the incomprehensible truths unveiled by the Spirit's "eruditio" as, simply, the promises that are hoped for in the future with *spes* and *fiducia*.[59]

The Subversion of Grace

What precisely is happening in Luther's thought is that, by the infiltration of the notion of promise, a subversion of grace is occurring in his theology. "Subversion" is the appropriate

---

58. WA 4.356.13 f. & 23-25: "affectum, non intellectum requirit fides . . . Sic enim fides non intellectum illuminat, immo excecat, sed affectum: hunc enim ducit quo salvetur, et hoc per auditum verbi." For the mature reformer, "the ears are the organs of the Christian man." Faith does not get the kind of "ears" Luther has in mind, nor is faith really "ex auditu," until the *intellectus* as a special, cognitive gift of the Spirit ceases to be the *definiens* of faith. As long as this spiritual *intellectus* is what faith really is, outward hearing is a *signum tantum* of the *res* that must be given at the same time (*simul*). This is the medieval, sacramentally-modeled manner of speaking.

59. WA 4.275.21-25 (Gl. Ps. 97:9: "Bonum est sperare in domino"): "Sic Ierem. 17[:7]: '. . . Benedictus homo, qui confidit in Domino et erit Dominus fiducia eius.' Hoc autem 'confidere' est pure spiritualia et eterna a Domino sperare contemptis omnibus, que sunt in mundo et vita ista, etiam in mortem usque." The problem now is not to understand what God is saying, but rather to hold it fast, to believe it, in spite of all the *contraria* of living. This helps explain the shift from *intellectus* to *affectus*. Perhaps it also explains Luther's satisfied comment that he has found an "easy" *intellectus* of Psalm 142 (WA 4.443.21 f.).

word because Luther never resorts to overt attack (who would attack grace?), and because it is not always explicit, as, for example, in this passage contrasting knowledge and faith: "Knowledge (*scientia*) is of present and past things; faith is properly of future things . . . For we know things that are being done, and that have been done; we believe future things that are being promised, as Abraham believed the promising God." [60] For what is *intellectus* if not *scientia*-plus-grace, which knows "present and past things," that is, the spiritual relationships that pertain between the events of the Old Testament and those of the New, whereby one discerns that the Old Testament is literally about Christ and the Church? And that the *gesta Christi* signify our *conformitas Christi*?

That is changing now. Grace-as-*intellectus* is being thoroughly undermined, at least at the point of simple understanding: the theologically loaded dichotomy of "word" and "meaning" has been broken down. Therefore, faith is not the grace of *intellectus,* but the trust of future things that are promised. But even more striking, perhaps, is the way in which the medieval doctrine of grace is being undermined on the question of the relation of merit and grace, and also regarding the understanding of the sacraments themselves. In both contexts, the infiltrator is promise. In these two areas, the possibility of direct influence from medieval thought is much more likely than in the hermeneutical questions raised in this study. Although a detailed investigation of these problems is inappropriate here, I wish at least to indicate the direction that such a study could take, for it could have as a central motif the subversion of grace.

The Situation Before Grace. — The problem of merit, it must always be remembered, was not worked out *in abstracto* but in the context of the sacrament of penance. The Nomi-

60. WA 4.322.18–21: "scientia presentium et preteritorum, fides futurorum proprie . . . Scimus enim que fiunt et facta sunt, credimus que futura promittuntur, ut Abraham credidit deo promittenti."

nalist doctrine of the *facere quod in se est* is frequently called "semi-Pelagian" because it held that man, on the basis of his natural endowments, could work himself into the sphere of sanctifying grace.[61] The language of the *facere quod* prior to grace begins to appear in Luther's *Dictata* with disturbing frequency, especially in its later part. The "sola gratia" theme, on the other hand, seems in fact to be stronger at the beginning than at the end. What is going on? Has Luther accepted the Nominalist doctrine, because he likes the notion of promise that appeared with it?[62] That may be part of the story. More important, though, is that the apparent nominalistic semi-Pelagianism which seems to be cropping out in Luther is simply another sign of the subversion of the medieval doctrine of grace — a subversion that comes about precisely through the instrumentality of the promise.

How does this happen? It happens when, and because, Luther shifts his model for faith from Christ to the Old Testament believer. The Old Testament believer does not have "grace" at all! A second problem worse than the first is created. Christ has "too much" grace (all there is, in fact, and no sin); the Old Testament faithful don't have enough (none, in fact). The old hermeneutical divide made it so. But that divide is no longer in effect. Promise has emerged to break it down, to put theological *res* and spiritual goods in the Old Testament word and faith itself.

61. See Oberman, *Harvest*, Ch. 5, and the profile of Biel's doctrine of justification, pp. 175 ff
62. Robert Holcot, it will be recalled, asserted that on the basis of God's infallible *pactum* man is assured that his efforts will not be in vain (it is improbable, by the way, that Luther read Holcot). Biel does not allow the *pactum* to "bind" God in this prejustification situation, where his sheer *misericordia* must be protected; the *pactum* is appealed to by Biel only in the context of *meritum de condigno*, where God owes it to himself, as it were, to honor his promise. But Luther has strictly and clearly excised *meritum de condigno* from his theology already (WA 4.17.4-26 and, more explicitly, 278.7-14 & 32-35).

The stage is set for a collision between Luther's idea of promise and the doctrine of grace, and its occurrence creates a dilemma. Must Luther not relent, and give up his new-found Old Testament model for faith; on this point is it not just as inappropriate as the Christ model? No! Must he not then, as a result, break down the utter uniqueness of the New Testament dispensation by saying that the Old Testament people did in fact have grace? In a way, yes, as has already been shown.[63]

The coming solution is that promise — not merit or grace — is the sole ground of the "facere quod in se est" which is *petitio*. Following is the *Dictata's* most eloquent expression of that idea, made all the more interesting by the fact that the first word of the Psalm text ("Preveni") immediately recalls the issue of prevenient grace (the *locus classicus* of the whole Pelagian question). The text, Ps. 118:147, reads, "I have come early, with untimely haste, and cried out, for in thy words I have greatly hoped." Luther writes: "How can he precede (*prevenire*) God by crying out? And not merely precede, but even 'with untimely haste'? *For it was not yet the day and time of grace, but still premature* and exceedingly early in the morning, when the night of the law was just barely beginning to be over, and the dawn of the new law was near. Thus [it is as though he says] Although I am in a time not yet ripe for crying out, and the spirit is not yet given, who may cry out; and *though grace and the Gospel are not revealed* — nevertheless I cry out. I do it *because I have your promises*. 'In your words I have greatly hoped.'

"For you have promised Christ and his grace; therefore I come early, even before it is given and delivered. And however much I may be unworthy, still you are true, you who have promised. Therefore, I do not come early and cry out because you are a debtor to me, or because I have merited or become worthy of so great a gift (for then I would not be 'coming early,' but would be coming legitimately, demanding my due),

---

63. WA 4.375.4 f.: "iste populus . . . non erat sine . . . gratia."

but because I have hoped in your word. Your mercy in promising has made me daring, so that I ask unseasonably, before any merit." [64]

Luther makes immediate application — *moraliter,* appealing to the Gospel promise just as he did in his exegesis of Ps. 113:1, the promise of Christ ("he who asks, receives."): "Therefore, even though our merits are mute, yet confident and daring we greatly hope in his words, from the mercy of him who promises . . . For if we should approach with merits, then we would not be 'coming early'; in fact, we would not be receiving, but would have already received, and then we would not have to 'cry out,' but would have to give thanks." [65]

64. WA 4.375.14–28 (Sch. Ps. 118:147: "Preveni immaturitate et clamavi: quia in verba tua supersperavi"): "Quomodo potest prevenire deum clamando? Sed non simpliciter prevenit, immo 'in immaturitate.' Nam *nondum erat dies et tempus gratie,* sed adhuc immaturum et valde mane, quando iam fere incipiebat nox legis finiri et prope erat ortus nove legis. Ideo licet sim in tempore nondum apto ad clamandum, nondum datus spiritus, qui clamet, *non revelata gratia et euangelio*: nihilominus clamo, et hoc, quia promissa tua habeo. 'In verba tua supersperavi.' Promisisti enim Christum *et gratia* eius: ideo prevenio quidem *ante datam* et exhibitam, sed utcunque indignus sim, tu tamen verax es, qui promisisti. Neque ideo prevenio et clamo, quia debitor mihi sis, aut ego meruerim aut dignus tanto munere (quia tunc non prevenirem, sed legitime venirem debita poscens), sed quia speravi in verba tua. Misericordia tua promittentis fecit me audacem, ut ante merita et intempestive peterem." (Italics mine.) Repeatedly, it is the promise, rather than grace, that is now being opposed to merit: for example, WA 4.284.3–5, 288.10–12.

65. WA 4.375.31–38: "Ita moraliter nos omnes semper prevenimus immature, quia ad ea, que nondum habemus, in que nos proficiendo extendimus, sumus indigni et gratis accepturi. Sed quid promisit: 'qui petit, accipit: qui querit, invenit': ideo tacitis meritis nostris, de misericordia promittentis confisi et audaces in verba eius supersperamus . . . Si enim cum meritis accederemus, iam non preveniremus, immo non acciperemus, sed iam accepissemus: ideo non clamandum esset, sed gratia agende." (Italics mine.) The contrast of Luther to the tradition is striking here. He alone draws an immediate analogy between the historical and religious situation of the Old Testament petitioner and that of the Christian. Some, following Augustine, suggest as one alternative for a literal interpretation the prophesying (Hugo) and petitioning (Perez only) of the pre-advent *ecclesia* (Augustine). As Hugo says, "dicitur quod prevenit tempus gratie

It is a curious accident of history that the direction in which Luther is going here is toward an ancient figure whose name has appeared often in this book, but whom none of our cast of characters, save Augustine, had read: Tyconius himself. For Tyconius, in his exposition of the third rule, had drawn a qualitative distinction between "Promises and the Law" in the Old Testament itself, using Paul as his guide.[66] But nobody had read Tyconius, and Augustine had felt it necessary to revise his Third Rule in terms of "Spirit and Letter" — that is, law and grace — because he felt Tyconius' theology of promise and law was not adequate to the Pelagian controversy. In making this revision, however, Augustine "buried" Tyconius and established for the whole Middle Ages the doctrine of grace that Luther inherited and which now he is beginning to undermine.[67] Thus, Augustine's reproach of Tyconius now threatens to fall upon Luther, too. Is Luther's promise theology adequate to the Pelagian problem? However one wishes to

---

desiderando adventum christi et prophetando de eodem. Unde sensus est: *Preveni* tempus gratie. *Et clamavi* desiderando adventum christi et prophetando de ipso; *immaturitate* . . . i.e. toto tempore quod fuit ante adventum christi, quod respectu temporis gratie dicitur nox." For Hugo, then, the Old Testament religious situation is contrasted with the Christian situation as night to day; no present relevance of that situation is even considered.

66. See Tyconius, *Liber Regularum* III, "De Promissis et Lege" (pp. 12–31). For example: "semen autem Abrahae non carnale sed spiritale, quod non ex lege sed ex promissione est" (p. 13). "Videmus legem ad promissionem non pertinere nec aliquando alteram in alteram inpegisse sed utramque ordinem suum tenuisse. Quia sicut lex numquam fidei obfuit, ita nec fides legem destruxit" (p. 14). Regarding him who is captive to the law of the members: "[non] aliquando liberari potuit nisi sola gratia per fidem" (p. 15). Finally, "conditio infirmat promissionem" (p. 22). The whole chapter is in this vein and merits further attention.

67. There is no doubt that Augustine was yet to wield heavier influence on Luther, who apparently did not give the anti-Pelagian writings close study until he turned to his next lecture course, on the Romans (see Lohse, "Die Bedeutung Augustins," pp. 124–127). If an intrinsic conflict does indeed exist between Luther's nascent theology of promise and the Augustinian doctrine of grace, the confrontation of the two in the Romans lectures would be an extremely interesting study.

answer, it should be clear that Luther has added a new dimension to the discussion by the virtual substitution of *promissio* for *gratia*.

The Sacraments. — The subversion of the medieval doctrine of grace must also have serious repercussions in the area of sacraments. Again, this is happening because of the efficacy Luther is finding in the "naked" word of promise. Only one text need be brought to bear here, a sort of parable that Luther injects into his programmatic "promise-advent" schema already discussed (Ps. 113:1).

In the middle of this remarkable scholion, Luther adapts for his own use a very common medieval parable: "It is as though a prince or a king of the earth should promise 100 florins to a robber or a murderer, if only that person — when a time and place had been established — having prepared himself, would expect him. In this situation it is evident that that king is a debtor out of his own gratuitous promise and mercy, without any merit on the part of the other; nor would the demerit of that one nullify what the king had promised." [68]

This is a variation on a common example which appears frequently in the systematic exposition of sacramental theology to clarify the relation of the New Testament sacramental rite to the gracious effect that comes with it. In Biel, for example, it functions to illustrate the argument that the sacraments are truly "causes" of the sacramental effects which God, on the basis of his covenant or promise to the Church, produces when they are exhibited.[69] Biel's version of the parable runs: "Thus,

68. WA 4.261.35-39: "sicut si princeps vel rex terre suo latroni aut homicide promitteret centum flo., tantummodo ut ille tempore et loco statuto eum expectaret paratus. Hic patet, quod rex ille debitor esset ex gratuita promissione sua et misericordia sine merito illius, nec demerito illius negaret, quod promisit." I cannot prove that Luther knew the medieval parable referred to. It was a rather common one, however, and a well-educated theologian of that day might be expected to have read it. Moreover, even if Luther invented his parable *de novo*, the comparison is instructive. The parable does not appear in any of the medieval treatments of Ps. 113:1.

69. Biel, IV *Sent.* d.1 q.1 a.1 not.3 E: "posset faciliter dici: quod

if a king should decree that one who has a leaden denarius stamped with the king's seal, should receive from the treasury 100 florins, then that denarius, presented at the treasury, is the cause of the reception of the 100 florins, not from the nature of lead, but solely by the will of the king." [70] Thus, for Biel and his medieval predecessors, the worthless token, solely on the basis of the gracious covenant of God with his Church, becomes an effective sign of the sacramental *res* — a visible sign of invisible grace. There is no intrinsic relationship between the token and the grace given; rather, grace is extrinsic to the token, existing solely in virtue of the will of God, and guaranteed by his *promissio* to the Church.

In Luther's adaptation, the "visible token" — the lead penny — has disappeared; all that one can grasp is the word of promise. The appropriate response is "expectatio," faith in the promising God. Having the promise is already "having everything, although in a hidden way." [71] Again, this represents a subtle but inexorable undermining of the medieval viewpoint. Why? Because in place of Biel's token, which represents the New Testament sacrament, Luther has placed nothing but the Old Testament promise.

Penance and Forgiveness. — Finally, an undermining of grace is occurring in the doctrine of penance. Its examination will bear out the thesis, stated earlier, that Luther's approach

---

sacramenta sunt vere et proprie cause effectus sacramentis, quem deus ex pactione sua cum ecclesia ad eorum exhibitionem producit, et ita salvarentur omnes auctoritates sanctorum [that is, those who taught that the New Testament sacraments cause grace]."

70. IV *Sent.* d.1 q.1 a.1 not.3 E: "ut si rex statueret quod habens denarium blumbeum signo regis signatum, reciperet de camera regis 100 florenos. Denarius ille presentatus ad camera regis causa est receptionis 100 florene, non ex natura blumbi, sed sola voluntate regis." The parable appears also, for example, in Bonaventura, Thomas (twice, rejecting its import), Durandus, and Occam, in support of the sacramental theory normally held in the Franciscan tradition.

71. WA 4.376.15 f.: "in verbis per fidem abscondite sunt res non apparentes, ideo habens verba per fidem habet omnia, licet abscondite."

to the seven penitential Psalms indicated important changes in his exegetical principles. It is now possible to delve deeper into those changes, and to show how the promise of the Old Testament has become of fundamental importance for reshaping the interpretation of these Psalms.

As already shown, Luther equated the penitent with the Old Testament believer, for to be in sin is the same as being "sub lege." Both persons petition for the advent of Christ — in flesh or (for the penitent) in the present. But what specifically is the spiritual advent? In the sacrament of Penance it receives concrete content: the penitent's plea for the spiritual advent is a plea to hear that his sins are forgiven.[72]

The petition cannot be made *in* grace, since it is *for* grace.[73] The grace desired is the forgiveness of sins (not *caritas* or anything else). The remarkable thing is that Luther is here on the very threshold of the "discovery" of absolution as the concrete word which is itself the answer to the penitent's prayer,

72. WA 4.444.17–445.1 (Gl. Ps. 142:8): "*Auditam fac mihi*, i.e. fac ut audiam et sentiam per internam inspirationem, *mane* cito et ante omnia *misericordiam tuam*, i.e., quod remissa per eam sint peccata mea: *quia in te speravi*, quia nullus alius preter te peccata remittit." The marginal gloss on "peccata mea" (444.39–445.26): "Q.d. Da mihi pacem conscientie mee, ut te mihi misertum esse sentiam. 'Auditui meo da gaudium et letitiam' [Ps. 50:10]. Et 'mane' dicit contra 'vespere,' quasi dicat: non caducam et presentis vite, sed crastinam et futuram, que est in spiritu, misericordiam quero."

73. WA 4.301.22–25 (Gl. Ps. 118:147): "indignus sit exaudiri, qui nondum est in gratia: tamen [quasi dicat] 'nimius ardor et desiderium gratie et misericordie cogit me prevenire, maxime quia in verba tu speravi: promisisti enim petentibus gratiam, licet sint indigni.'" Jetter exemplifies the host of scholars eager to "save" Luther when he begins talking about man's *dispositio* for grace: "The disposition is not our striving for grace, but our striving in grace" (*Die Taufe*, p. 246 n. 4). The above text, and several others (for example, WA 4.375.14–28, discussed earlier, and given in n.64 above), show that this comment could hardly be more off the point, since the situation under discussion is that of the Old Testament person who has a problem just because he is "not yet in grace." It is not grace, but only the promise, that stands against merit; see also the "nuda promissio misericordie" of WA 4.329.29, in its context, and the setting of the last penitential Psalm, 142, especially at WA 4.443.24–26.

to be received with faith: the word of forgiveness.[74] Absolution is not mentioned explicitly, but Luther's interpretation suggests it, and perhaps assumes it: one prays to hear the spoken word of forgiveness, and to sense and feel (*sentire*) by the Spirit's *inspiratio* that his sins are indeed forgiven.[75]

Luther regards with wonder the Old Testament petitioner who asks only for a word, the Gospel.[76] He goes on to allude to the things "hidden" in the words, reminding the reader at first of that grace "hidden" in the sacramental signs — until he reminds his readers that the hidden thing is not grace but the future itself which God will bring.[77] Luther now contrasts the Old and New Testaments as follows: the Old Testament promises a word (*iustitia*), while the New promises a *res* (*premium eternum*).[78] "Grace" in all this — grace in the traditional sense — has no particular role among the theological ideas now in force. Thus, promise and *pactum*, rather than grace, are opposed to merit throughout the exposition.

The significance of this reorientation in Luther's thought has not generally been appreciated by Luther scholars trying to explain away the apparent "Pelagian" direction of Luther's thought.[79] A frequent *apologia* offered for Luther was to ex-

---

74. Bizer, *Fides*, pp. 102–114, dates this discovery 1518, with Luther's *Resolutiones disputationum de indulgentiarum virtute* (WA 1.522–628).

75. In WA 4.444.17–445.1, given in n. 72, it may be that both the "hearing" and the "sensing" are "per internam inspirationem," but I think it more likely that only the latter is. The ears seem to be coming into their own; they receive and understand the message, and the Spirit confirms it.

76. WA 4.376.13–15: "Mira est enim hec petitio, non nisi verba peti a deo, non res, sed signa rerum. Quis enim pro verbis tam anxie unquam clamavit?"

77. WA 4.376.15 f.: "Sed quia in verbis per fidem abscondite sunt res non apparentes, ideo habens verba per fidem habet omnia, licet abscondite."

78. WA 4.458.4–10.

79. Axel Gyllenkrok labeled the scholion on Ps. 113:1 as among "the worst rocks of offense" for Luther scholars (*Rechtfertigung und Heiligung* [Uppsala, 1952], p. 40 n. 2). It was no problem to Gyllenkrok himself, since he judged this Luther still "medieval." Most scholars saw Luther's

plain that he had not yet encountered — or at least studied — Augustine's anti-Pelagian writings,[80] which are so much in evidence in the next exegetical writing of Luther's (on Romans); and that therefore his anthropology had not properly been straightened out. The problem with this approach, however, was that in general it failed to see that the classic terms of the Augustine-Pelagius debate — grace, merit, and free will, which had not changed for a thousand years — were already being altered by the introduction into the discussion of the word of promise. Luther's real answer to the Pelagian question cannot properly be assessed without consideration of this new element.

adherence to the *facere quod in se est* doctrine as his last surviving link with Nominalism and took it as their task to show that Luther did not really adhere to it any more. See, for example, Karl Holl, *Luther* (*Gesammelte Aufsätze* I [Tübingen, 1921]), p. 132 n. 6, and Vogelsang, *Luthers Christologie,* p. 70. Vogelsang argues that the *facere quod* is present only "terminologisch," although "sachlich" it has been overcome by Luther's tropological hermeneutic. Vogelsang would be hard put to explain, then, why tropology is more characteristic of the early *Dictata,* while the *facere quod* business appears more frequently in the later part. Rudolf Hermann rightly recognized the redemptive-historical framework of the passage and labeled the *dispositio* as essentially "Adventsgesinnung (*Luthers These "Gerecht und Sünder zugleich"* [Gütersloh, 1930], pp. 240 f.). Wilhelm Link disposed of the *dispositio* too conveniently by asserting that it is simply God's promise (*Das Ringen Luthers um die Freiheit der Theologie von der Philosophie* [München, 1955], pp. 198 f.). Lief Grane argues that Luther's uniqueness comes through in his understanding of man's *Dasein* as "always preparation" ("Vorbereitung"; *Contra Gabrielem* [Gyldendal, 1962], p. 299). But he gives no explanation for the fact that Luther's favorite authority for this outlook is Bernard of Clairvaux: see *WA* 3.105.19–22; 4.350.14–16, 364.17 f.; 55/2.64.5 f. (1516). For a proper interpretation of this text one should affirm at the outset that, far from being an offensive remnant of medieval theology, this text is one of the most important and pregnant indicators of a new theology. Like the Nominalist ideas it finds helpful, it is indeed subversive of the medieval doctrine of grace – but that is exactly what makes it new.

80. But see Lohse, "Die Bedeutung Augustins," for evidence of Luther's familiarity, before 1515, with the main outlines of Augustine's anti-Pelagian position.

CONCLUSION

In his first course as a professor in Bible, Luther's task was to provide an interpretation of his text that would be both learned and edifying for his Christian audience. Although the text was an Old Testament book, his first response was to abandon it, in effect, in favor of the New Testament. He outdid the whole tradition, from Augustine to Faber, both in his christological interpretation and in setting up an opposition between the "historical" sense and his "prophetic" interpretation. As he was at length to discover, however, he could not carry through this plan and at the same time do justice to the Old Testament text, for "all its goods" were not in present grace and spirit, but in future "words and promises." When Luther awakened to this fact and began hearing the testimony of pre-advent Israel, the result was not only the theological recovery of the Old Testament but the eloquent first themes of an emerging Reformation theology.

Promise played a critical role in every step of that Old Testament recovery and became the heart of the new theology. The new *sensus propheticus* became the word of the Old Testament prophet addressed to his own people (not to Christ or, occultly, to Christians), exhorting them to future hope on the basis of the testimonies. A new normative-literal sense — *testimonium* or promise — became all-embracing for the whole Bible, outweighing in importance the traditional *doctrina* and *lex*. A future-oriented hermeneutical structure, based on God's promise and three advents of Christ, began to threaten the traditional fourfold structure, whose dynamic of signification presupposed a future that was dark and unknown, save to an elite few. The "hermeneutical divide" between letter and spirit was lifted out of its traditional law-grace, Old Testament-New Testament terms and planted in the Old Testament itself, whose "spirit" now appeared *simul* in its letter, that is, in its inviolable promise of the future, unconditioned by the law of Moses and the failure of Israel.

Out of the theological and historical limbo of "umbra" to which the people of Israel had been consigned in most medieval exegesis, a "remnant" emerged, which Luther called the "faithful synagogue," and which became the concrete example to which even the Christian church itself should conform. The word of promise, and faith as *expectatio,* gradually undercut tropology as the "sensus ultimatus" of Luther's exegesis, allowing the letter — the clear and naked words of the text — to take on a theological significance not accorded them before, and requiring not grace as *intellectus* and *caritas,* but faith. It was the word of promise, not *conformitas christi* via tropological signification, that led Luther away from medieval theology to the exclusive *"sola* fide" and *"solo* verbo" of Reformation theology.

It is clear that opposing Luther in this development was the mainstream of the medieval hermeneutical tradition — its hermeneutical theory (with no future import in its letter), its understanding of letter and spirit (in Old-New Testament terms), and its overall description (*figura*) and evaluation ("carnal") of the Old Testament, its word and its faith. It is also clear that Luther began his course in agreement with these earlier views, as he labored under the guidance of the best names in the tradition. And the most curious thing is what happened between Luther and Nicholas of Lyra. It was the "judaizing" Lyra, together with his rabbis, whom Luther had singled out for special attack in his preface, written in the summer of 1513. But in the end, it was Lyra to whom, in spite of himself, Luther would have to return, at least insofar as the historical and pre-Christian situation of the Old Testament author became the "letter" — that is, insofar as the Old Testament became the text that Luther was actually interpreting. Conversely, his early favorite Faber Stapulensis, perhaps the most Christ-minded of all Luther's exemplars, had eventually to be abandoned, even though his technical assistance continued to be welcome in Luther's next course, on the Romans.

Where, then, did Luther get his new hermeneutic and the structural members of a new theology? The best explanation for this recovery of the Old Testament, and for the theological adjustments that went with it, is that it came about from trying to exegete the Old Testament text itself. Among all of Luther's sources, the Old Testament itself seems to have been the one that finally cut through the "prophetic" morass of his rich but confusing christological interpretation. At Psalm 118 the Old Testament addressed him with its *testimonia, eloquia, petitio,* and *spes* and finally induced him to take theological account of it. The Old Testament led him to see that he was still "as if" (*ac si*) an Old Testament man, insofar as he had not yet attained, and God had not yet given, that which had been promised. Indeed, it was the Old Testament that unveiled the real situation of the Christian church as like the situation of the "faithful synagogue"; even the Church was not yet the "reale quid Israel" but a *testimonium* and promise of the eschatological Israel. In the Old Testament he found the "simul" that characterizes authentic Christian existence which, subjected to all the contradictions (*contraria*) of real life, must grasp, as its entire good, the words and promises of God.

The medieval hermeneutical tradition, by contrast, was beset with ideas that worked against the Old Testament functioning theologically in the canon. The *sensus litteralis* tended to be reduced to the *sensus historicus,* especially as regards the Old Testament, and hence irretrievably past. The *historia* by itself, and therefore the words that narrated and interpreted it, bore no message for any time beyond its own — and what it said to its own time even tended to be deceiving because it was *figura.* The letter was without spirit, without theological meaning for the future. And thus, for the situation in which the Christian exegete found himself centuries later, it was "unedifying."

Earnest attempts were launched to make the historical and literal sense the foundation and norm of interpretation, and with some remarkable results, especially in the Victorine school, Thomas, Lyra, and Burgos. But the fourfold hermeneutical structure programmatically distracted medieval exegetes from expecting anything of theological value to appear in the Old Testament letter. A little *lex,* a little *doctrina* — that was about all. The value was in the spiritual senses. *Allegoria* for what is to be believed concerning Christ and the Church, *tropologia* for what is to be done in Christian life, *anagogia* for heavenly mysteries to which Christians tend — these carried all the theological freight. This meant that the New Testament, which was universally acknowledged to be the spiritual meaning and goal of the Old, became its "true" letter, the text and source for all its theological and spiritual content.

The fact that the *sensus litteralis* only signified the future, but did not yet reach out to embrace it in any certain declaration of the divine intention, became the most severe problem for Luther's peculiar use of tropology. For the way he interpreted it, its whole efficacy depended on what God intended to do with the person, not on what the person could do. Luther believed Christ's cross and resurrection signified and in some sense caused, *tropologice,* his own repentance and forgiveness. Although in penitential self-annihilation he could perhaps discover himself being conformed to the cross, the rest had to be conjecture. How was one to know whether God was really committed to carry this *conformitas Christi* through cross and hell to the *gaudium, libertas,* and *certitudo* that lay beyond? Did God work as tropolgy and anagogy worked?

The letter of Scripture was no help for Luther precisely

because it supposedly spoke of nothing but Christ. The letter — even the promises — were actually addressed to Christ; they only "signified" Luther. But then he began to notice the literal word about the future — the *testimonia dei*, the *promissiones* in which God's word was addressed to his people. And Luther could find in the letter the response as well: the *petitio*, the sighing and joy and certainty that God had really laid his own honor on the line, committed himself, so that faith might not be betrayed.

Discovering this, Luther discovered "his" Gospel: the promising word. "Gospel" would no longer be called "grace"; the Gospel was a certain kind of word. Furthermore, grace was not required to make the words "spiritually" intelligible and operative, for they were all too unambiguous and clear in themselves. The old dichotomy of "word" and "meaning," modeled on the sacramental sign and *res*, and described in terms of killing letter and life-giving spirit, lost its predominant role.

And now — to the consternation of many Luther scholars — a new kind of *facere quod in se est* seemed to appear (a new Pelagianism?). Grace was being subverted; its traditional vocabulary and conception had become ill-suited to express Luther's new understanding of words and the emerging theology of promise. Grace as supernatural and invisible *res* had little place in the theological picture, just as it could have no place in honest explication of the Old Testament, which had become Luther's real text in historical (that is, pre-grace) terms.

The change in fundamental hermeneutical structure seemed to be undermining the Augustinian doctrine of grace that Luther had inherited from the Middle Ages, and the effect of this subversion became visible in the contexts of both justification and sacraments. In neither of these central areas of theology could the old categories and language any longer bear the weight of what Luther had been learning.

APPENDIX

BIBLIOGRAPHY

INDEX

APPENDIX. Occurrences of *Pactum* and *Promissio* in the *Dictata*

The following tables list by page and line all occurrences of *pactum* and forms of the verb *pango*, as well as *foedus, promissio*, and forms of the verb *promitto* which appear in Luther's *Dictata super Psalterium*. For the first fifteen Psalms, I use the new critical edition (*WA* 55/1 and 2); for Psalms 16–150, I use *WA* 3.108.31 – 4.462.26. Occurrences in the *Adnotationes* to Faber's Psalter, 4.463 ff., are not included here.

PANGO, PACTUM	FOEDUS [1]
\multicolumn{2}{c}{WA 3 [2]}	

PANGO, PACTUM	FOEDUS [1]
144.24	
282.5,15	
289.3 (twice),5,6,7,8,10	
(*not* 368.20: read *preterita* for *pacta*) [3]	
	395.13 *federati*
489.20	
491.10	
497.1,2 (twice), 4	
508.27	
(558.7: in the Ps. text, Ps. 77:57)	558.18

1. Whenever a relevant word occurs that is not a form of the noun *foedus*, it is also listed.
2. There are no occurrences in *WA* 55/1 and 2.
3. So Meissinger, *Luthers Exegese*, p. 8, confirmed by a personal letter from Dr. Reinhard Schwarz (Tübingen, Oct. 9, 1965), one of the editors of the new edition.

WA 3 (cont.)

583.8	
	607.14
626.5	626.5 with *Bundt*
629.24	629.24

WA 4

37.29 (quoting Isa. 55:3)	
40.15	
41.2,21 (quoting Jer. 31:32), 28,29	
44.13	
49.4	
	85.22
92.27	
165.20	
201.23 (quoting Num. 25:12 f.)	201.23 (quoting Num. 25:12 f.)
203.16	
(244.19: *pactum* occurs in Jer. 32:40, cited but not quoted)	
262.7	
300.11 (quoting Prov. 2:17)	
312.41	
329.35	
344.2,3	
350.13	350.13
443.31	

PROMISSIO	PROMITTO

WA 55/1

50.7

WA 55/1 (cont.)
    80.19
    86.17

WA 55/2 [4]
    3.16
    10.7
    15.9
    76.16

WA 3
    113.31
    119.27,29

123.9
    128.19
138.6
    150.11
164.26   164.2
    167.3,11
    171.6
    183.7,8,9,10
    199.16,17,33
    207.34
    209.33
226.15   226.8,11
234.13
237.13   237.10 f.,12
238.1
241.13
242.1
243.3

4. All the occurrences in WA 55/2 are in material that scholars agree comes from 1516. See the summary of Gordon Rupp, *The Righteousness of God* (London, 1953), p. 130 n. 6; the Weimar editor's introduction, WA 55/1, p. 16*.

278 | APPENDIX

245.5 f.[5]	WA 3 (cont.)
	274.5
	274.7 f.
	279.3
	284.25
	289.5
295.34	
	299.27
	302.15
310.30	
(312.23: in the Ps. text, Ps. 55:9)	312.22
313.1	313.27
	317.11
318.16	318.15
	(329.34 *polliceretur*)
332.11	
	335.1
	341.18
	347.26
	351.17,35,36,38
	353.32
	359.10
	364.20
	377.3 (three times),33
382.26	382.18 f.,29
	384.34
387.38 (quoting Acts 2:33)	
393.15	
	400.1
	412.18 (twice),33,34
(436.35 *promissor*)	436.37
	437.1,7

5. The *f.* always indicates a divided word, not a second occurrence.

APPENDIX | 279

   WA 3 (cont.)
     452.11
     461.4
     476.17 f.
     477.25
     479.23
     497.5
     502.20
506.14 f.
     548.28
     549.3
553.38
554.20
557.10
558.2
561.7   561.12
     568.37
     572.16
577.21
     585.12
590.13
605.6
     609.20
     612.33
631.10
633.25

   WA 4
     2.20,23,35,39 f.
     6.14
     8.40
13.8   9.23 f.
13.12 (quoting Lyra) 13.6,7,8 f.,9,14,15,17
      (twice),19,21,25,26
     14.20,23,24,34

	WA 4 (cont.)
	15.2,8,9,13,15,17 (twice), 19,21,28 f.
17.23,36	17.11,14,16,18,31,37
	21.29
	22.10,11,32
37.32	37.5,9,12
	38.5,29
	39.18
40.1,15	
41.14,17,20	41.3,15
	43.16
	46.22
50.20	
	70.25
73.2	
	74.14 f.
79.32	79.28
	92.4
100.24	
	101.16
	104.26
	105.40
	116.22 f.
	117.31,32 (twice)
	118.1,18
	120.28
	121.9
	124.7
	127.16,17,18,20
	140.26
	144.4,22 (quoting Rom. 1:2)
	159.11 (twice)
160.17	

WA 4 (cont.)
                    163.2
                    164.14
                    165.36 f.
                    189.36 f.
193.23   193.11,13,17,19,33,36,37
195.37 f.   195.13,38
197.1   197.2
201.1,10,32   201.1,5
                    203.15 f.
204.17
                    215.17
                    216.32
                    218.26
                    220.11 (twice)
                    231.27
                    236.24
                    237.37
                    244.18
                    245.18,33,36
251.26,27   251.1,5
                    256.30
                    258.6,8,10
260.2
261.33,38   261.26,29,36,39
262.1,6,12,28   262.2,7,20,23
                    266.18
                    271.25
                    272.17
                    273.30
278.21 (quoting Gal. 3:22)
                    284.4 [6]

6. All occurrences listed from here to 391.25 (inclusive) belong to the exegesis of Psalm 118. They constitute more than one-fourth of all occurrences in the *Dictata*.

	WA 4 (cont.)
	285.11
	286.3,4,34
287.3 f.,4	287.2 f.,5,8
288.11	288.11
	289.11
	290.13
	291.3,9
	294.10
	295.17
	296.9,13,15,16
	298.1,2,7,10,36 f.
	301.4 (twice),24
	302.8,15,18
303.25	303.3,22,26,34,38,39
	304.7,35,37
	305.20
	306.15 (quoting Gal. 3:23)
	310.27
312.41	
	320.35
	322.21 (twice),22,22 f.,26
	324.37
	325.24,25
329.29	329.35
330.24	
	331.25 f.,32
332.15	332.11,19 f.
	333.32
	334.28,29
	335.39
	337.3
	341.28,31 (twice),32
	343.10,36
344.26	344.2,3

WA 4 (cont.)

	345.21
346.28	346.26
347.4	347.37
348.1	
	350.27
	360.6,7,9,28,29,31,32
	361.33
	364.37,38 (twice)
	365.2
373.6	373.9
	375.5 f.,21,22,24,27,33,34
	376.8,34
	377.26
	379.15,27
380.36	380.16
	381.40
382.7	382.35
	388.30 f.
389.21	389.20 f.,22 f.,25,29,29 f., 37,38
391.24 f.,25	391.8
393.38	
396.26	396.11
398.37	398.10
	399.25
400.4	
	402.25,32
	403.5
408.25	408.26
	410.5
	412.36 f.
	413.6
	419.8,11,24
	421.5,5 f.,23

WA 4 (cont.)
$422.1^{8},33$
423.31
426.20
$431.6,12$
432.24
435.3^{2}
443.30
$443.^{8},9,31$
446.3
451.9
452.36
453.33 $453.20,34$ (twice)
457.3^{8} 457.12 (twice)
461.5

BIBLIOGRAPHY

PRIMARY SOURCES

Altenstaig, Johannes. *Vocabularius theologie.* Hagenau, 1517.
Augustine. *De doctrina christiana libri quattuor,* in CSEL 80. Vienna, 1963. (Trans. D. W. Robertson. *On Christian Doctrine.* New York, 1958.)
———. *Ennarrationes in Psalmos,* in CChr 39 and 40. Turnholti, 1956.
———. *De spiritu et littera liber unus,* in CSEL 60. Vienna, 1913. (Trans. John Burnaby. *The Spirit and the Letter,* in LCC 8. Philadelphia, 1955.)
Bernard of Clairvaux. *Sermones in adventu domini,* in PL 183.
Biblia . . . cum glosa ordinaria, et litterali moralique expositione [= Postilla] Nicolai de lyra, necnon additionibus [Pauli] Burgensis, ac replicis Thoringi [Matthias Doering]. Basle, 1502.
Biel, Gabriel. *Canonis Misse Expositio,* ed. H. A. Oberman and W. J. Courtenay, 4 vols. Wiesbaden, 1963 ff.
———. *Collectorium in quattuor libros sententiarum.* Basel, 1512.
Bonaventura. *De reductione artium ad theologiam,* in *Tria Opuscula.* Quaracchi, 1938.
———. *Liber IV Sententiarum,* in *Opera Omnia* I–IV. Quaracchi, 1882–1902.
Cassian, John. *Conlationes* XXIIII, in CSEL 13/2. Vienna, 1886.
Cassiodorus. *Expositio in Psalterium,* in CChr 97 and 98. Turnholti, 1958
Doering, Matthias. *Replicae.* See *Biblia.*

Duns Scotus, John. *Ordinatio,* in *Opera Omnia,* ed. P. C. Balić, I. Civitas Vaticana, 1950.

——. *Quaestiones in IV Libros Sententiarum,* in *Opera Omnia,* Vivès ed., VIII–XVI. Paris, 1891–1895.

Durand de Saint-Pourçain, Guillaume. *Commentaria in IV Libros Sententiarum.* Lyon, 1562.

Faber Stapulensis, Jacobus. *Quincuplex Psalterium.* Paris, 1513.

Gerson, Jean Charlier de. *De sensu litterali Sacrae Scripturae,* in *Oeuvres Complètes,* ed. P. Glorieux, III. Paris, 1962.

Gregory of Rimini. *Super Primum et Secundum Sententiarum.* Venice, 1522 (reprinted New York, 1955).

Hugo de S. Caro Cardinalis. *Biblia Latina cum postilla.* Basel, 1504.

Hugh of Saint Victor, *Didascalicon de studio legendi.* A critical text ed. C. H. Buttimer. Washington, D. C., 1939. (Trans. Jerome Taylor. *The Didascalicon.* New York and London, 1961.)

——. *De sacramentis Christianae fidei,* in PL 176. (Trans. R. J. Deferrari. *On the Sacraments of the Christian Faith.* Cambridge, Mass., 1951.)

——. *De scripturis et scriptoribus sacris,* in PL 175.

Isidore of Seville. *Sententiarum Libri* [*de summo bono*], in PL 83.

Lombard, Peter. *Glossa Psalterii,* in PL 191.

——. *Libri IV Sententiarum,* 2 vols. 2nd ed., Quaracchi, 1916.

Luther, Martin. *Dictata super Psalterium,* in WA 55/1 and 2 (Weimar, 1963) for Pss. 1–15; WA 3 and 4 (Weimar, 1885 f.) for Pss. 16–150.

——. Marginal Glosses on Augustine and Lombard, in WA 9.

Nicholas of Lyra. *Postilla.* See *Biblia.*

Paul of Burgos. *Additiones.* See *Biblia.*

Perez of Valencia, James. *Centum ac quinquaginta psalmi Davidici.* Lyon, 1514.
Prierias, Silvester de. *Aurea Rosa super evangelia totius anni: Tractatus primus.* Venice, 1582.
Thomas Aquinas. *Commentum in quattuor libros sententiarum,* in *Opera Omnia* VI and VII. Parma, 1858.
———. *Quaestiones Quadlibetales,* in *Opera Omnia* IX. Parma, 1859.
———. *Summa Theologiae,* ed. Commissio Piana, 5 vols. Ottawa, 1953.
Totting, Henry, of Oyta. *Quaestio de sacra scriptura et de veritatibus catholicis,* ed. Albertus Lang. Münster, 1953.
Tyconius. *The Book of Rules* [*Liber Regularum*], ed. F. C. Burkitt (*Texts and Studies,* ed. J. A. Robinson, III, no. 1). Cambridge, 1894.
William of Occam. *Quodlibeta Septem.* Strassbourg, 1491 (reprinted Louvain, 1962).
———. *Super IV Libros Sententiarum,* in *Opera Plurima* III and IV. Lyon, 1495 (reprinted London, 1962).

SECONDARY SOURCES

Medieval Studies

Brown, R. E. *The 'Sensus Plenior' of Sacred Scripture.* Baltimore, 1955.
Caplan, Harry. "The Four Senses of Scriptural Interpretation and the Medieval Theology of Preaching," *Speculum* 4 (1929), 282–290.
Denzinger, Henricus. *Enchiridion Symbolorum,* 32nd ed. Freiburg, 1963.
Dobschütz, Ernst von. "Vom vierfachen Schriftsinn," in *Harnack Ehrung* (Beiträge zur Kirchengeschichte ihrem Lehrer Adolf von Harnack zu seinem siebzigsten Geburts-

tage [7. Mai 1921] dargebracht von einer Reihe seiner Schüler). Leipzig, 1921, pp. 1–13.

Ebeling, Gerhard. *Evangelische Evangelienauslegung.* München, 1942.

———. "The Hermeneutical Locus of the Doctrine of God in Peter Lombard and Thomas Aquinas." *JThC* 3 (1967), 70–111.

———. "Hermeneutik," *RGG*³ III (1959), 242–262.

Hahn, Fritz. "Zur Hermeneutik Gersons," *ZThK* 51 (1954), 34–50.

Hailperin, Herman. *Rashi and the Christian Scholars.* Pittsburgh, 1963.

Hanson, R. P. C. *Allegory and Event.* London, 1959.

Haubst, Rudolf. *Die Christologie des Nikolaus von Kues.* Freiburg, 1956.

Landgraf, Artur. "Die Gnadenökonomie des Alten Bundes nach der Lehre der Frühscholastik," *ZKT* 57 (1933), 215–253.

Lubac, Henri de. *Exégèse Médiévale: les quatre sens de L'Écriture.* Paris, 1959–1964.

Mailhiot, M.-D. "La pensée de S. Thomas sur le sens spirituel," *Revue Thomiste* 59 (1959), 613–663.

Oberman, Heiko A. " 'Facientibus quod in se est Deus non denegat gratiam.' Robert Holcot O.P. and the Beginnings of Luther's Theology," *HTR* 55 (1962), 317–342.

———. *Forerunners of the Reformation: The Shape of Late Medieval Thought Illustrated by Key Documents.* Translations by Paul L. Nyhus. New York, 1966.

———. *The Harvest of Medieval Theology.* Cambridge, 1963.

———. " 'Iustitia Christi' and 'Iustitia Dei': Luther and the Scholastic Doctrines of Justification," *HTR* 59 (1966), 1–26.

———. "Quo Vadis? Tradition from Irenaeus to Humani

Generis," *Scottish Journal of Theology* 16 (1963), 225–255.

O'Malley, John W. "A Note on Gregory of Rimini: Church, Scripture, Tradition," *Augustinianum* 5 (1965), 365–378.

Pépin, Jean. "S. Augustin et la fonction protreptique de l'allégorie," *Recherches Augustiniennes* 1 (1958), 243–286.

Pontet, Maurice. *L'Exégèse de S. Augustin Prédicateur.* Paris, 1944.

Posthumus Meyjes, G.H.M. *Jean Gerson: zijn Kerkpolitiek en Ecclesiologie.* The Hague, 1963.

Rosenthal, Frank. "Heinrich von Oyta and Biblical Criticism in the Fourteenth Century," *Speculum* 25 (1950), 178–183.

Smalley, Beryl. "The Bible in the Middle Ages," in D. E. Nineham, ed., *The Church's Use of the Bible, Past and Present.* London, 1963, pp. 57–71.

―――. "Gilbertus Universalis, Bishop of London (1128–34), and the Problem of the 'Glossa Ordinaria,'" *Recherches de Théologie Ancienne et Médiévale* 7 (1935), 235–262; 8 (1936), 24–60; 9 (1937), 365–400.

―――. *The Study of the Bible in the Middle Ages,* 2nd ed. Notre Dame, 1964.

Spicq, P. C. *Esquisse d'une histoire de L'Exégèse Latine au Moyen age.* Paris, 1944.

Strauss, Gerhard. *Schriftgebrauch, Schriftauslegung und Schriftbeweis bei Augustin.* Tübingen, 1959.

Synave, P. "La Doctrine de S. Thomas d'Aquin sur le sens littéral des Écritures," *Revue Biblique* 35 (1926), 40–65.

Torrance, T. F. "Scientific Hermeneutics According to St. Thomas Aquinas," *Journal of Theological Studies* 13 (1962), 259–289.

Vignaux, Paul. *Justification et prédestination au XIVe siècle:*

Duns Scot, Pierre d'Auriole, Guillaume d'Occam, Grégoire de Rimini. Paris, 1934.
———. *Luther Commentateur des Sentences*. Paris, 1935.
Werbeck, Wilfrid. *Jacobus Perez von Valencia: Untersuchungen zu seinem Psalmenkommentar*. Tübingen, 1959.

Luther Studies

Bauer, Karl. *Die Wittenberger Universitätstheologie und die Anfänge der deutschen Reformation*. Tübingen, 1928.
Beintker, Horst. "Neues Material über die Beziehungen Luthers zum mittelalterlichen Augustinismus," *ZKG* 68 (1957), 144–148.
Bizer, Ernst. "Die Entdeckung des Sakraments durch Luther," *EvTh* 17 (1957), 64–90.
———. *Fides ex Auditu*, 3rd ed. Neukirchen, 1966.
Boehmer, Heinrich. *Luthers Erste Vorlesung*. Leipzig, 1924.
Bornkamm, Heinrich. *Luther und das Alte Testament*. Tübingen, 1948.
———. "Iustitia Dei in der Scholastik und bei Luther," *ARG* 33 (1942), 1–46.
———. "Zur Frage der Iustitia Dei beim jungen Luther," *ARG* 52 (1961), 16–22, and 53 (1962), 1–60.
Brandenburg, Albert. *Gericht und Evangelium: zur Wortheologie in Luthers erster Psalmenvorlesung*. Paderborn, 1960.
Ebeling, Gerhard. "Die Anfänge von Luthers Hermeneutik," *ZThK* 48 (1951), 172–230.
———. *Evangelische Evangelienauslegung*. München, 1942.
———. "Hermeneutik," *RGG* [3] III (1959), 242–262.
———. "Luthers Auslegung des 14.(15.) Psalms in der ersten Psalmenvorlesung im Vergleich mit der exegetischen Tradition," *ZThK* 50 (1953), 280–339.

———. "Luthers Auslegung des 44.(45.) Psalms," in Vilmos Vajta, ed., *Lutherforschung Heute.* Berlin, 1958, pp. 32–48.

———. "Luthers Psalterdruck vom Jahre 1513," *ZThK* 50 (1953), 43–99.

———. "The New Hermeneutics and the Young Luther," *Theology Today* 21 (1964), 34–46.

Grane, Lief. *Contra Gabrielem: Luthers Auseinandersetzung mit Gabriel Biel in der Disputatio Contra Scholasticam Theologiam, 1517.* Gyldendal, 1962.

Gyllenkrok, Axel. *Rechfertigung und Heiligung in der frühen evangelischen Theologie Luthers.* Uppsala, 1952.

Hägglund, Bengt. *Theologie und Philosophie bei Luther und in der occamistischen Tradition.* Lund, 1955.

Hahn, Fritz. "Faber Stapulensis und Luther." *ZKG* 57 (1938), 356–442.

———. "Die Heilige Schrift als Problem der Auslegung bei Luther," *EvTh* 10 (1951), 407–424.

Hermann, Rudolf. *Luthers These 'Gerecht und Sünder zugleich': eine systematische Untersuchung.* Gütersloh, 1930.

Herntrich, Volkmar. "Luther und das Alte Testament," *Luther-Jahrbuch* 20 (1938), 93–124.

Holl, Karl. "Luthers Bedeutung für den Fortschritt der Auslegungskunst," in *Luther* (*Gesammelte Aufsätze zur Kirchengeschichte,* I), 7th ed. Tübingen, 1948, pp. 544–582.

Iserloh, Erwin. "'Existentiale Interpretation' in Luthers erster Psalmenvorlesung?" *Theologische Revue* 59 (1963), 73–84.

Jetter, Werner. *Die Taufe beim jungen Luther.* Tübingen, 1954.

Link, Wilhelm. *Das Ringen Luthers um die Freiheit der Theologie von der Philosophie.* München, 1955.

Lohse, Bernhard. "Die Bedeutung Augustins für den jungen Luther," *KuD* 11 (1965), 116-135.
Maurer, Wilhelm. "Kirche und Geschichte nach Luthers Dictata super Psalterium," in Vilmos Vajta, ed., *Lutherforschung Heute*. Berlin, 1958, pp. 85-101.
Meissinger, K. A. *Luthers Exegese in der Frühzeit*. Leipzig, 1911.
Metzger, Günther. *Gelebter Glaube: Die Formierung reformatorischen Denkens in Luthers erster Psalmenvorlesung, dargestellt am Begriff des Affekts*. Göttingen, 1964.
Müller, Gerhard. "Die Einheit der Theologie des jungen Luther," in F. W. Kantzenbach and Gerhard Müller, eds., *Reformatio und Confessio*. Berlin and Hamburg, 1965, pp. 37-51.
Müller, Gerhard. "Neuer Literatur zur Theologie des jungen Luther," *KuD* 11 (1965), 325-357.
Oberman, H. A. " 'Facientibus quod in se est Deus non denegat gratiam.' Robert Holcot O.P. and the Beginnings of Luther's Theology," *HTR* 55 (1962), 317-342.
———. " 'Iustitia Christi' and 'Iustitia Dei': Luther and the Scholastic Doctrines of Justification," *HTR* 59 (1966), 1-26.
———. " 'Simul Gemitus et Raptus': Luther und die Mystik," in Ivar Asheim, ed., *The Church, Mysticism, Sanctification and the Natural in Luther's Thought*. Philadelphia, 1967, pp. 20-59.
Pelikan, J. *Luther the Expositor*. St. Louis, 1959.
Pinomaa, L. *Register der Bibelzitate in Luthers Schriften in den Jahren 1509-1519*. Mimeographed, Helsinki, 1952.
Prenter, Regin. *Der Barmherzige Richter: Iustitia dei passiva in Luthers Dictata super Psalterium, 1513-1515*. Copenhagen, 1961.
———. *Spiritus Creator*. Trans. J. M. Jensen. Philadelphia, 1953. For footnotes, see the German edition, München, 1954.

Preus, James S. "Old Testament *Promissio* and Luther's New Hermeneutic," *HTR* 60 (1967), 145–161.
Raeder, Siegfried. *Das Hebräische bei Luther untersucht bis zum Ende der ersten Psalmenvorlesung.* Tübingen, 1961.
Rost, Gerhard. "Der Gedanke der Gleichförmigkeit mit dem leidenden Christus in der Frömmigkeit des jungen Luther." *Lutherischer Rundblick* 11 (1963), 2–12.
Rupp, Gordon. *The Righteousness of God: Luther Studies.* London, 1953.
Saarnivaara, Uuras. *Luther Discovers the Gospel.* St. Louis, 1951.
Saint-Blancat, Louis. "Recherches sur les sources de la théologie Luthérienne primitive," *Verbum Caro* 8 (1954), 81–91.
———. "La Théologie de Luther et un nouveau plagiat de Pierre d'Ailly," *Positions Luthériennes* 4 (1956), 61–81.
Scheel, Otto, ed. *Dokumente zu Luthers Entwicklung (bis 1519),* 2nd ed. Tübingen, 1929.
———. *Martin Luther vom Katholizismus zur Reformation,* II. 3rd and 4th eds. Tübingen, 1930.
Schwarz, Reinhard. *Fides, Spes und Caritas beim jungen Luther unter besonderer Berucksichtigung der mittelalterlichen Tradition.* Berlin, 1962.
Schwarz, W. *Principles and Problems of Biblical Translation: Some Reformation Controversies and Their Background.* Cambridge, England, 1955.
Stange, Carl. *Die Anfänge der Theologie Luthers.* Berlin, 1957.
Vignaux, Paul. *Luther Commentateur des Sentences.* Paris, 1935.
Vogelsang, Erich, ed. *Der junge Luther (Luthers Werke in Auswahl,* ed. Otto Clemen, V). Berlin, 1955.
———. *Die Anfänge von Luthers Christologie nach der ersten Psalmenvorlesung.* Berlin and Leipzig, 1929.
Volz, Hans. "Luthers Arbeit am lateinischen Psalter," *ARG* 48 (1957), 11–56.

INDEX

Abraham, 109, 115, 206, 207, 208
Absolution, 263-264
Acceptatio, 2, 3
Advent(s) of Christ: historical, 19, 20, 114, 116, 156, 163, 171, 172, 173, 178, 179, 210; and value of OT, 20, 156, 210; eschatological, 22, 114, 170, 237; spiritual, or tropological, 170, 178, 225, 236-237, 263
Affectus, 255
Allegory, *allegoria*, 21, 26, 31, 36, 41; OT as, 15, 84, 104, 106, 109, 112, 115-117; history as, 122; place of, in hermeneutics, 240-241. *See also* Fourfold sense
Amor, 42, 46, 123. *See also Caritas*
Anagogy, *anagoge, anagogia*, 21, 22, 26, 36, 40-41, 58; in Luther, 146n, 148, 170. *See also* Fourfold sense
Analogy, analogies, 46, 94, 172-173, 209-210
Anselm of Laon, 26
Aquinas, Saint Thomas, 46-60, 80, 90, 99, 111, 122; justification by grace in, 49, 128; and Scotus, 62-65; and Lyra, 67; and Prierias, 134; and Faber, 140
Articles of faith, 92
Assurance, 234
Augustine, Saint, 9-23, 53, 89, 95, 102, 103, 108; and Tyconius, 11, 12, 228, 260; and Lyra, 68-69; and Luther, 149, 253, 265
Authority: as hermeneutical criterion, 73, 74-75; of Church, 76-77, 82, 90, 98, 101; of events, 99

Baptism, 13n, 118, 130, 131
Bede, 26
Bernard of Clairvaux, 178n, 192n, 265n
Bible: as wholly edifying, 13; aimed at faith and love, 28, 36, 52; uniqueness of, 29-30, 34, 56; has own logic, 80; clarity/obscurity of, 253
Biblicism, 34, 77
Biel, Gabriel, 123-132 *passim*, 261-262
Bonaventura, 40-46, 123; on law, 43-45, 125; on OT and NT sacraments, 130-131
Burgos, Paul of, 86-101, 103, 106, 136, 145n

Caritas, 17, 20, 42, 121, 122, 157, 243-244; as goal of interpretation, 13, 189; distinguishes new from old law, 41-42, 48, 161, 163; excited by promise, 46, 47, 123, 157, 161; in Christ, 116, 231; and eternal reward, 126-127
Catholic truth, 75-76
Certitude, 95, 219-220
Christ: key to OT, 4, 32-33, 83; history of, as significative or sacramental, 34, 57, 99-100, 117-118, 236, 239-240; signified in OT, 57; his promise to Church, 59, 75-78; as literal sense of OT, 68; as *fundamentum* of Scripture, 93-94, 97; establishes literal sense, 96-97, 98; as promised in OT, 108-109, 179-180, 195,

214; without faith or hope, 116, 231; as *comprehensor*, 116, 231, 233; and unity of Scripture, 120, 121; as content of Psalms, 141, 146; as *veritas*, 157; as Psalms speaker, 146–147, 167, 168, 172n, 174, 213; as literal sense of Psalms, 173, 228, 234; as goal of exegesis, 195; his own faith, 229, 230–233; as promiser, 250–251. See also Advent(s) of Christ; Tropology

Christological exegesis, 4, 68, 74, 106; in Burgos, 93–98; in Perez, 103, 108–110, 113–117; two kinds of, 116, 200n; of Psalms, 143–147, 154, 177, 195, 246. See also Christ

Church, 35, 36; as allegorical sense of Christ, 57; as source of normative word, 57, 58; heir of Christ's promise, 59, 75–77; authority of, 76, 77, 79, 81, 83; signified by NT, 77, 236; as Psalms speaker, 169, 171; conformity of, to synagogue, 220–225; as testimony, 224–225

Circumcision, 118, 130, 131–132, 211n

Commandment(s). See Law

Conformitas, imitatio (Christi), 113, 197, 248, 256

Contingentia, 62–65

Covenant, *pactum, testamentum*, 124, 215; in Nominalism, 2, 129–132; of grace, 129–130; and sacramental causality, 130–131, 162, 261–262; relation of old and new, 132, 201–204; *pactum Christi*, 202, 213; eternal, in OT, 207, 208, 211, 215, 264. See also Promise

Cross, 239, 248

David: as prophet, 65, 67, 110, 138, 146–147, 154, 167–168, 169, 173; as figure of Christ, 115; as Christ, 201, 213
Dionysius the Areopagite, 41, 124
Disposition, 193
Doctrina, 13, 16–17, 32, 34, 36, 58–59, 70, 141, 189, 190
Doering, Matthias, 96, 106, 107
Dogma, 93
Double literal sense: in Lyra, 67–69, 84–85; in Totting, 73–74; in Gerson, 81; in Perez, 110; in Faber, 139. See also Literal sense
Durandus of Saint-Pourçain, 128

Ebeling, Gerhard, 5, 100n, 143n, 146n, 147n, 181, 190, 200n, 226, 227, 228, 234–235, 240n, 245n, 250–251n
Eruditio, as spiritual understanding, 164, 167, 168, 243, 255. See also *Intellectus*, Spiritual understanding
Eucharist, 241. See also Sacrament(s)
Events. See Historical events

Faber Stapulensis, Jacobus, 137–142, 176; and Luther, 145, 147, 173, 228
Facere quod in se est, 125n, 127, 129, 194, 257, 258
Faith: as assent, 59; Christ's own, 116, 229, 230–233; medieval understanding of, 156–157; formed by love, 157; as *affectus*, 182; in promise, 183, 187, 208–209, 232, 248, 251; alone, 210, 229, 247–248; tropological, 233–235; and *intellectus*, 250, 255, 256; of future things, 256. See also Old Testament faith
"Faithful synagogue," 172, 173,

174, 211, 212–225; as remnant of Israel, 215–217; occurrences of term, 216n; as model for Christianity, 217, 220–225, 233, 248, 251

Figura, 15, 18, 19, 20, 32, 49, 63, 84

Figurative interpretation, 10, 11, 12, 13, 14n, 17, 18, 19, 25, 84

Forgiveness, 262, 263–264

Fourfold sense of Scripture: in Cassian, 21; in Augustine, 21n; in Hugh, 26–28; in Bonaventura, 41, comprehended by divine intention, 54; on NT basis, 55, 57–58, 99–100, 236, 240; in Gerson, 83–84; Luther and, 174, 227, 240–242; logic of, 235–239. *See also* Spiritual sense(s)

Franciscan tradition, 2, 40, 130–131, 162

Fundamentum. *See* Christ; Literal sense

Future: knowledge of, 65–66; relation to promise, 77, 117, 121, 185, 221, 222–223, 264; and OT word, 111, 192, 198; as "spirit," 190; faith in, 210, 256

Gerson, Jean, 79–85, 176; and Burgos, 91, 92, 93, 96, 97, 101; and Perez, 105, 107, 112; and Faber, 140–141; and Luther, 146n, 148

Gospel: and promise, 2, 5; and law, 38–39, 45, 132, 208; as law spiritually understood, 43, 45, 48–49, 121, 125, 163, 235; as sacramental, 242

Grace: and hermeneutical theory, 9; and law, 39, 125; signified in OT, 40; as *intellectus*, 44, 256; defines new law, 48; and justification, 49, 121, 127; and understanding Scripture, 95; subversion of, 128, 255–265; accompanies the Word, 242–244, 254–255; prevenient, 258

Grammatical sense of Scripture, 14, 106, 138–139, 147, 182, 183. *See also* Literal sense

Gregory of Rimini, 78n, 82, 92

Heilsgeschichte. *See* History of salvation

Heresy, heretics, 80, 177, 185

"Hermeneutical divide," 16, 42, 71, 99; and advent of Christ, 20, 32, 163; Luther shifts, 197, 200–211, 246–247, 257

Historical events: as significative, *figurae*, etc., 37, 56, 63, 84, 108, 117, 135, 169; in Scotus, 64–65. *See also* Old Testament history

Historical sense (*sensus historicus*) of Scripture, 52, 176; in Hugh, 28; as *fundamentum*, 35; in Lyra, 70; in Burgos, 89–90; in Faber, 138–139; in Luther, 144–145, 180, 183

History: and doctrine, 99–101; and revelation, 100

History of salvation, *Heilsgeschichte*, 20, 25, 37, 54, 55, 57, 83

Holcot, Robert, 129, 130

Hope, 17, 19, 27, 28, 204; and anagogy, 22, 36; under promise, 219–220

Hugh of Saint Victor, 24–37; on scriptural senses, 26–28, 146n; on literal sense, 29–31, 35; on OT interpretation, 31–34, 35

Humilitas, 116, 228–229, 229n

Imitatio. *See Conformitas*

Incarnation. *See* Advent(s) of Christ

Intellectus, 167, 172n, 237–238, 243–244, 250, 255, 256. *See*

also *Eruditio*; Spiritual understanding

Intention of author: determines sense of text, 54, 69, 73, 90, 91, 126, 133-134, 135, 137-138, 139-140, 214; and spiritual sense, 106-107; and promise, 111, 117; regarding the law, 125-127

Isidore of Seville, 24, 68, 99

Jews, 106, 158, 159, 190, 204-205; and Jesus, 96, 97, 98; synagogue, 135; in OT interpretation, 147-148, 165, 173, 185; as heretics, 177. See also "Faithful synagogue"; Old Testament people

Justification: in Nominalism, 2, 124-130; in OT, 42, 211n; by grace, 49, 121, 122, 128; by faith, 120, 121, 122, 128, 229; and tropology, 226-227, 236-237, 250; and sacrament, 239-240

Law, 12, 16, 17, 42-45, 128-129, 132, 201, 210; as (killing) letter, 11-12, 39, 42, 44, 49, 128; of love, 17; of works, 19; in the testaments, 20-21, 39, 120; and grace, Spirit, etc., 20-21, 99, 127; spiritual understanding of, 25, 38, 43, 45, 48-49, 121, 125-127, 163, 164, 235; and gospel, 132, 208; and Christ, 191, 223; as preparation, 204. See also Letter and spirit

Letter and spirit, 11, 42, 108, 144; as law and grace, 11n, 12n, 25, 36, 48-49, 70, 99, 260; as OT & NT, 15, 23, 36, 42, 70, 246; in Hugh, 24-25; in Lombard, 38-39; in Bonaventura, 42-43; in Thomas, 48-49; in Lyra, 70; in Burgos, 99; in Perez, 106-107; as word and meaning, 107, 252; in Faber, 139; in Luther, 148; as law and promise, 200. See also Law

Literal sense (*sensus litteralis*) of Scripture: as plain meaning, 12, 13, 14, 34, 80, 81; two levels of, 14, 36; in Hugh, 28-31; as *fundamentum*, 35, 67-68, 81, 84, 93-95, 97, 139, 180; in Aquinas, 51-57 *passim*, 69, 134; and theological proof, 52-53n, 68, 73-74, 80; in Lyra, 67-69; and Church, 79, 80, 81, 83; heretical claim to, 79-80; as "carnal," Jewish, etc., 80-81, 105, 106; *logicalis* and *theologicus*, 81-82; in Burgos, 86-101 *passim*; and Christ, 96, 98, 228, 234; in Perez, 104-105; in Prierias, 133-136; in Faber, 137-139. See also Double literal sense; Grammatical sense; Intention of author; Normative literal sense; Prophetic sense

Lombard, Peter, 38-40, 228

Love. See *Caritas*

Lyra, Nicholas of, 61-71; and Totting, 73-74; and Gerson, 80, 81, 84-85; and Burgos, 88, 97; and Perez, 107; and Faber, 139; and Luther, 145, 182n, 189n, 248n

Marcion, 3, 6, 10, 84

Merit: *condignum*, 3, 129, 130, 257n; *congruum*, 125, 129, 130, 256-257; opposed, 258-259, 264

Moral sense of Scripture, 171, 173, 177, 178, 198n, 226, 259; displaces tropology, 248n, 250, 259. See also Tropology

Moses, 6, 65, 67, 164

Mystical theology, 22, 28, 146n

Normative literal sense of Scripture, 4, 14, 15, 27, 52, 55, 77, 104, 106; in OT, 18; in NT, 36, 70, 100-101; shift in locus of, 56-57; in Church, 59-60, 84; in Totting, 73-75; redefined by Gerson, 80, 84; in Burgos, 91-92, 100-101; as intention, 126; as *testimonium*, 184-191
Necessary truths, 63, 64
New Testament: as true sense of OT, 16, 20, 25, 34, 39, 45, 52, 54, 57, 70, 83, 140-141; spiritual sense of, 34-35, 57, 77, 236; basis of fourfold interpretation, 100, 236
Nicholas of Lyra. See Lyra

Occam, William of, 62
Old Testament: role in canon, 3, 10, 15, 20; as letter, 15-16; theological value of, 16, 32, 45, 52-53, 79, 98, 112, 132, 140-141, 147, 156, 163. See also Allegory
Old Testament faith, 6, 77-78, 98; as inferior, 19, 79, 165; as exemplary, 113-114, 115, 207-209, 220-222, 257, 258; in Christ, 114, 117. See also Faith; "Faithful synagogue"; Old Testament people
Old Testament history, 4, 33, 52, 98, 121; as *figura*, *umbra*, etc., 4, 23, 31, 32, 33, 35, 36, 45, 78-79, 112, 119, 156. See also Historical events
Old Testament-New Testament relation, 112, 123-124, 200n; as letter and spirit, 15, 23, 36, 42, 70, 246; unity of, 38-39, 119-121; difference in promises, 40, 47, 156, 264; sacraments compared, 40, 118, 124; in Aquinas, 46; and *caritas*, 48; seen via *pactum*, 132, 202
Old Testament people: contrasting conceptions of, 4, 19-21, 45, 49, 127-128; ignorance of, 33, 36, 45, 212-213; "special persons," 43, 45, 48, 128, 212-213; without grace, 49; as figures of Christ, 113, 115; as models for Christians, 113-114, 115, 197, 207-209

Pactum. See Covenant
Pelagianism, 11, 257, 258, 260, 264-265
Penance, 166, 240, 262-264
Penitential psalms, 166-175 *passim*, 263; as prayer of Christ, 167
Perez of Valencia, James, 102-122, 176, 235
Petition, 191, 198; Psalms as, 113, 171, 173, 178, 179, 182, 184, 186; occurrences of *petitio* in *Dictata*, 217n; as *facere quod in se est*, 258
Potentia absoluta, ordinata, 64, 126
Prierias, Sylvester, 133-137, 176
Promise, *promissio*: 2, 4-6, as normative part of Scripture, 13, 18-19, 59, 76; relation to anagogy, 22; devalued, 50, 157-158; accounts for future, 77, 111; theological import of, 111; differs from *figura*, 112, 200n; in Nominalism, 129-130; relates hermeneutics and theology, 155; evokes petition, faith, 182-183; synonymous with *testimonium*, 184; as normative sense of Scripture, 184-191, 195; and advents of Christ, 192-195; promise to Christ, 201, 230, 233, 245, 246;

and faith, 209, 232, 247–248, 251; and sacrament, 211n, 251n, 261–262; certitude in, 219; displaces grace, 261; opposes merit, 264
  New Testament: of *eternalia* or *spiritualia*, 36, 40, 41, 47; evokes love, 41–42, 46, 47, 123, 157, 161; of Christ to Church, 59, 75, 76–78, 87, 137
  Old Testament, 16–19, 23, 112, 205, 207–211 *passim*; of *temporalia*, 17, 35–36, 40, 41, 47, 158–159, 204–206; of Christ or NT, 18, 20, 108–109, 179–180, 195, 214; of grace, 19; as prophetic message, 180, 214; as inviolable, 206–207
Prophecy, prophets, 65–66, 109–110, 159–160, 180, 198, 213, 214, 252
Prophetic sense (*sensus propheticus*) of Scripture: Christ as, 144–147, 154, 228, 234, 246; and historical interpretation, 154, 180; as Church speaking, 168, 169; change in meaning of, 171, 173, 176–183, 226
Providence, 30, 54

Quadriga. See Fourfold sense

Rashi, 24, 70
Reformation theology, 1–2, 4–6, 62n, 226–227, 246, 249
Remnant of Israel, 212, 215–216. *See also* "Faithful synagogue"
Res. See Signum
Res sacramenti, 243
Richard of Saint Victor, 41
Righteousness, 249

Sacrament(s), 2–3, 49, 159; causality in, 2–3, 130–131, 162, 261–262; and hermeneutics, 37, 240–241; of OT and NT, 40, 118, 124, 130–132, 211n; justifying, 49, 239; and promise, 211n, 251n, 261–262
Scientia, 21, 62–63, 256
Scotus, John Duns, 62–65, 123
Scripture. *See* Bible
Signification: of words (*signa*), 29–30, 36–37, 51; of things (*res*) or events, 29–31, 33, 34, 36, 51, 54, 55, 56–57, 84, 111
Signum and *res*, 13, 51, 59, 174–175
Simul, 162, 209, 242, 252
Singularia, 63
Speech. *See* Word(s)
Spirit, Holy, 4, 181; in OT, 48, 109–110, 146–147; in Church, 57, 59, 79, 90–91; author of Scripture, 73; and understanding Scripture, 95, 107, 139, 141, 160; and literal sense, 96, 139
Spirit and letter. *See* Letter and spirit
Spiritual sense(s), 12n, 14, 16, 51–52, 80; in Cassian, 21; in Aquinas, 55–57; valid for proof, 74–75, 102–103, 106; relation to literal, 86, 92, 93–95, 134; as existential category, 95–96, 106–107, 160–161. *See also* Allegory; Anagogy; Fourfold sense; Spiritual understanding; Tropology
Spiritual understanding: of the law, 25, 36, 38–39, 42–44, 48, 125, 163; and Christ's advent, 32, 163, 165; of Scripture, 95; in Luther, 163–165, 167, 172, 183. *See also Eruditio; Intellectus;* Letter and spirit
Stapulensis. *See* Faber
Sufficiency of Scripture, 91

Synagogue, 178. *See also* "Faithful synagogue"; Jews

Testament. *See* Covenant; Old Testament; New Testament
Testimony, *testimonium*: and faith, 183; as Scripture's normative meaning, 184–191, 195, 222, 248; and hope, 219–220; Israel and Church as, 222, 224–225. *See also* Promise
Theology, 62–65; *theologia crucis*, 240n
Thomas. *See* Aquinas
Totting of Oyta, Henry, 73–79, 87, 88, 96, 101
Tradition, 1, 3, 5, 58–59, 74–75, 78, 97, 101
Tropology, *tropologia*, 226–245 *passim*; in Cassian, 21, 22, 26; in Hugh, 26–27, 36; in Bonaventura, 41; in Perez, 113–115; of Christ and Christian, 167, 168, 170, 174, 197, 226–227; nature of faith in, 233–235; Luther's rationale for, 236–237; displaced by "moral" interpretation, 248n, 250; failure of, 249. *See also* Fourfold sense; Moral sense
Trust, 256
Turmerlebnis, 5, 246
Tyconius: rules of, 9, 10, 11, 99, 103; third rule of, 11, 12, 24, 68, 70, 99, 108, 109n, 149n, 260; first rule of, 228, 245, 249

Veritas, 157
Victorine school, 24
Visio dei, 65–66

William of Occam, 62
Word(s) of Scripture: of OT, 6, 52, 159–160; signification of, 29, 159; function of, 36–37, 57, 58, 192, 198, 229–230; univocity of, 51, 53; normative, 59; and meaning, 107, 252–253; of promise, 111, 209, 247–249; and grace, 162, 208; as causative, 238, 241, 254; as sacramental, 239–245; unique qualities of, 252–255; clarity of, 253; of forgiveness, 264

DATE DUE

NO 3 0 96			

BR 6556
333.5
.B5   Preus, James S.
P7   From shadow to promise.
1969

HIEBERT LIBRARY
Fresno Pacific College - M. B. Seminary
Fresno, Calif 93702

DEMCO